Tourism

Tourism looks set to replace oil as the most important global industry as countries capitalise on the high returns it offers, often at the expense of the environment, communities and individuals. James Elliott explores the ways in which governments of both developed and developing countries manage this diverse and volatile industry.

Using case studies from the UK, Australia, Vietnam and Thailand, and referring to the USA, this wide-ranging book covers key aspects of tourism management at all levels of government. Topics include:

- tourism organisations
- policy making and planning
- central and local government involvement
- public and private sector management
- environmental control and sustainable development.

Accessible information boxes and excerpts from official documents, combined with historical and economic overviews, are employed to provide a framework from which to evaluate and analyse why and how governments are involved in managing this complex and highly competitive sector.

James Elliott is a Senior Lecturer in Public Administration at the University of Queensland, Australia.

Tourism

Politics and public sector management

James Elliott

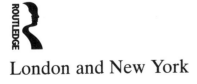

London and New York

First published 1997
by Routledge
11 New Fetter Lane, London EC4P 4EE

Simultaneously published in the USA and Canada
by Routledge
29 West 35th Street, New York, NY 10001

© 1997 James Elliott
James Elliott has asserted his moral right under the Copyright, Designs and
Patents Act, 1988, to be identified as the author of this work.

Typeset in Times by Keystroke, Jacaranda Lodge, Wolverhampton
Printed and bound in Great Britain by TJ International Ltd, Padstow,
Cornwall

British Library Cataloguing in Publication Data
A catalogue record for this book is available from the British Library

Library of Congress Cataloging in Publication Data
Elliott, James
    Tourism: politics and public sector management / James Elliott.
    Includes bibliographical references and index.
    1. Tourist trade – Government policy. I. Title.
  G155.A1E427 1997
  338.4′791–dc21   96–52245

ISBN 0–415–07157–7 (hbk)
ISBN 0–415–07158–5 (pbk)

Contents

Series editor's preface
Public Sector Management series

Tourism, as Professor Elliott explains, is one of the fastest growing industries in the world. Governments in countries at all stages of development are increasingly dependent on it, but it is of special significance in countries intent on achieving sustainable development. This leads to general questions about the role of governments in various countries, questions about what governments conceive to be their particular responsibilities in relation to tourism, and questions about the relationship of tourism to public sector management. In the longer term there are also questions about the consequences of the development of tourism for citizens. It is increasingly apparent that people at all levels of society and in all occupations are affected in one way or another by this fast growing and important industry. Consequently, Professor Elliott's book, which examines all levels of government in relation to tourism, is timely and welcome.

Because tourism is such a relatively new sphere for public sector management, the problems associated with it are only just becoming apparent. At one extreme, the development of tourism may be associated with the growth of the mass media and international marketing, which contribute to its vigorous growth. However, at the other extreme, issues of crime, drug use and sexual disease, including AIDS, may be seen in a new light because in some areas their growth has been associated with the expansion of tourism. Both these relationships are considered in this book, which is concerned with what tourism is and how tourism relates to other phenomena and responsibilities in both the public and private sectors of the economy.

The scholarly literature in this field is still in its infancy and Professor Elliott's monograph is an original and significant contribution to it. There can be few other scholars who can match his breadth of experience and depth of study, reflecting the many years he has devoted to this aspect of public sector management. His wide-ranging knowledge is well illustrated in the comparative material contained in his book, which focuses on the United Kingdom, Australia, Thailand and Vietnam. However, the book also draws attention to the experience and sometimes the peculiarities of managing the tourist industry in other countries. This study is therefore a particularly welcome addition to the Public Sector Management series because it looks at some of the global contexts and applications of public sector management in relation to the new and fast growing tourist industry.

Richard A. Chapman
Professor of Politics,
Durham University

Illustrations

Preface

This book is about how governments manage tourism, one of the fastest-growing industries in the world, which, by the turn of the century, will have replaced oil as the largest industry in the world. It is about politics, policies, different kinds of governments and their organisations; it is about how governments manage their relations with industry. There can be conflict between the industry and local people and conservationists about tourism development, the destruction of the environment and the use of power. Public sector management is required to stop the abuse of power, achieve sustainable development, and protect the people and national resources. There are principles which managers may follow, and this book is concerned about how these principles are followed in the practice of management.

Many of the sources for this study are drawn from public bodies, Parliament, Congress, government ministries and departments, local government and public agencies such as the tourism boards. These sources are important, for they give insights into and contain the formal objectives of governments, management and tourism, and the criteria by which they can be evaluated. Parliamentary and congressional reports and the increasing academic literature on tourism from several disciplines are also valuable sources. With the use of the framework provided by the book, local material and experiences can be collected and used to study management and its impact on local tourism areas. Any framework, however, should be used in a flexible manner, for in practice tourism is a dynamic activity and there is considerable interaction between sectors and organisations.

This book is the result of many years' direct experience and research into tourism and the countries mentioned. It will be a valuable text for a wide range of courses, including tourism, management, national and local government, politics, public policy and environmental studies, and it will also be of interest to the general reader.

Acknowledgements

I am grateful to the numerous public officials and managers from the tourism industry in many countries who have supplied the information on which this book is based. Thanks especially to the Tourism Society of London and English Tourist Board for permission to reproduce material and to my research assistant in Tokyo, Yoichi Kato.

Jim Elliott

Acronyms and abbreviations

AAT	Airport Authority of Thailand
ABTA	Association of British Travel Agents
AGIIT	Australian Government Inquiry into Tourism
AIA	Australian Incentive Association
AIDS	acquired immune deficiency syndrome
ANA	All Nippon Airlines
ASEAN	Association of Southeast Asian Nations
ATC	Australian Tourist Commission
ATIA	Australian Tourism Industries Association
ATTA	Association of Thai Travel Agents
BA	British Airways
BAA	British Airports Authority
BHRCA	British Hotels, Restaurants and Caterers Association
BITOA	British Incoming Tour Operators' Association
BOAC	British Overseas Airways Corporation
BOI	Board of Investment (Thailand)
BTA	British Tourist Authority
CBI	Confederation of British Industry
CEO	chief executive officer
DTI	Department of Trade and Industry (UK)
EC	European Community
EIA	environmental impact assessment
ESD	ecologically sustainable development
ETB	English Tourist Board
EU	European Union
FIRB	Foreign Investment Review Board (Australia)
GATT	General Agreement on Tariffs and Trade
GDP	gross domestic product
Gov	Government (UK)
HC	House of Commons (UK)

ICAO	International Civil Aviation Organisation
IMF	International Monetary Fund
ITOA	Inbound Tourism Organisation of Australia
JICA	Japan International Cooperation Agency
JNTO	Japan National Tourist Organisation
NESDB	National Economic and Social Development Board (Thailand)
NGO	non-governmental organisation
NTA	National Tourist Administration
NTO	National Tourist Office, National Tourism Organisation
PSM	public sector management
Qantas	Queensland and Northern Territory Aerial Services
QTTC	Queensland Tourist and Travel Corporation
R and R	rest and recreation (USA)
RTA	Regional Tourist Association
RTB	Regional Tourist Board
RTO	Regional Tourist Organisation
SCCI	State Committee for Cooperation and Investment (Vietnam)
TAT	Tourism Authority of Thailand
THF	Trust House Forte
TIC	Tourist Information Centre (UK)
TOT	Tourism Organisation of Thailand (predecessor of TAT)
UK	United Kingdom of Great Britain and Northern Ireland
UNDP	United Nations Development Programme
USA	United States of America
USTS	United States Travel Service
USTTA	United States Travel and Tourism Administration
VAT	value added tax
WTO	World Tourism Organisation (WTO as used in this book); World Trade Organisation (established 1995, succeeded GATT)

1 Introduction

This chapter explains the basic methodology of the book, covering:

- why governments are involved in tourism;
- who are the most important participants in tourism management;
- how public sector management (PSM) operates in practice;
- what are the results and impacts of the PSM of tourism; and
- the comparative nature of tourism and PSM.

This book is about how governments manage and mismanage tourism. It is about politics; that is, the use of power by public organisations in their management of tourism. The main instrument used by governments is public sector management (PSM) which includes all types of public organisations ranging from national government departments to small tourism units managed by local governments. The processes of management are also analysed, from the formulation of policy by political leaders to its impact on local communities. Management in this book always refers to PSM unless otherwise stated.

There are two main concerns underlying the approach of this book to the PSM of tourism. One is termed *principles*, the other *practice*. Principles are the justification for the use of power by governments. They give legitimacy to the actions of managers, and citizens have expectations that the principles will be followed. The second main concern, on which the book concentrates, is the actual practice of management, how public managers and their organisations behave at the different levels of government from federal and national to local. Attention is given to formal values, attitudes, objectives, roles and relations between governments and tourism and its industry, but also to informal practices.

THE FRAMEWORK OF WHY, WHO, HOW AND WHAT

Governments and tourism are large and complex areas to study and, in order to help in the identification, analysis and evaluation of the most significant factors, a framework is used based upon four main questions: why, who, how and what.

Why are governments so important to tourism? Why do governments get involved in tourism management? Why does tourism have to be managed? It is suggested that governments have responsibilities which require them to get involved in policy areas such as tourism. There are principles which managers should follow and there are objectives which governments wish to achieve for political, economic and moral reasons. Some issues and problems can only be managed by governments.

Who are the main participants in the tourism policy system? Who are the significant policy makers, public sector managers and power holders in the public sector and industry? Which are the most important organisations?

How is management actually carried out, how do managers manage? How do participants operate and behave, how does the system work in practice, how is policy formulated, implemented and managed, how are objectives achieved and by what means? How does PSM manage in political and power systems of great complexity at both the formal and informal level?

What are the impacts of tourism? What are the results of management in practice and performance? Has there been success or failure? What have been the most significant issues? Have principles been followed, objectives achieved? What are the lessons for tourism PSM?

WHY GOVERNMENTS ARE INVOLVED IN TOURISM

The importance of governments

Governments are a fact in tourism and in the modern world. The industry could not survive without them. It is only governments which have the power to provide the political stability, security and the legal and financial framework which tourism requires. They provide essential services and basic infrastructure. It is only national governments which can negotiate and make agreements with other governments on issues such as immigration procedures or flying over and landing on national territory. Governments have power, but how

Box 1.1 Public sector management and tourism: framework for analysis

	Principles What *should* be done? Ideal behaviour, theory, model	Practice What *is* done, practice not principles
	Principles: public interest, public service, effectiveness, efficiency, accountability	Actual behaviour
Why involved	Responsibility of government and PSM, moral, legal, professional principles Political culture, expectations Power of government Public objectives	Economic objectives Economic pressure Political objectives formal and informal Tourism has to be managed Need to respond to problems and demands
Who involved	Government and people Those affected by policy PSM Industry and interest groups	Policy makers, politicians, managers Power holders Industry Those affected
How involved	According to political culture, PSM principles PSM tourism norms Partnership with industry Formal process	Policy systems, formulation and implementation Power networks Management process Formal and informal
What results	Objectives, effectiveness Serve public interest and people Protect environment and community Efficiency	Success or failure Objectives achieved Impact Efficient, effective PSM

they use this will depend upon many factors including political culture, the political and economic power holders and their perception of the tourism industry. There are different types of government, including national, state and local, and they can be either active or passive in tourism management and in the use of their powers. Governments can assist tourism by the provision of services; they can also control the industry and its activities in order to ensure that activities and safety standards are maintained in the public interest. These are all legitimate functions of governments which they are expected to perform for the public good. How these functions are performed and the success or otherwise of government depends upon the quality of its public sector management (PSM). Governments perform their functions through PSM. PSM includes all managers in all governments and public organisations whose duties affect tourism in some way. The public services provided, such as immigration or clean public beaches, are part of the total tourism product and can either add or detract from its attractiveness.

The importance of tourism

Governments have become involved in tourism mainly because of its economic importance. In periods of industrial and economic decline, world recession, massive unemployment and a growing gap between the rich and poor, tourism is one of the few growth industries; it is also able to provide the scarce foreign currency which most governments desperately need. Tourism is one of the largest industries in the world and, according to the World Tourism Organisation (WTO), tourism has replaced oil at the top of the list in terms of foreign currency movements, or at the latest it will do so by the year 2000. In 1995, there were a total of 567 million international tourist arrivals compared to 25 million in 1950. For several countries and governments tourism is the single most important economic activity. Chapter 2 examines the economic importance of tourism and its historic growth. Table 1.1 shows the World's forty top tourism destinations and indicates which are the most popular countries for tourism.

Tourism is more than an industry and an economic activity, it is a universal dynamic social phenomenon touching most countries of the world and affecting their people. The social effects of tourism can be profound, especially in developing countries; local communities can be transformed for good or ill. Living standards and the quality of life can be raised by the inflow of finance, new employment and

Table 1.1 The world's top 40 tourism destinations: international tourist arrivals (excluding same-day visitors); (thousands of arrivals), 1995

Rank 1985–95		Countries	Arrivals 1995 (000)	% change 1995/94	% of total 1995
1	1	France	60,584	–1.2	10.7
2	2	Spain	45,125	4.4	8.0
3	3	United States	44,730	–1.7	7.9
4	4	Italy	29,184	6.2	5.1
13	5	China	23,368	10.9	4.1
6	6	United Kingdom	22,700	7.9	4.0
11	7	Hungary	22,087	3.1	3.9
9	8	Mexico	19,870	16.1	3.5
23	9	Poland	19,225	2.3	3.4
5	10	Austria	17,173	–4.0	3.0
7	11	Canada	16,896	5.8	3.0
16[1]	12	Czech Republic	16,600	–2.4	2.9
8	13	Germany	14,535	0.3	2.6
10	14	Switzerland	11,835	–3.0	2.1
14	15	Greece	11,095	3.6	2.0
19	16	Hong Kong	10,124	8.5	1.8
15	17	Portugal	9,513	4.2	1.7
22	18	Malaysia	7,936	10.3	1.4
26	19	Thailand	6,900	11.9	1.2
21	20	Netherlands	6,526	5.6	1.2
28	21	Turkey	6,512	7.9	1.1
24	22	Singapore	6,422	2.5	1.1
17	23	Belgium	5,224	–1.6	0.9
18[2]	24	Russian Federation	4,796	3.3	0.8
55	25	South Africa	4,676	20.0	0.8
35	26	Macau	4,623	3.0	0.8
25	27	Ireland	4,398	2.1	0.8
54	28	Indonesia	4,319	7.8	0.8
20	29	Bulgaria	4,125	1.7	0.7
32	30	Tunisia	4,120	6.8	0.7
38	31	Argentina	4,101	6.1	0.7
46	32	Australia	3,771	12.2	0.7
40	33	Korea (Republic)	3,753	4.8	0.7
36	34	Puerto Rico	3,297	8.4	0.6
33	35	Norway	2,880	1.8	0.5
41	36	Egypt	2,872	21.9	0.5
27	37	Romania	2,750	–1.6	0.5
29	38	Morocco	2,579	–25.6	0.5
–	39	Bahrain	2,483	9.4	0.4
39	40	Taiwan (prov. of China)	2,332	9.6	0.4
	Total 1–40		**496,039**	**3.4**	**87.4**
	World total		**567,402**	**3.9**	**100.0**

Source: World Tourism Organisation (WTO), 1996
Notes:
1 Former Czechoslovakia
2 Former USSR

educational opportunities, and the revitalisation of local traditions and cultures. Tourism can be a source for peace and better international understanding between different peoples by bringing them more closely together economically and socially and building up friendships.

Problems of tourism

Governments are drawn into tourism because of the importance of the industry and because of its problems, and its at times controversial impact. Strong resentment and opposition have arisen in both developed and developing countries over the adverse effects of tourism. Tourism has been criticised for its destructive impact on local and traditional communities and cultures and on areas such as the coastline of Spain, the beaches of Thailand and Mexico, the national parks of the United States, and the historic cities of Europe. It is claimed that resorts, golf courses and marinas have been developed for the wealthy at the expense of the poor and the environment. These are highly political issues and raise questions about the use of power and who gets what, when and how. Such issues require the intervention of PSM as a public service to find acceptable solutions and to support the public interest.

Another problem of the tourism industry is its highly competitive nature and volatility in both domestic and international markets. PSM should be aware of these problems and be prepared to try to alleviate them. It should not be adding to the problems by too much intervention, too many regulations and controls, thus becoming part of the problem instead of the solution.

Tourism is vulnerable and can easily be affected by changes in public policy and public perceptions. PSM assistance can be needed. The industry is also sensitive to events outside its control, including national disasters or political events such as the 1991 Gulf War and the French nuclear tests in the South Pacific in 1995. Management, both public and private, must be prepared to take swift decisions to help the industry at times of crisis.

Problems are caused by mass tourism especially during the peak seasons. The tremendous increase in air traffic and the great strains placed on airports and their infrastructure require action by governments. Management is influential in the difficult decisions involving huge capital investment to solve such problems. Airlines and airports are discussed in Chapter 7.

Tourism is a dynamic industry which is always changing and there are always new challenges and problems. This study, however, is concerned with the more permanent factors, such as principles, values or needs, or factors which are important in organisations such as power, politics and leadership. How effectively and efficiently management uses these factors to solve problems is a test of that management.

Principles

Governments have responsibilities and there are principles suggested on which their management activities can or should be based. PSM has been given power to meet its responsibilities in tourism within general principles. These principles will require PSM at times to intervene in tourism, but the same principles will also control that intervention. The general principles which are normally accepted internationally are *public interest, public service, effectiveness, efficiency* and *accountability*. Managers interpret the principles according to their own national political and administrative systems.

One of the main differences between the public and private sectors is the binding nature of those principles on public sector managers. While the private sector has its own principles and priorities, its managers have much more freedom than their public counterparts. Public managers may possess power and resources but these can only be used according to the law and accepted principles, otherwise their use is illegal or illegitimate.

The actual behaviour may depart from the principles, and there can be conflict between principles and the various legitimate demands being placed upon managers. The successful manager will be able to balance these conflicting demands. Managers in the private sector, if they understand these principles, will be able to work more effectively with the public sector and so achieve a better result for their organisation. Adherence to principles makes for higher quality management which is more responsive to society and the needs of industry. In the actual practice of management there is always a danger of politicians, public and private organisations and managers becoming self-serving and failing in their official responsibilities. Public organisations and resources can be used for private purposes. There can be financial corruption but more insidious is organisational corruption, where public objectives and principles are displaced by private objectives. Principles and their enforcement are a safeguard against political and managerial abuse and corruption. Principles are necessary to evaluate organisations and management.

WHO IS INVOLVED IN TOURISM MANAGEMENT?

Governments at all levels, from national and federal governments, through to local governments at the village level, can all be involved in the management of tourism. PSM includes all public organisations such as national civil services and government ministries and departments, statutory authorities, public bodies and the organisations and officials of state and local governments. Tourism ministries and departments and national tourism organisations (NTOs) are particularly important. The line between the public sector and private sector is not always clear. Some public sector organisations, such as publicly owned airlines, compete with private organisations in the market and there are joint ventures with ownership divided between the public and private sectors. Tourism is used in a wide sense, including the tourism industry and the many service industries which are grouped together as the tourism industry. Most of the industry is in the private sector but it also includes profit-making organisations in the public sector. Profit-making organisations range from large multinational hotel chains to single-owner guest houses or restaurants.

There are numerous organisations which are part of the tourism community but not part of the profit-making tourism industry. These include interest or pressure groups and non-governmental organisations (NGOs). These organisations include national and local groups which have interests in a wide range of issues such as social, economic, environmental and moral problems. Tourism is a people-based activity, affecting the tourists, domestic and international, the people in the industry, and all those in the host community who are affected by tourist activity in some way or another. Yet a key issue in politics and PSM and among all the people and organisations is who are the main power holders?

Government is a power holder but it is involved with tourism not only as an industry but as an educational and cultural experience for both the tourists and the host community. Tourism not only has an economic impact but also affects the natural environment and local culture. While most tourism is provided and controlled by the private sector, the public sector has a crucial role to play in providing the necessary policy guidelines, and the environment, infrastructure and management needed in both the economic and non-economic spheres.

Box 1.2 Who is involved in tourism management? Tourism policy community

Legislative branch	Congress/Parliament: lower and upper houses, elected representatives
Executive branch government	National, state and regional. government Public sector management Ministries/departments: ministry of tourism Statutory authorities/ business enterprises: national tourism organisation; development agency, public regulatory bodies Environmental protection agencies, advisory and consultative bodies, joint ventures with private sector
State government	Elected assemblies
Local government	Departments, enterprises and PSM, elected councils
Interest/pressure groups	Non-governmental organisations, economic, social and environmental groups
Industry	Hotels, travel agents, airlines, trade unions, theme parks
Political parties, public opinion, mass media	
Judicial branch	Courts: constitutional, national, local
International organisations	World Tourism Organisation, United Nations Development Programme (UNDP), European Union Economic institutions, World Bank, IMF, Asian Development Bank

HOW MANAGERS MANAGE

How PSM is involved and actually manages in practice will vary with the political culture of the country and the strength of the principles operating in any specific situation. Managers are involved in tourism through organisations and networks, through problem solving and both formally and informally. They are also involved because of principles and moral responsibilities but these can be overlooked in the pressure and stress of actually managing. PSM is important, for it is at the management level that expertise is found, information is available, and from where advice and policy formulation and actual implementation must come and where much power lies. This is the level which interacts directly with the political and industrial leaders and conveys the information and understanding which each group requires.

Governments have gradually accepted the importance of tourism at least economically, but they have been much slower to accept their responsibilities for the problems posed by tourism development. In theory PSM is under the control of the government, but in practice it is not possible to say where the power of government ends and the power of PSM begins. In the management of tourism it is all part of a continuum. There is also pressure upon government and management alike to respond to economic needs and demands within the nation, including the demands of tourism.

Politics and power

No study of management and tourism can neglect the reality of politics and power. Politics is about the striving for power, and power is about who gets what, when and how in the political and administrative system and in the tourism sector. Principles and control systems are there to try and ensure that power is used in the public interest and that proper and legitimate procedures and objectives are followed. PSM in particular must manage within the political environment, taking into account the political ideology, power conflicts and the priorities of governments and ministers as well as policy objectives. Managers must operate within the political culture, but they also have power, because of their control over resources and their position, to advise and influence ministers and policy. There is also the politics of the bureaucratic culture and administrative system, including infighting between management agencies. Tourism PSM within that system is responsible for fighting for the tourism industry to ensure that tourism gets what it needs. There are various power networks covering the political, public and private sectors in which, for PSM to be effective, it must be an active participant. Managers will strive to protect their own position, departments and minister but they are also responsible for wider economic and national considerations.

Complexity and interdependence

In the real world of PSM tourism no clear lines of demarcation can be drawn between principles and practice, the why, who, how and what, politics and power, formulation and implementation of policy, the public and private sector, or formal and informal factors. The world of politics, PSM and tourism is extremely complex and the various principles and issues all intermingle and affect one another. For example, there are different levels of government – national, state and local – and a multiplicity of public organisations ranging from government departments to public airlines. In the private sector, there are also airlines, and organisations ranging from large international resorts in Thailand to a one-person travel agency in a small town in England, to the management of the Grand Canyon National Park in Arizona, United States, and a gambling den in Hong Kong. All these organisations with their various objectives are interrelated and dependent upon one another to a greater or lesser degree. The test of the good manager is to be able to understand this complexity, operate effectively and efficiently within the system, reconcile or balance conflicting objectives and so achieve PSM tourism objectives.

Formality and informality

Governments and PSM operate on formal and informal levels. For example, some administrative systems follow the Weberian ideal system (see Chapter 3) and stress formal principles and the importance of regulations and procedure being managed by the officials holding the formal power to ensure an efficient organisation. Managers work within a formal system and they accept the formal decisions of ministers, but they also have to be aware of the informal, unstated factors involved in the system and decisions. The informal factors, especially in the political sphere, can be more powerful than the formal. Power holders can go against formal principles by using their power informally to achieve their personal objectives. Good managers, however, will also use informal factors to achieve formal legitimate objectives. They also use and follow the formal official documents and reports, such as those quoted in this study. Formal and informal practices, management systems, plans, concepts, technology and policy all have to be put to the acid test of how fully objectives are achieved and what are the actual results.

WHAT RESULTS? PRACTICE AND PERFORMANCE

Management is important, for it is responsible for going beyond the words and promises of politicians. Too often statements are made and paper programmes and plans produced without any real action being taken. The justification for PSM in tourism management and the test of its validity, legitimacy, professionalism, effectiveness and efficiency are found in the results of its practice and performance. Practice is an evaluation of the actual practice of management. Performance is an evaluation of how successful management has achieved tourism objectives.

First, in terms of performance evaluation, what has been achieved for the people, how well have they been served? What have been the outputs of the programme? It is the actual impact of the policy which is ultimately important rather than intentions or formal objectives. How far does public policy affect the life of the people, physical, emotional and spiritual, what is the impact on community and environment? Second, in terms of practice evaluation, have the public interest and principles been followed? The public interest includes respect for the political and administrative system and the political culture of the society. PSM must manage within, and fulfil, the criteria required by the political, legal system, for management behaviour to be truly legitimate.

Third, what has been the achievement in terms of efficiency and effectiveness? Have objectives been achieved at the lowest possible cost? Have resources been used efficiently? Has there been a reasonable return on the public investment? It is not always easy to evaluate the success or failure of public policy or what the contribution of PSM has been. Policy or management objectives are not always clear, and they can also be contradictory. Situations, the environment and values can change, especially over time, and therefore the achievement of the original formal objectives may be counter-productive to what is perceived as the current public interest. Management may be very successful in increasing tourist numbers and their expenditure, but it could be at a heavy cost to the environment because of the excessive tourism development needed to cater for the greatly increased number of tourists. In the actual world it is often PSM which must try to reconcile the opposing power forces. This may mean that the principles or ideals must be sacrificed to reach a consensus and that a compromise proposal is the most effective and efficient way forward. In those situations the informal process may be the most effective for management.

The impact of policy and PSM is most important for the life of the people and tourism; management endeavours to monitor and control the system and impact through various mechanisms. Control and accountability is a key principle of PSM and are responsible for ensuring that other principles are followed. An ideal control system would evaluate both the impact and how successfully management has followed PSM principles, lessons would be drawn and improvements made. Management, however, is not always successful at monitoring or controlling organisations or projects and learning from the experience. Managers can formulate plans but fail to implement them. Although it is difficult to measure the performance of public managers in any particular policy area, their contribution is essential and cannot be provided by private management. The performance of the tourism industry is judged by profits and growth, but to be successful practice must be based on an understanding of, and work with, PSM organisations and principles.

The evaluation of public management performance is a difficult management task because of the complexity and variety of government and tourism industry organisations, processes and problems. It is made more difficult and stressful, or challenging, because it is performed under public scrutiny. Managers who are responsible for control are themselves under scrutiny and are accountable. The check-list in Box 1.3 reflects the complexity and difficulty of the task but also provides a tool to help to analyse and evaluate management's actual performance.

Box 1.3 Check-list for the accountability and evaluation of the public sector management of tourism

Why: It can be relatively easy to describe why governments are involved in and how they manage tourism, but to describe or analyse is insufficient. The real significance of PSM can only be assessed by an evaluation of its performance within the context of the political administrative systems. It is an evaluation of those systems and of the role of political leaders and PSM. It is an evaluation of the results achieved, and the performance of:

Who: 1 (a) politicians
      (b) political systems
   2 (a) managers
      (b) administrative systems.

How: 1 Effective, efficient in managing within
     (a) a democratic system and process
     (b) an administrative system and process.
   2 Allow freedom to the industry, stimulate participation of the private sector and local people in the politics and management of tourism.
   3 Criteria:
     (a) Effectiveness in achieving objectives
     (b) Efficiency in achieving objectives (at lowest possible cost)
      (i) Economic and public service objectives
   4 Ability to meet the challenges and overcome the problems facing tourism management.
   5 Making the best use of national and natural resources respecting the public interest.
   6 Protecting the natural and cultural environment and local communities.
   7 Having a commitment to a sustainable environment, and ecologically sustainable tourism development.

What: 1 Increase the number of overseas and domestic tourists.
   2 Successful operation in a competitive market situation.
   3 Financial objectives:
     (a) increase expenditure of foreign exchange
     (b) increase expenditure of domestic tourists (at national, state and local government levels).
   4 Ensure reasonable return on marketing, infrastructure, development and other public tourism expenditure.
   5 Spread tourism receipts and expenditure benefits to the poorer regions, giving better balance with the national capital and richer regions.
   6 Extend the tourism seasons to a longer period, preferably for the whole year.
   7 Employment:
     (a) Increase the number of people employed in tourism, and not just the unskilled
     (b) Ensure reasonable wages and conditions to workers, help them to reach their full potential.
   8 Add more depth and satisfaction to the tourism experience for hosts and guests.

A COMPARATIVE APPROACH

This study takes a comparative approach, for tourism has to compete in a world which is becoming increasingly interdependent. The tourism industry could not survive without international cooperation. There are many differences between countries, such as economic, political, social and cultural differences, public sector systems and the tourism product. This study does not underrate national differences but suggests that many of the issues and problems faced by tourism managers are similar even if the political systems in which they operate are different.

Whether in developed or developing countries the tourism industry must cooperate with government. Whatever the country or type of government the basic principles apply, and policies have to be formulated and implemented. Public management is required at all levels to assist in providing the tourism product. Marketing and control mechanisms, for example, are required in all systems. Countries are at different stages of economic development and have different political and administrative systems, yet they have similar experiences and problems in tourism. These can provide useful insights and lessons and help to deepen our understanding of how governments manage tourism. Such lessons can help in improving the management of tourism, and in preparing for and meeting the challenges of the future.

Tourism is highly competitive not just between countries but also between regions, national and international, and between local governments. This requires both public and private managers to be open, aware, responsible and competitive with other countries. Managers need to develop a comparative perspective. Generalisations can be drawn which can lead to the formulation of principles and possible models for tourism management. The government of Vietnam, for example, has spoken of the possibility of using the Thai model for its tourism development. A comparative approach is helpful because tourism is found in all countries and most governments are supporting it and are involved in its management.

FIVE COUNTRIES

Many countries are referred to in this study but five countries are given greater attention. They are drawn from the three most important tourism regions in the world and are very different, but they are successful tourism countries with many similar concerns. Reflecting a variety of political, economic and PSM systems, they are all trying to manage and develop tourism and solve its problems. It is more through the similarities than the differences that the study of tourism management is of national and international relevance.

The United States is the world's biggest earner from tourism. It has a federal type of government and a non-interventionist form of tourism management especially at the federal level. Several state and city governments, however, are very active in tourism management.

Australia, a 'new' country, also has a federal system but in recent years there has been a strong commitment to tourism growth and much more active public contribution. State governments are deeply involved in the promotion of tourism.

Britain is a unitary system with power centralised in London. It is typical of the 'old' successful tourism countries which have a historical and cultural appeal. In 1995 it was fifth in the top twenty. Ten of the top twenty world earners in 1995 were in Europe and have this type of tourism product. Europe is the world's leading tourism region, with 60 per cent of all tourists and 53 per cent of revenue.

Thailand was tenth in the top twenty in 1995 and is one of the most successful tourism countries in Asia, which is one of the fastest-growing tourism regions in the world. Thailand is no longer a developing, or Third World country, but tourism is still its largest single foreign currency earner. It has a democratic unitary system with power centralised in Bangkok and a traditional bureaucracy. Tourism is based on a dynamic private sector, but there is a well-established national tourism organisation.

Vietnam is very much a developing country and tourism is seen as one answer to its economic poverty. It is a one-party Communist state but is moving rapidly into a market-based economy. Tourism is a government priority sector with dynamic autonomous public enterprises operating in the regions and large cities. Vietnam is not one of the world's top forty tourism destinations but has had one of the highest tourism growth rates in the world in the 1990s. This rapid growth, however, is bringing many of the problems experienced in the other countries but especially in Thailand.

Why: most countries in the world, both developed and developing, regard tourism and its development as important because of its contribution to their national economies through foreign exchange, investment, economic stimulation, job creation and the development of poorer regions. In a number of countries tourism is the most important single foreign currency earner. A relatively poor country such as Nepal is as eager to attract tourists as a rich country like Switzerland. Even Japan, which has a large foreign account surplus, unlike many other countries, has used tourism not to increase its foreign exchange balances but to reduce them. The Japanese government has used its tourism management agency, Japan National Tourist Organisation (JNTO), to encourage the Japanese to travel overseas as tourists. All over the world there is concern about the environment, and governments are under pressure to become involved in the management of tourism to protect the environment.

Who is involved covers several similarities, including the widespread use of the independent statutory agency as the main public management organisation, such as the Tourism Authority of Thailand (TAT) and the English Tourist Board (ETB). PSM in both developed and developing countries has to deal with tourism ranging from luxurious tourism resorts to backpackers travelling on the cheap. The 'who' of tourism includes state and local governments and interest groups.

How tourism is managed will depend upon the political culture of the country and the ideology of its government. Tourism is a universal phenomenon which is supported by countries of all political persuasions, in the developed and the developing world, ranging from the United States, France and Tunisia to China, Cuba and Vietnam. How active a government is in tourism management will depend in part upon its political ideology and the importance it attaches to tourism. This will also vary within a country. For example, American political culture has limited the federal government's intervention in tourism, but some state governments such as those of Hawaii, Florida and Alaska are very active in tourism management.

What the impact of tourism has been and the economic returns, and how well it has been managed, vary between countries. In all countries, however, it has been a source of benefit but also of controversy, forcing the local PSM to react in various ways. Many historic cities of Europe complain of too many tourists as do some resort areas of South-east Asia. The management of tourism control has become a major issue in many countries.

SUMMARY

The public sector management of tourism is based on the importance of the following:

- governments and their role in tourism
- tourism to governments
- the practice and management of tourism by governments and organisations and the issues involved

- the principles and government responsibilities on which tourism management should be based
- an international perspective for the development of tourism.

The typology of *why, who, how* and *what* is applied to the actual *practice* of management. This book accepts the position that the public sector manager should follow certain *principles* because this is what the citizens require and expect from their managers. These principles can be used to evaluate, and hold managers accountable for their performance.

Chapter 3 discusses PSM, principles and practice.

Chapter 4 discusses the practice of politics and power as used by management from the centre as they *formulate* objectives, politics and priorities.

Chapter 5 illustrates the importance of formal and informal factors for management from the centre as they try to *implement* policy.

Chapter 6 shows the importance of effective management of tourism at the *local level* using case studies.

Chapter 7 discusses the complexity and interdependence of the *public and private sector*.

Chapter 8 shows how *control and accountability* are essential if the actual practice and performance of managers are to be evaluated, destructive aspects of tourism avoided and the public interest protected.

SUGGESTED READING

Useful journals include *Annals of Tourism Research* (USA) and *Tourism Management* (Britain). There are also publications from tourist organisations such as the World Tourism Organisation, the Australian Tourist Commission, the British Tourist Authority and, in the United States, from state tourist organisations. Each country has many books on politics and public management or administration. The following titles indicate the wide range of books available on tourism.

Edgell, D.L. (1990) *International Tourism Policy*, New York: Van Nostrand Reinhold. A US perspective also covering US tourism.

McIntosh, R.W., Goldner, C.R. and Ritchie, J.R.B. (1995) 7th edn, *Tourism: Principles, Practices, Philosophies*, New York: John Wiley. A comprehensive introductory textbook on tourism.

Pearce, D. (1992) *Tourist Organizations*, Harlow, Essex: Longman.

Outline of organisations including chapters on the United States, Germany, the Netherlands, Ireland and New Zealand.

Richter, L.K. (1989) *The Politics of Tourism in Asia*, Honolulu: University of Hawaii Press. Covers countries such as China, the Philippines, Thailand, India, Pakistan and Sri Lanka.

Williams, A.M. and Shaw, G. (eds) (1991) *Tourism and Economic Development: Western European Experiences*, London: Belhaven Press. Detailed chapters on tourism development in various European countries.

2 Why tourism?

This chapter explains:

- how tourism is defined
- the historical development of tourism
- the economic importance of tourism.

DEFINITIONS

Tourism can be defined in more than one way depending upon the basis of the study, such as geography, sociology, psychology or economics. For example, it can be defined as an industry or a series of industrial sectors such as hotels, restaurants and transport all loosely grouped together which provide services for tourists. It can also be defined as an experience from the tourist's point of view, an experience of relaxation and pleasure. For the host communities it can be viewed as pleasurable and profitable, or as a troublesome nuisance. In 1937 the League of Nations defined a foreign tourist as 'any person visiting a country other than that in which he normally resides, for a period of more than 24 hours'. Definitions are useful for governments and public sector managers and for the industry, and for statistical, legislative, administrative and industrial purposes. They are important for budgetary allocations, the evaluation of public sector management (PSM) performance, for policy formulation, and for policy resource and land-use planning. Definitions and statistics are an essential PSM tool. In 1993 the following definitions were accepted by the United Nations Statistical Commission, following the advice of the World Tourism Organisation (WTO). The terms used are 'tourism', 'visitor' and 'tourist'. 'Visitor' is the term normally used in tourism statistics and that includes all types of travellers engaged in tourism.

Box 2.1 Definition of 'tourism', 'visitors' and 'tourists'

Tourism: the activities of persons travelling to and staying in places outside their usual environment for not more than one consecutive year for leisure, business, and other purposes.
  Including:

1 domestic tourism, residents of a country travelling in their own country
2 inbound tourism, non-residents visiting a country other than their own
3 outbound tourism, residents of a country visiting other countries.

Three main categories of tourism:

1 internal tourism that is domestic and inbound tourism
2 national tourism which is domestic tourism and outbound tourism
3 international tourism which is inbound and outbound tourism.

Visitors: persons who travel to a country other than that in which they usually reside but outside their usual environment for a period not exceeding twelve months and whose main purpose of visit is other than the exercise of an activity remunerated from within the place visited.
  Including:

1 same-day visitors, who do not spend the night in a collective or private accommodation in the country visited
2 *tourists*: visitors who stay in the country for at least one night.

HISTORICAL REASONS FOR GOVERNMENT INVOLVEMENT IN TOURISM

Why: early times

Historically, travel has always depended upon PSM, as can be seen clearly by the central place occupied by administrators in successful empires such as ancient China, Egypt and Rome. Governments and their managers provided the environment for law and order and security, the means of exchange, coins for money to pay for services, all essential for trade and travel. Roads, bridges and harbours were provided. Stable government allowed the development of a wealthy class who could travel for leisure, religious and health purposes. Government officials administered laws, collected taxes, protected frontiers, stopped the spread of disease and kept the lines of communication open, as officials do today. The ease with which the Christian apostle Paul could travel around the Roman Empire is a testimony to the efficiency of its administrative system.

Trade has been an important reason for travel but so also have been religious attractions, and the Greek Olympics. Great numbers of pilgrims have always travelled to such religious sites as Kyoto in Japan, Benares in India, Mecca in Saudi Arabia and Christian sites in Medieval Europe. Public management is immediately involved because of the need to maintain security of travel and law and order among such large groups of people, apart from the possibility of raising revenue.

As in modern tourism, market demand in earlier times stimulated the private sector to provide services such as accommodation, food, entertainment and transportation (though most tourists travelled on foot). Local economies were also stimulated by the demand for souvenirs and relics to take home. Modern tourists, like the pilgrims of Chaucer's *Canterbury Tales*, have a specific place to visit and wish to see as many attractions as possible.

The attraction of Jerusalem and the wish to rescue the Holy Land from the Turks led to one of the biggest examples of overseas travel – the Crusades – from the eleventh to the thirteenth centuries. Christian governments encouraged thousands of Europeans to travel in the eight military expeditions for the recovery of the Holy Land from the hands of the Turks at no small cost to the national revenues. The experience of the travellers and the knowledge and mementoes they brought back helped to enrich and open up Europe. Likewise, from the seventeenth century onwards Europe was enriched by the knowledge and objects of art brought back from the Grand Tour. This was travel undertaken to the cultural centres of Europe such as France and Italy, by the sons of the aristocracy and wealthy to complete their education. The Grand Tour took many months, and involved the employment of tutors and servants and helped poorer local economies. It stimulated further overseas travel, and the upper classes and future government leaders gained a better understanding of foreign countries. The wealthy encouraged the development of health spas and watering places. A settled government with a good administrative system allows the growth of the wealthy classes who can afford the time and money to engage in leisure activities and travel.

Why: modern times

The growth of travel and tourism relied upon a dependable system of transportation, such as appeared on the introduction of steamships and railways in the nineteenth century. Modern tourism was also helped by the growth of urbanisation, industrialisation, affluence and education, and the desire to visit attractive places in the country, by the sea and overseas. Even if steamships and railways were privately owned and managed they still had to be assisted and regulated by government. PSM was involved in the provision of docks and piers and other infrastructure, and in the regulation of ships and trains for safety as well as for a source of government revenue. National and local governments were keen to encourage trade and tourism, and public organisations such as the British Board of Trade actively helped the private sector. Public officials, however, were less active in preventing the destruction caused to the natural and historic environment by the construction of the railways and new resort towns. Public authorities were deeply involved in managing special events such as the first Great Exhibition held in the Crystal Palace in Hyde Park in London in 1851, and similar events in Vienna in 1863 and Paris in 1878 and 1889. Governments have also strongly supported events such as the modern Olympics for political reasons and because they attracted large numbers of tourists who helped the national economy. PSM involvement in tourism increased with special events such as the Festival of Britain in 1951 and Expo '88 in Brisbane, Australia, in 1988.

How: the private sector

The private sector, however, was and is still the basic sector in tourism and normally the most dynamic and responsive to market demand and the changing environment. In nineteenth-century Britain Thomas Cook was a good example of that entrepreneurial drive. He organised his first excursion train in Britain from Leicester to Loughborough in 1841, overseas to Holland, Germany and France in 1855, and the first package tour, in 1863, to Switzerland. He was a hard-working, innovative leader, able to recognise growing demands for travel and to supply what was required: enjoyable safe travel with minimum problems at a reasonable price. Cook was also a successful manager who established a world-wide, efficient organisation effective in producing the services now required. His organisation was efficient in its expertise, communication, coordination and leadership, all factors essential to bring together the many diverse elements for the successful tourism product and experience. These included security, travel tickets and hotel vouchers for a variety of destinations, including the United States, and the new destinations available with the opening of the Suez Canal in 1869. In 1871 Cook opened an office in New

York and became the leading tour operator in the 1880s and 1890s. His travellers' cheques were introduced in 1873; those of American Express in 1882. Cook's innovative tourism included a round-the-world trip for 220 guineas at about the same time as Jules Verne was arranging his Around the World in Eighty Days. External factors also helped Cook in his business, such as the growing interest in natural scenery inspired by writers such as Wordsworth on the English Lake District, and the development of travel guidebooks and, later, photography.

For Cook travel was not just an economic activity aimed at making money; it also had a social or moral dimension. He wanted to get the English working classes away from the squalor of the industrial cities into which they had flocked and from the problems of health and alcohol generated there, and enable them to enjoy the clean air of the seaside. Cook also supported the right of the rising middle and professional classes and of women to travel overseas for educational and recreational purposes.

How: public sector management

The success of Cook and others and the overall growth of tourism, however, would not have been possible without the support of governments and PSM. Governments provided the environment for security, the growth of affluence and leisure time, and the laws and financial system necessary for tourism. The infrastructure provided by the British Empire and commercial networks of public post and telegraph, the provision of roads, ports and railways, were also essential. In the United States the expansion of the railways and the introduction of dining cars, the Pullman sleeping cars, railway restaurants and hotels boosted the tourist industry. By the 1880s there were over fifty railways in Canada and the United States. The United States set the pattern for the twentieth century with the hunt for the sun and the introduction of resorts. In the 1890s the resort hotels of southern California and Florida were already very popular for winter vacations in the sun. The year 1903 saw the beginning of the Hawaii Visitors Bureau. Governments gradually accepted the responsibility for public safety and health, leading to various regulations for railways and shipping. Government intervention, however, was limited; passports, for example, were not required until the First World War. Depending upon the political culture, governments varied in their involvement with the industry in the provision of services such as railways and hotels. Some governments, as in the Australian states, provided guest houses and travel bureaus as an offshoot from the railway departments. Several governments around the world, starting with the United States in 1872, began to create national parks in areas of outstanding natural beauty. New Zealand had its Department of Tourist and Health Resorts in 1901. Several local governments in tourism areas provided amenities for tourists such as piers, concert halls, parks, picnic areas and toilets, and at the same time they provided the infrastructure of sewage, water, garbage collection and roads. Tourism, including day trips, was an important economic activity for local areas.

After the First World War, the key factor which was to dominate governments' interest in, and intervention into, tourism for the rest of the century became clear. Tourism was seen as an important provider of foreign currency and support for the nation's balance of payments. Yet in Britain, for example, the travel account was in deficit as in 1929.

Britain 1929		Expenditure (£)
Overseas tourists	692,000	22,445,000
British tourists	1,033,000	32,794,000

In Australia the number of tourists was small, testifying to the distances from Europe and the United States and the cost of travel over such long distances. The world recession also affected numbers.

Australia	*1926*	*1930*
Overseas tourists	24,759	22,186
Australian tourists	24,560	24,569

Even in this period there were those, such as the economist Ogilvie (1933), who were critical of governments and the poor quality of official statistics. Similar criticisms about statistics in Australia in the 1970s led to the establishment of the Australian Bureau of Tourism Research. In a prophetic comment about Britain, Ogilvie said: 'The nation of shopkeepers is already in large measure a nation of innkeepers but it knows little of it, because of the many defects of our official passenger statistics.'

To try and increase the number of foreign tourists to Britain the 1926 Come to Britain Movement was sponsored by the Secretary to the Department of Overseas Trade and Winston Churchill,

Chancellor of the Exchequer. In 1929 the government supported the establishment of the Travel Association of Great Britain and Ireland and gave a grant of £5,000. The importance of travel was recognised by the grant of Royal patronage to the Association. Its slogan was 'Travel for Peace', and its objectives were:

1 to increase the number of visitors to Great Britain and Ireland,
2 to stimulate demand for British goods, and
3 to promote international understanding.

However, the underlying main objective was to improve the balance of payments position.

Governments had also generally come to accept that they had some responsibility for the health of workers, not least because healthy workers were more efficient. In the United States the Fair Labor Standards Act of 1938 brought in the forty hour week. The British Amulee Report of 1938 led to the Holidays with Pay Act, providing a two-week holiday with pay for workers. Holidays helped workers to be more healthy and efficient. The two-week annual holiday came into effect after the Second World War and proved a great boost for tourism.

How: post-Second World War

After the war, in the United States there was a tremendous growth in tourism, which required federal government intervention. The pressure on outdoor recreation areas required action by the US Forest Service and the National Parks Service and the establishment of the Outdoor Recreation Resources Review Commission in 1958. Increasing growth in car and air travel, especially with the arrival of jumbo jets, led to further government regulation and federal funds being made available for highways and the establishment of government corporations such as Amtrack to keep some railroads in operation. State governments in states with a large tourism industry became more active.

The British government after the war, unlike the US government, was particularly concerned to boost foreign tourists, especially from the United States, in order to gain US dollars. The Travel Association stated: 'There is also an increasing awareness on the part of all sections of the community of the importance of the tourist industry as a factor in national and European recovery.' As a part of the Association in 1947 a British Tourism and Holiday Board was established, with most of its budget coming from public funds. In the same year the White Paper on Britain's Four Year Plan made specific mention of tourism's importance for the country's economic future. The US Marshall Plan to help Europe after the war envisaged tourism being a dominant factor in economic progress, and this was given specific mention in American legislation on the subject. The government tried to improve the position of the foreign tourist in Britain, and in 1949, for example, established an Inter-departmental Working Committee of the Civil Service to upgrade reception facilities. In 1953, while sweet rationing continued in Britain, arrangements were made for confectionery to be sold off the ration in the departure lounges of international airports. Under the Conservative government rationing ended in 1954, by which time Britain had a £2 million surplus balance on tourism plus the income from British carriers, adding a welcome £3 million to the balance of payments. The US dollar was the most important segment of the balance. Yet the tourism industry was outspoken about the problems caused by government controls over the industry which did not allow them to compete on a more equal basis. In the 1980s similar criticisms were made of government in Australia about the lack of a 'level playing field' for tourism. British tourism had, however, made a remarkable recovery after the war, and by 1948 was 2.5 per cent above the peak of 1937. Even in 1946 there were 200,000 visitors, in 1960 it was the fourth largest export earner, and in 1962 with 2 million visitors, the largest single US dollar earner. There was some criticism, as for example in 1957 when a tourist advertisement was criticised as putting Britain forward as an 'old curiosity shop', yet it was the history and culture which helped to attract the American tourists. The tourism balance, however, moved into deficit with so many British people travelling overseas, and the government in 1966 imposed a £60 limit on the travel allowance which the British tourist could spend overseas.

What: control and impact

PSM was not only involved in the financial aspects of tourism but also in control and regulation of the motor vehicles and airlines which have revolutionised travel in recent decades. Most major governments were directly involved in the airline business through government ownership of national airlines such as BOAC in Britain and Qantas in Australia. Private interests and the national political culture in the United States discouraged government ownership of airlines but allowed government regulation. The development of

charter flights, cheap package tours and the jet airliner brought overseas travel to the masses but was devastating to domestic tourism
and local government, especially in the seaside towns. Sea travel also
suffered, and by 1957 passengers travelling by air over the Atlantic
outnumbered those travelling by sea.

Spain in particular became the destination of mass tourism, with 50
million visitors per year, 1½ times its population. Northern Europeans
looking for sea, sand and sun on cheap package tours transformed
southern Spain into one of the biggest tourism regions in Europe.
Tourism growth was strongly supported by the Spanish government,
which provided the infrastructure and allowed massive private development. The government sought foreign currency but also political
acceptability after its support of the Fascist powers during the war.
Public authorities responded readily to the developers and economic
forces, and the gains in foreign currency and employment were
considerable. There was, however, little sense of public responsibility
for the protection of natural resources, so financial gains were at the
cost of extensive destruction of the natural environment and damage
to the communities of the tourism regions.

Thailand from the 1970s was to undergo the same experience with
the same kind of government policy and PSM behaviour. Switzerland,
on the other hand, one of the oldest and most successful tourism
countries in the world, has been able to retain its natural beauty and
life style partly because conservative governments at both federal
and local level controlled and limited tourism development.

Why: responsibility

Historically, PSM has been involved in travel and tourism from
the earliest times for normative and empirical reasons. Obviously
there have been many changes over time in the nature of travel and
tourism, not least in political culture and technological innovation,
but management still has the same basic responsibilities. It accepts
the responsibility in the public interest of providing control management of tourism to ensure public safety. One of the first objectives
of governments has always been to raise revenue. This has been used
partly for the provision of infrastructure or government services
and subsidies. Good governments and PSM have always striven to
protect the public interest, to serve the public efficiently and effectively, and to maintain control of both the public and private sectors
of tourism.

ECONOMIC REASONS FOR GOVERNMENT INVOLVEMENT IN TOURISM

Governments became involved in tourism historically, and are still involved in the management of tourism today, mainly for economic reasons. This is true of governments at all levels: they all expect their economies to benefit from tourism. Tourism is seen as a major industry and a boost to the economy generally, partly through the results or 'flow on' of the multiplier effect. In the United Kingdom, 'The Government fully recognised the great economic and employment contribution and potential of tourism and seek to encourage the development, growth, and international competitiveness of the UK tourism industry' (UK House of Commons 1985/86, HC 106).

Internationally tourism is now one of the largest industries in the world and one of the fastest growing. According to the WTO, tourism receipts in 1993 constituted a higher proportion of the world exports than all other sectors, other than crude petroleum/petroleum products and motor vehicles and related parts. International tourism receipts have been growing faster than world trade. In 1950 they were worth US\$ 2.1 billion and in 1995 US\$ 372 billion, and in the same period, 1950–95, tourist arrivals rose from 25 million to 567 million (see Figure 2.1). Tourism receipts are more important than tourism arrivals, and countries can be in contrasting positions: in 1995 Australia ranked thirty-second in terms of arrivals but fifteenth in receipts, while Hungary was seventh in arrivals but only fortieth in receipts.

National governments in particular are trying to increase international tourism in order to boost the national economy and to improve their foreign exchange position. Tourism economic activity is seen as having a multiplier effect by helping other sectors of the economy. Many countries have foreign exchange deficits, and inbound tourism expenditure helps to rectify the deficit. Japan, on the other hand, is in the unusual position of being criticised for large foreign exchange surpluses and so is encouraging outbound tourism to cut the surplus. Countries can also have deficits on their tourism account where their nationals are spending more overseas than foreign tourists are bringing into the country, as in the United Kingdom in 1995 (see Table 2.1). This tourism deficit makes a foreign exchange deficit worse.

For some countries tourism is the single most important foreign currency earner, as in Thailand where tourism replaced rice exports in 1983 as the number one earner. Tourism was the industry which

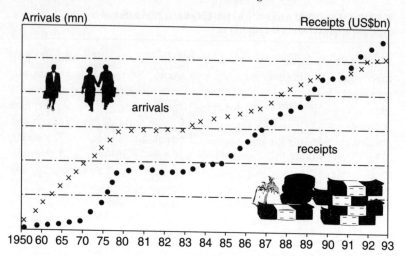

Figure 2.1 Development of international tourism arrivals and receipts world-wide, 1950–93

helped Spain to solve its economic problems after the Second World War. In Australia, it represents about 12.6 per cent of export earnings, exceeding all other industries except metal ores and minerals. It constitutes 11 per cent of the Australian GDP annually and employs 6.6 per cent of the workforce (*Insight* 1996). Britain, for example, in 1992 had a record number of tourists. Despite the recession and expensive pound, 18.5 million visitors spent £7.9 billion (US$12.18 billion) up from 17.1 million visitors spending £7.4 billion (US$11.41 billion) in 1991. In Britain, tourism makes up almost one-third of the service export earnings and is a considerably larger industry than manufacturing sectors, such as food, motor vehicles and aerospace.

The United States is the tourism country with the largest foreign currency earnings, in 1992 of US$53,861 million, with an average growth rate between 1985 and 1992 of 12.09 per cent. In 1981, for the first time it achieved a surplus on its foreign travel account with more being spent in the United States due to a fall in the value of the dollar. One of the main objectives of the US government is to achieve and maintain such a surplus, which it started to do again in 1989. Travel and tourism in 1992 generated more than US$51 billion in federal, state and local taxes. In 1994/95, however, the United States was one of the few countries to record a drop in tourism receipts of 3.4 per cent (see Table 2.2).

Unlike many industries, tourism is a growth industry, which also makes it attractive to governments. Traditional industries in the

Table 2.1 The world's top 40 tourism spenders: international tourism expenditure (excluding transport)

Rank		Country	Expenditure (m US$) 1995	% change 1995/94	% of total 1995
1985	1995				
2	1	Germany	47,304	9.0	14.7
1	2	United States	44,825	2.9	13.9
4	3	Japan	36,737	19.6	11.4
3	4	United Kingdom	24,625	11.0	7.6
5	5	France	16,038	15.6	5.0
10	6	Italy	12,366	1.5	3.8
7	7	Netherlands	11,050	0.6	3.4
8	8	Austria	9,500	1.8	2.9
6	9	Canada	9,484	–18.8	2.9
17	10	Taiwan (prov. of China)	8,596	9.0	2.7
12	11	Belgium	7,995	2.7	2.5
9	12	Switzerland	6,543	3.4	2.0
25	13	Korea Rep.	5,919	44.8	1.8
14	14	Sweden	5,109	4.7	1.6
11	15	Mexico	4,950	–7.7	1.5
21	16	Spain	4,750	13.4	1.5
15	17	Australia	4,574	5.4	1.4
16	18	Norway	4,185	6.5	1.3
24	19	Singapore	4,113	12.2	1.3
18	20	Denmark	3,778	5.4	1.2
39	21	China	3,483	14.7	1.1
42	22	Thailand	3,403	17.1	1.1
20	23	Brazil	3,120	5.9	1.0
28	24	Israel	3,118	7.7	1.0
23	25	Argentina	2,538	1.5	0.8
13	26	Kuwait	2,250	4.8	0.7
27	27	Indonesia	2,198	15.7	0.7
44	28	Portugal	1,819	6.7	0.6
22	28	Finland	1,819	5.3	0.6
19	29	Malaysia	1,791	3.1	0.6
32	30	South Africa	1,749	4.2	0.5
30	31	Ireland	1,613	2.4	0.5
26	32	Venezuela	1,518	6.2	0.5
36	33	Greece	1,187	5.5	0.4
35	34	New Zealand	1,185	7.6	0.4
58	35	Egypt	1,120	5.0	0.3
54	36	Hungary	965	4.3	0.3
38	37	Turkey	904	4.4	0.3
41[1]	38	Czech Republic	864	3.8	0.3
33	39	Puerto Rico	814	2.1	0.3
50	40	Colombia	793	4.9	0.2
Total 1–40		**310,691**	7.3	96.4	
World total		**322,228**	6.7	100.0	

Source: World Tourism Organisation (WTO), 1996
Note: 1 Former Czechoslovakia

Table 2.2 The world's top 40 tourism earners: international tourism receipts (international transport excluded), 1994/95

Rank 1985	1995	Country	Receipts (m US$) 1995	% change 1995/94	% of total 1995
1	1	United States	58,370	−3.4	15.7
4	2	France	27,322	6.6	7.3
2	3	Italy	27,072	13.1	7.3
3	4	Spain	25,065	14.7	6.7
5	5	United Kingdom	17,468	15.1	4.7
6	6	Austria	12,500	−5.0	3.4
7	7	Germany	11,922	7.5	3.2
12	8	Hong Kong	9,075	9.1	2.4
31	9	China	8,733	19.3	2.3
22	10	Thailand	7,556	31.1	2.0
16	11	Singapore	7,550	6.8	2.0
8	12	Switzerland	7,250	−4.2	1.9
9	13	Canada	7,048	11.7	1.9
74	14	Poland	7,000	13.8	1.9
25	15	Australia	6,875	15.4	1.8
10	16	Mexico	6,070	−3.9	1.6
15	17	Netherlands	6,050	7.8	1.6
34	18	Korea Rep	5,579	46.6	1.5
14	19	Belgium	5,250	1.3	1.4
42	20	Indonesia	5,233	9.4	1.4
18	21	Turkey	5,021	16.2	1.3
23	22	Portugal	4,500	10.1	1.2
27	23	Argentina	4,306	8.5	1.2
19	24	Greece	4,150	6.3	1.1
37	25	Malaysia	3,500	9.8	0.9
32	25	Taiwan (prov. of China)	3,500	9.0	0.9
20	26	Denmark	3,350	5.5	0.9
23	27	Japan	3,250	−6.5	0.9
21	28	Sweden	2,930	3.7	0.8
30	29	India	2,754	21.6	0.7
33	30	Egypt	2,700	95.1	0.7
24	31	Israel	2,554	12.7	0.7
-	32	Macau	2,500	−7.0	0.7
55[1]	33	Czech Republic	2,497	27.0	0.7
36	34	Norway	2,385	10.6	0.6
29	35	Philippines	2,340	2.5	0.6
50	36	Cyprus	1,850	8.8	0.5
35	37	Puerto Rico	1,824	5.0	0.5
41	38	Ireland	1,800	2.0	0.5
45	39	South Africa	1,595	12.0	0.4
57	40	Hungary	1,575	10.3	0.4
		Total 1–40	**329,869**	**7.6**	**88.5**
		World total	**372,585**	**7.5**	**100.0**

Source: World Tourism Organisation (WTO)
Note: 1 Former Czechoslovakia

developed countries, such as iron and steel, coal, textiles, engineering and motor vehicles, have declined, and in other countries the financial return from basic commodity production, minerals, and agriculture have dropped. Tourism, however, is still growing and expanding especially in the booming economies of South-east Asia.

Table 2.3 International departures, Asia

	Millions 1993 (1st half)	*Change from 1992%*	*As percentage of total population*	
			(1991)	*(1992)*
South Korea	1.1	10.3	4.3	4.7
Singapore	1.0	16.3	45.6	68.9
Taiwan	2.3	12.5	16.7	20.8
Thailand	0.72	25.2	1.8	2.2
Hong Kong	1.2	16.3	35.3	38.4
Japan	5.5	5.4	8.6	9.6

The small proportion of the population who travel to foreign countries in the new, increasingly affluent countries gives some indication of the potential growth of the market. Market demand has also grown with the relative decline in the cost of international tourism, with the development of wide-body jet airliners and a greater range of package tours. The supply of tourism products has also increased, with distant destinations and a more diverse range of holidays available. Governments – for example, in the Far East and the Pacific islands – are now eager and in a position to attract an increasing number of European tourists. Continually increasing competition from overseas markets is a challenge to national and local governments and the industry to try and improve the domestic tourism product.

Domestic tourism

International tourism is the glamour side of the industry but in fact domestic tourism provides most of the revenue. In the United States, for example, it is about 90 per cent and is particularly strong in states such as Hawaii, Florida and Nevada. Tourism is the third largest retail industry in the United States and one of the top three sources of revenue in forty-six states. Direct revenue from tourism is important for the economies of US state and local governments, such as bed and sale taxes, individual and corporate income taxes, alcohol and entertainment taxes and fees for camping, parks, highways and other services. In Britain in 1990, of the £25 billion spent on tourism, £10.5 billion was from domestic tourists and £5.2 billion from day trippers. This expenditure can be a big boost for local economies, and while towns and cities have attracted 53 per cent of domestic trips, they have only gained 45 per cent of domestic tourism spending. Therefore, there is competition among local governments to attract tourists to their areas. Domestic tourism is also important in Australia: in 1991–92 it amounted to A$18.14 billion of the total tourism expenditure of A$26.6 billion.

Employment

Governments and PSM see tourism as one of the main providers of employment especially in times of recession and when other industries are declining. Tourism is a labour-intensive growth industry and is important in providing jobs partly for the highly skilled but more for the less skilled. In the poorer regions of a country the provision of jobs by tourism can be very significant. The rate of unemployment is a central political consideration and can affect the popularity and electoral chances of governments.

This was recognised in 1985 by the British Thatcher government, which reorganised the political and public sector management of tourism by moving one of its most important ministers and the management of tourism from the Department of Trade and Industry to the Department of Employment. Nearly 1.5 million people were working in industries directly related to UK tourism in 1990, about 7 per cent of all employment. Between 1980 and 1990 employment grew 26 per cent. In Australia in 1996, tourism provided 500,000 to 600,000 jobs, with more new tourism-related jobs being added each year. By the year 2002, travel and tourism is expected to surpass health care to become the largest employer in the United States. In all countries governments have seen tourism as important not only for boosting the number of jobs but also boosting the economics of the poorer regions and helping to redress regional imbalances.

Investment

Another reason for government support of tourism is that it can attract investment, both domestic and foreign, which will stimulate the economy. Foreign investment is particularly important to developing countries but also in other countries where domestic investors are reluctant to invest in tourism. Foreign investment can speed up development, raise standards in the industry, bring in new ideas, technology, contacts and markets. Unlike other investments it stays in the country, hotels cannot be removed like primary and other production. Foreign tourism investment in Australia is second only to real estate investment. In the period 1985–89 foreign tourism investment approved totalled A$9,521 billion. In the three years to 1992 Japanese investment accounted for about 70 per cent of approvals. The Japanese are large tourism investors in other areas such as Hawaii.

There are also criticisms of the economic and other effects of tourism development and foreign investment in the industry, and the lack of government and administrative control and clear policy. It is suggested that in tourism economic benefits only go to a few, while the taxpayer is subsidising tourism through the provision of infrastructure such as roads, sewage disposal, water supplies and airports. The cost of land, labour and commodities can be pushed up for the local people while profits can leave the area and the country. Foreigners can be seen as dominating or controlling local resources and the industry, while catering mainly to foreign nationals and importing foreign labour and goods. It is possible that foreigners have access to cheap capital and so are able to outbid any local investor. This is one reason why governments are trying to measure the costs and benefits of tourism more carefully and also to control and monitor foreign investment through organisations such as the Australian government's Foreign Investment Review Board.

SUMMARY

There is now an international definition of tourism defined through the World Tourism Organisation which is useful for PSM. Tourism can only be fully understood by means of a knowledge of its historical and economic background. Many factors influential in the past still have influence today. Historically governments have become involved in managing visitors or tourism since early times. Government intervention then and now was motivated by the desire to raise revenue and to meet their public responsibilities in areas such as safety and health. The acceptance of tourism as being important economically has led to the provision of government grants to help the private sector in marketing but has also brought about more public management involvement. Private sector initiative has been an essential factor in the growth of tourism.

Tourism has grown rapidly in economic importance, especially since the Second World War, and this has been gradually recognised by governments. More recently tourism has been recognised as making a significant contribution to employment, investment and regional development and as a stimulant to the general economy.

How governments have managed the historic and economic development is discussed in the following chapters, but first, in Chapter 3, there is a discussion of PSM.

SUGGESTED READING

Ball, A. (1991) *The Economics of Travel and Tourism*, Melbourne: Longman Cheshire.

Burkart, A.J. and Medlik, S. (1981) 2nd edn, *Tourism: Past, Present and Future*, London: Heinemann. Includes a useful historical section.

Holloway, J. (1994) 4th edn, *The Business of Tourism*, London: Pitman. Chapters on history, economics, the industry and public sector tourism.

Mathieson, A.R. and Wall, G. (1982) *Tourism: Economic, Physical and Social Impacts*, London: Longman.

Swinglehurst, E. (1982) *Cook's Tours: The Story of Popular Travel*, Dorset, England: Blandford Press. Illustrated history of this famous tourist company.

Turner, L. and Ash, J. (1976) *The Golden Hordes: International Tourism and the Pleasure Periphery*, New York: St Martin's Press. Very readable, wide-ranging, with good historical coverage.

Towner, J. (1994) *A Historical Geography of Recreation and Tourism*, London: Belhaven Press.

3 Public sector management and tourism

This chapter explains:

- what is the public sector and its environment
- the principles of public sector management (PSM)
- the Weberian ideal type of bureaucracy
- the factors important for the PSM of tourism
- what happens in practice and recent changes.

The term 'public sector' covers the whole range of public organisations from national government ministries and departments to government business enterprises and local government tourism departments. Just as tourism is an extremely diverse and complex industry so also is the public sector, with its wide range of organisations of tremendous variety, linked together in complex structures and relationships. In this study PSM is taken as being similar to the more traditional term 'public administration', and is applied to the management or administration of the whole of the public sector, national, state and local. There are various definitions which can be given to these two terms and to the term 'bureaucracy'. New meanings are always being added as different aspects of management are stressed. The definitions, however, are all concerned with the functioning of the public sector with its responsibility to serve the public interest and as it works to achieve public objectives (Dunsire 1973; Hughes 1994; Wilson 1989).

Public management is taken in the widest context as it has to manage tourism which is an industry and activity of tremendous diversity. Public servants or civil servants are the officials serving governments directly; officials of statutory agencies such as national tourism boards are not civil servants but are public officers employed by an organisation in the public sector. Either group can have tourism responsibilities but both are taken as part of PSM. Whether public management takes a more traditional administrative approach to tourism or a managerial approach will often depend upon power and political factors in the system and current managerial trends. As McIntosh *et al.* state:

> The managerial approach is firm oriented (microeconomic), focusing on the management activities necessary to operate a tourist enterprise, such as planning, research, pricing, advertising, control, and the like. . . . Products change, institutions change, society changes; this means that managerial objectives and procedures must be geared to change to meet shifts in the tourism environment.
>
> (1995: 17)

This study, however, takes a wider view of PSM responsibilities and activities. Managers will try to achieve tourism objectives and will change to meet the demands of the market, but they will go beyond the market to serve the society as a whole and follow public sector principles. Figure 3.1 illustrates the complexity of the management of tourism. Managers must manage within the political and industrial environment with its power relationships and formal and informal factors.

WHY: POLITICAL ENVIRONMENT AND PRINCIPLES

Environment

Governments are the legitimate holders of power in the political system and are responsible for making policy and establishing policy guidelines. PSM must operate within the constitutional, legal and political environment established by governments.

First, 'Government refers to the institutions and processes whereby societies make and enforce decisions which are binding upon their members' (Stewart and Ward 1996: 2).

PSM is responsible for managing organisations to achieve government objectives, and is also involved in formulating and implementing public policy.

Public policy is, second 'A purposive course of action followed by an actor or set of actors in dealing with a problem or matter of concern' (Anderson 1984: 3).

Management must operate within a political system whether at the international, national or local government level. Decisions about tourism are taken in the context of a political system. A political

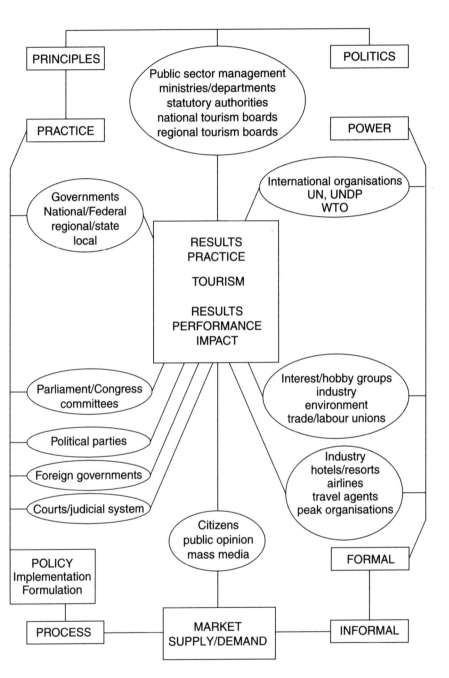

Figure 3.1 Tourism: the political, administrative and industrial environment

system can be liberal, democratic or totalitarian, it can be left or right politically, but in practice all types of regimes have supported or sponsored tourism. The dominant ideological and philosophical beliefs and values of the political system will determine how far governments will intervene in the economic system, what will be the role of the private sector, and how much support and finance will be given to tourism.

Third, 'A political system is any persistent pattern of human relationships that involves, to a significant extent, power, rule or authority' (Dahl 1970: 6).

The politicians in a political system desire power and this can make their input dynamic but also irrational and impermanent, for in any situation they will usually act to retain or acquire power. In contrast, management ideally is rational, permanent, formal and efficient. However, in practice politics operates within management and organisations leading to power struggles just as there are among politicians. The power holders in any political or administrative system are important because, fourth; 'Power is the capacity to overcome resistance, the capacity to change the behaviour of others and stop them from getting what they want. It determines who gets what, when, and how' (Lasswell 1951: 287).

PSM is in a position to have that kind of power in tourism, to determine who gets, what, when and how.

Principles

PSM is involved in the political system and society because there are certain general principles which should be followed and governments are responsible for implementing them. These are *normative* principles, which ideally should be followed but are sometimes departed from in practice. How closely the principles are followed and how they are interpreted will vary according to the national political culture and the government of the day. They are interrelated and in practice they can sometimes even contradict one another, but success in dealing with contradictions is one test of the good manager. The implementation and enforcement of principles and the protection of the moral basis of the state is ultimately the responsibility of government and public managers. For this study five general principles are applied.

The *public interest*, or public good, is one main principle. It is a basic responsibility of public sector managers to manage for public interest and not for any private or particular political or business interest.

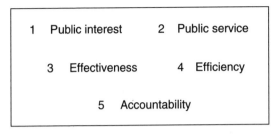

Figure 3.2 Five general principles

They must strive to attain the goals of their organisation but do so within the ideals of the political and administrative system and in terms of democracy, openness and equity. PSM goals involve ethical goals related to a concern for the community. Public needs and demands should always be met first, before private demands. Private sector managers, on the other hand, respond to the demands, and strive to achieve the objectives, of their private organisations. Managers of private companies in the tourism industry are required to look after the interests of their company and none other. Public sector managers have a much wider responsibility to the whole society and not just to their organisation or tourism sector. The formal processes, regulations and systems of accountability which are found in the public sector are there to ensure that the behaviour of public managers is in the public interest and that they do not abuse the trust and considerable power which has been given to them.

It is not always easy to know exactly what is the public interest, or what section of the public should get priority. PSM, however, operates within the context of legislation, government policy statements and objectives, and accepted international and national values. There are standards which should be followed of truth, integrity, impartiality and correct procedures and there is the rule of law and the due process of law. Following the public interest could involve managers in a very open policy-making system with people being consulted and encouraged to participate in policy areas such as tourism development.

PSM may support the development of a tourism resort by private developers but the first duty is to act for the public and in the public interest at both the national and local levels. Supporting the development of the resort may be quite compatible with the public interest economically but managers should take into account the non-economic costs as well. The ideal situation is when the public and private sector are working together in partnership and serving both the public and private interest. Within the political and administrative system care needs to be taken that sectional or departmental interests do not replace the public or national interest.

The second general principle – that of *public service* – is related to the principle of the public interest but it is more specific and directed. It requires management to take positive action to meet the needs of the society and to provide the necessary public service. This principle suggests that the basic role of managers should be service to the people and this should be the basis for their management of tourism. Service is about managing organisations, achieving public objectives and applying rules for the benefit of the public. PSM has a responsibility not just for achieving economic objectives and responding to market demands but also for social objectives, social justice and equity. In the United States, Wilson (1989: 132) points out that 'equity is more important than efficiency in the management of many government agencies'. He also discusses the multiplicity of constraints on public agencies as they strive to meet public service objectives. The private sector has the narrower basic objectives of increasing profits and the return on investment. If there is a commitment to public service, there will be as much attention given to the fair distribution of wealth as to the creation of wealth by groups or individuals. A different value system is applicable to PSM which places constraints upon its behaviour. It should always support the social good and act against unfair exploitation. Power is given to managers to be used in the service of the people, such as protecting those least able to protect themselves; for example, an aboriginal community threatened by tourism development. Managers obviously work for a salary package, but at the management level of the public sector they at least should also be motivated by service to the community. Tourism is market driven for economic gain but the public interest demands that PSM should also be service driven. Managers should act positively to curb an unbridled free market so that public resources are not squandered, or public squalor created for the many by the excesses of the few. All principles have to be interpreted in practice by governments and PSM in the context of the national political and administrative culture. How much or how little management does in the area of public service will depend upon the political ideology and values of those with power and will be influenced by interests, debate and controversy in the society and policy community.

Third *effectiveness* is taken as the achievement of the goals and objectives of the organisation. This is the prime responsibility of PSM and a test of their effectiveness. If objectives are not achieved, the competence and value of the manager or organisation must be in doubt unless the objectives set were unrealistic or unattainable. The most effective policy is one which achieves all its objectives. Managers must ensure that they do not lose sight of their formal objectives and that they are not replaced by informal private objectives. They should also take care that the actual task of managing the organisation does not displace the effective achievement of organisational objectives. Tourism is so important economically that it requires effective PSM, but also because it is so potentially destructive.

Efficiency is the gaining of the best possible value from the expenditure of public money. Efficiency is 'the extent to which maximum output is achieved in relation to given costs or inputs, and effectiveness is used to refer to the extent to which overall goals are achieved' (Chapman 1988: 60). Like any private sector manager, the public sector manager has a responsibility to be efficient; there must be a commitment to obtaining the maximum results at the lowest possible costs. Too often the public sector is accused of wasting public money. It is the responsibility of PSM to be efficient and to ensure that there is no basis for these accusations. Managers must be efficient in directing and controlling their organisation, resources, finance and personnel.

The fifth general principle, that of *accountability*, is one of the strongest principles to operate in the public sector and enforces the four principles already mentioned; it covers the public responsibilities of PSM, including behaviour, performance and finance.

> Accountability is the fundamental prerequisite for preventing the abuse of delegated power and for ensuring instead that power is directed toward the achievement of broadly accepted national goals with the greatest possible degree of efficiency, effectiveness, probity and prudence.
>
> (Canada 1979: 21)

Within the concept of accountability are the functions of control, monitoring, answerability and evaluation, where ministers and those responsible are expected to answer for their activities to the public and to the elected representative body. Management is responsible for its activities to a range of bodies, including the departmental minister, the government, Parliament, the public, the media and various accounting and control mechanisms within the public sector, such as the auditor-general. Traditionally it is the minister or government which must answer to the Parliament or people for the behaviour of

PSM, but there is also the direct accountability of managers. This accountability can operate through a hierarchical system in which the manager is responsible to the manager above, as in the Weberian bureaucratic system.

In their respective countries managers must follow the constitution, the laws of the land and the government of the day. The loyalty required here is not always clear cut and there can be conflicts, but in a liberal democratic system the manager is expected to follow the laws and conventions which protect the public interest. Ideally there should be no conflict between the wishes of the government of the day and the public interest and so no conflict for public sector managers.

WHO: MULTIPLICITY AND DIVERSITY

A whole range of public organisations directly and indirectly are involved in tourism management and they are found at all levels of government, national, state, regional and local. Parliaments and courts can be included as public organisations, but public sector managers are normally responsible either for government departments headed by ministers or for agencies responsible to ministers. There is also a multiplicity of other organisations, such as statutory authorities headed by appointed boards and managed by full-time executives. There can be regulatory and marketing boards, and government business enterprises. In tourism it is common to find a public statutory board managing the tourism industry and marketing tourism on behalf of governments. Some government enterprises can take the company form, such as a national government-owned airline. At the local government level a local concert hall or park can be managed by a department or an official of the local council. Thus a multiplicity of organisations related to tourism are managed by public sector managers on behalf of governments, parliaments and the people and also on behalf of the tourism industry. In Britain, a good example of this multiplicity, which has increased in recent years, is given in the following memorandum:

> Tourism covers a wide variety of economic activities, mainly in the services sector. The Secretary of State for Trade and Industry has sponsorship responsibility for only some of these activities – essentially hotels and residential catering, privately owned tourist attractions and travel agents, although some other sectors for which he has sponsorship responsibility, a good example being the

non food retail trade, benefit from tourism. Other Departments directly concerned are the Department of the Environment (planning and land use, local government, inner cities, environmental protection, sport and recreation, historic buildings and ancient monuments), Department of Transport (aviation, shipping, roads, railways, signposting), Office of Arts and Libraries (museums, galleries). Department of Education and Science and Department of Employment (education and training for tourism occupations) and the Ministry of Agriculture, Fisheries and Food (pubs, restaurants, food retailing, and advice on developing farm tourism). The regulatory activities of the Home Office (liquor licensing, shop hours, fire regulations) also impinge directly on the tourism industry, as do fiscal policies (the Treasury) and matters within the control of local authorities such as parking, litter and the provision, management and control of tourist attractions, including camping sites, piers, museums, art galleries and historic buildings.

(UK, Commons 1985, HC 106, Memorandum
from Department of Trade and Industry)

HOW: FORMAL, INFORMAL AND CHANGES

The Weberian ideal type

Max Weber, one of the most famous writers on bureaucracy, put forward an ideal type of management based on a legitimate legal authority system, aspects of which are still found in most modern PSM systems. He believed that this ideal – a rational form of administration – was inevitable and would produce continuity, precision, discipline, strictness and reliability. The bureaucracy could be used by elected representatives in the public interest and for the public good.

These characteristics are still important for obtaining effective and efficient PSM. Management functions are continuous and there is a continuity in management and managers which is not found among politicians. There are specific tasks to perform and managers have the authority to perform them within set rules. The work requires training and skill. Offices are organised on a hierarchical basis with each official being responsible to a more senior manager within the organisation. Managers should not use their position or the resources of the organisation for their own personal benefit. PSM is very much based on written documents because of its public nature and system of accountability. The bureaucratic system is considered to be more

Box 3.1 The Weberian ideal type: characteristics or principles

1 The staff members are personally free, observing only the impersonal duties of their offices.
2 There is a clear hierarchy of offices.
3 The functions of the offices are clearly specified.
4 Officials are appointed on the basis of a contract.
5 They are selected on the basis of a professional qualification, ideally substantiated by a diploma gained through examination.
6 They have a money salary, and usually pension rights. The salary is graded according to position in the hierarchy. The official can always leave the post, and under certain circumstances it may also be terminated.
7 The official's post is his sole or major occupation.
8 There is a career structure, and promotion is possible either by seniority or merit, and according to the judgement of superiors.
9 The official may appropriate neither the post nor the resources which go with it.
10 He is subject to a unified control and disciplinary system.

(Albrow 1970: 44)

efficient because of these characteristics and the rationality and consistency which they impart to the organisation. There are weaknesses in the Weberian type of bureaucracy, such as its rigidity, stress on regulations and its neglect of informal factors which can be damaging to the tourist industry. Weber was also concerned about how to control the power of the bureaucracy. The system is still a useful normative tool to help analyse the management of tourism.

Politics, controls and informal factors

In practice PSM can operate very differently from the Weberian ideal type. Rational behaviour and the following of principles is not always the norm and both public and tourist interests can suffer. Normative principles are there to guide and control the behaviour of PSM, but there are other factors which can be more influential. These factors may rarely or never be found in the operation of private sector management.

Politics

One of the biggest differences between the public and private sector is the *political environment* in which PSM must operate. Managers, because they are public officials, are ultimately responsible to and dependent upon ministers for their legitimacy. The objectives and policy which managers must manage are established by governments and ministers but these are not always clear and can be contradictory. Political considerations can take precedence over rational policy and consistency. Caiden (1991: 30) puts it more strongly: 'In the public sector, political values have always overridden managerial values.' Long-term management objectives in practice can be displaced for short-term political advantage, but managers should always follow the legitimate political leaders and the requirements of the democratic system. The system, however, could allow for PSM objections to political corruption or abuses through whistle-blower legislation. Managers are expected to be anonymous and to take a back seat in the public arena compared with the public exposure of the minister and political leader. There are also the politics of public organisation in which managers engage in power struggles to 'determine who gets what, when and how' (Lasswell 1951: 287).

Controls

Controls and constraints are imposed by the public interest and community considerations and the public expectation that certain principles will be followed. For example, managers are expected to support social justice and equity principles as well as to follow legal and official formal rules and regulations. Procedures and long-drawn-out processes also act as a control device, and can conflict with social justice considerations and with market demand. The controls and constraints operating on PSM are much stronger and wider than those operating on private managers. Managers must operate within a process and environment which emphasises accountability, there is more scrutiny and answerability to various bodies, including Parliament. Their freedom to manoeuvre is much less than that of the private sector because of this control system. There is less freedom to manage finance and personnel and to make decisions. Outside bodies place more constraints on public managers. Budgetary and personnel quotas can be rigid compared to the private sector. Managers must be aware of public opinion, the media and interest groups and if necessary amend their behaviour. In the development of a tourism resort PSM principles may require the fullest possible participation of the local people in the policy-making process, even if this is not conducive to efficiency and effectiveness.

Informal factors

Managers should never forget the power of informal factors which can be used to assist or hinder the work of any organisation, or political or policy system. Factors can include individual or organisational self-interest as opposed to the public interest, morale, group loyalty, ambition, the survival instinct, empire building and secrecy. These make the task of managers and the achievement of objectives more difficult and can lead to internal conflict and displacement of goals. In practice, managers can displace the formal tourism goals with their informal personal goals of building up their own power. The pressure on managers, or the corporate culture of the organisation, can encourage managers to neglect formal objectives, to spend too much time on managing the organisation and too little time on achieving the formal objectives of the organisation. An inordinate amount of time can be spent on people management and defending departmental interests. It may be a formal requirement that swift decisions are given to tourism requests but the amount of time spent on paper work, meetings, formal procedures and informal consultation can make decision making very slow. To achieve effective management of the tourist industry, public managers cannot rely entirely upon formal factors but must also utilise the informal factors.

Changes

PSM is always subject to change, and in recent years has been going through considerable changes with the introduction of what has been called 'managerialism'. This has seen the introduction of many elements from the private sector in the belief that this would make the public sector more efficient. Cost cutting has been the main objective, but there is also a new emphasis on efficiency and effectiveness. Greater freedom has been given to managers and they have been given contracts or positions based upon their work performance. The idea has been to try and manage public agencies as much as possible like private organisations responding to the market and with the introduction of the user pay principle. Public tourism marketing agencies were expected to charge for their services. Organisations were expected to pay their way and operate commercially, by making profits, responding to competition and achieving measurable targets. Whenever it has been possible public sector organisations, or some of their activities, have been privatised, so leaving a much smaller traditional public sector. Government airlines and hotels, for example, have been privatised. There has been considerable deregulation. The changes envisaged that government tourism ministries or divisions would concentrate on policy formulation, while implementation and marketing would be left to the private sector and local government. Much of the push for managerialism has come from right-wing politicians, but it has also been taken up by many of socialist persuasions as a stimulus to better economic performance and a less costly public sector. It is an international trend, and aims to make use of modern management techniques. Tourism and PSM are not divorced from political and management trends or fashions.

Box 3.2 provides a guide to the practice of public sector management of tourism which can be used in analysing the actual behaviour of managers.

Box 3.2 Guide to the practice of the public sector management of tourism

Why:

1   Tourism is very important to governments economically and politically, and this is recognised by managers who provide the necessary support. Tourism could not survive without public sector assistance.
2   Managers need to be aware that tourism not only has economic effects but also has social impacts both positive and negative. Tourism, especially development, can have wide repercussions and be very controversial; therefore managers need to be sensitive and monitor and regulate policy implementation carefully. Managers at all levels of government should be open to community inputs.
3   Managers are responsible for the implementation of principles and policy and the efficient management of public resources, ensuring that there is balance between the various costs and benefits and a reasonable return on the public investment.
4   Managers should recognise that only the industry can provide the qualities for a dynamic competitive tourism.

Who:

5   The public management of tourism requires a considerable amount of freedom and flexibility. There is accordingly a good case for the establishment of an autonomous public agency.
6   Such an agency, outside the national civil service, allows for the appointment and the building up of expert staff who have skills in marketing and other specialities and allows for management on a continuous, regulated basis.

---

7 Management at the local government level is vital, as this is normally where the impact of tourism is directly experienced.

How:

8 Tourism is very diverse, and there are a great number and diversity of public and private organisations; therefore tourism PSM must have excellent communication, cooperation and coordination and be open to different ideas and inputs, whilst avoiding duplication and wasteful competition.

9 Because of the interdependency of the various sectors and organisations, managers must be able to secure trust, establish good relations and act as bridge agents between the various organisations.

10 Managers should be able to get the support of political and community leaders for tourism development, using development in a wide sense and not just as physical or land-use development;

11 Managers should be prepared to act as stimulators and catalysts.

12 Managers should be able to manage long-term and short-term policy programmes and public tourism organisations at all levels of government. They should have that wider perspective which is able to manage tourism objectives within the context of national objectives.

13 Managers should recognise that tourism involves politics, power and conflict.

What: industry

14 Managers should be skilled not only in dealing with public sector officials but also with private sector managers and with the environment in which each operates. They will be prepared to prevent or resolve conflict between the two sectors.

15 The industry is very competitive and changing all the time; managers need to be aware of this, and to be flexible, responsive and swift in their reaction and to be change orientated.

16 Managers should ensure that the industry has the fullest possible freedom to respond to the demands of the market without damaging essential public interests. The public sector must not become too regulatory and rigid but strive to meet the needs of industry and balance them with society's needs.

What: control

17 Managers should accept that control is an important responsibility of public management.

18 Because of its dependence on the public sector for support and development among other things tourism is open to special pleading or corruption. Managers should ensure that a high standard of integrity is maintained at all times.

19 Management should accept that the impact of tourism is the crucial test of management performance.

SUMMARY

Public sector management is a complex activity and operates in an environment of government, public policies, political systems and power. Yet it is expected to be concerned with principles such as the public interest, public service, effectiveness, efficiency and accountability.

Among the multiplicity of organisations some try to follow the rational Weberian ideal but have to contend with the irrationality of politics, various controls and informal factors. Management, however, like tourism is always changing, and not least at this time with the introduction of the new PSM or managerialism. What happens in practice is always the most important, and a suggested guide to practice is offered. The next five chapters examine practice and performance using the principles and framework questions of why, who, how and what.

SUGGESTED READING

Useful journals for PSM/public administration and public policy include *The Australian Journal of Public Administration*, *Public Administration* (United Kingdom) and *Public Administration Review* (United States).

Annals of Tourism Research (1983) Special issue on Political Science and Tourism, vol. 10, no. 3.

Hall, C.M. (1994) *Tourism and Politics: Policy, Power and Place*, Chichester, England: John Wiley. An excellent introduction to the politics of tourism.

Hennessy, P. (1989) *Whitehall*, London: Fontana Press. Very readable account of British public administration and politics.

Hughes, O.E. (1994) *Public Management and Administration: An Introduction*, London: Macmillan. Chapters on new public management, public policy and public enterprise.

Peters, B.G. (1995) 4th edn *The Politics of Bureaucracy*, White Plains, NY: Longman. A structured, analytical discussion of comparative public administration.

Richter, L.K. (1985) 'State-sponsored tourism: a growth field for public administration?' *Public Administration Review* 45, 6: 832–9.

Stewart, R.G. and Ward, I. (1996) 2nd edn, *Politics One*, South Melbourne: Macmillan. An introductory textbook to Australian politics, administration and policy making.

Wilson, J. (1989) *Bureaucracy*, New York: Basic Books. Comprehensive; an outstanding textbook on American bureaucracy and politics.

4 Management from the centre

Formulation

This chapter explains:

- why governments are involved in the management of tourism from the centre
- who are the actors, or which are the institutions engaged in tourism at this level, including cabinets, ministers, ministries and the policy community
- how the system of tourism policy making is managed
- what the results are in one system: the United Kingdom.

Management from the centre is essential if there is to be any unity, coherence and development in a country, for the centre is where most of the power lies. The nature and complexity of modern societies require effective and efficient management from the central government, not least in the formulation of policy. The full-time professional managers (civil servants or public officials) have the responsibility to manage the system but the ultimate responsibility lies with the elected political leaders of national and state governments. Historically it can be seen that tourism could not survive without government and their provision and management of services, which are essential for tourism.

As the British Tourism Society (1989) stated: 'a successful tourist industry depends upon the effective undertaking of essential national tasks within a framework of national policy and coordination which, although they are currently lacking in Britain, could be provided within the existing legislation'.

UK governments have agreed that the public sector has an essential role to perform, but have seen this role more in providing a supportive environment for tourism than a dominant leadership role from the centre.

WHY: RESPONSIBILITIES, IDEOLOGY AND OBJECTIVES

It is necessary for national and state governments to be involved in sectors such as tourism for public objectives to be achieved and for such sectors to survive and prosper. It is only these governments which have the legitimacy and power to establish needed national objectives and policies, and to direct and control the many diverse bodies involved in tourism. These governments have the responsibility as well as the resources to perform these functions. 'The Government's job is to provide a framework in which enterprises can flourish, in tourism as in other industries' (UK, Department of Employment and Central Office of Information, *Tourism in the UK* 1992: 5).

National and state governments, as the central policy-making bodies, have the power to 'make and enforce decisions which are binding upon their members', they have *responsibilities* which are interpreted by ideologies and together help to shape *objectives*.

Responsibilities

Each government will have its own set of responsibilities and priorities which will reflect national needs and political culture, and the perception of these responsibilities will change over time. It is the function of PSM to manage the system so that these responsibilities of governments are fulfilled.

Stability and security

Governments have a basic responsibility to ensure the survival of the nation. They must also provide the basic law and order which is required, for without stability there cannot be a viable tourism industry. This is shown quite clearly in situations in which unrest or violence in a society causes a dramatic fall in tourism, as has been experienced in countries such as Egypt, Fiji, the Philippines and Sri Lanka. Britton (1983: 3) argues that a 'destination must be accessible, it must be politically and socially stable'. In Fiji following the 1987 *coup* and the subsequent political turmoil there was a significant fall in the number of tourists. The government accepted that peace and order was essential to attract and keep tourists, and in 1992 the Fijian tourism minister was claiming that all was now well and that the recent elections had brought democracy and stability. The economically poor but beautiful island country of Sri Lanka established a successful tourist industry in the 1970s with an average growth rate per annum from 1976 of 24 percent, reaching 407,000 tourists in 1982.

From 1983 the government was not able to ensure stability because of the fighting with the Tamil Tigers. By 1987 there were only 180,000 tourists. In the 1990s a curtailment of violence and good management brought numbers up, and in 1991 there were 317,000 tourists. The tourism managements systems of Europe have been able to meet the challenges posed by the terrorist threats in Europe in 1986 which led to a big drop in the number of American tourists, as well as the devastating effects on tourism of the Gulf War of 1991.

Governments must provide a stable management system, policies and a control system to assist in the survival and development of the tourism industry, even in a system as strong in free enterprise as that of the United States. As one American writer expressed it: 'In order to plan for and provide rational order to such a diverse and dynamic industry, it is necessary to provide policies to assist the decision makers in this complex industry' (Edgell 1990: 7).

Standard of living

The responsibility to help raise the living standards of the people comes mainly through economic development. This needs to be positively balanced, with long-term development and not just short-term growth. As tourism is one of the fastest-growing industries in the world and as other industries decline, it can be argued that governments have a responsibility to encourage tourism development. As a British minister responsible for tourism said: 'Governments would ignore at their peril an industry which is so far reaching, so fast growing and has such potential' (UK Employment Secretary, April 1991). Economic growth is normally given high priority by governments. The public service principle suggests that there should be a fair distribution of resources in society between the various groups and regions. Tourism can help to achieve these objectives by providing economic development in the poorer regions.

Government responsibilities include providing for the social conditions of the people, their health and well-being. The resources of the nation should be protected, including areas of natural beauty, historic sites and buildings. Attempts should be made to eradicate poverty, as Thailand and Vietnam are trying to do, by the stimulation of tourism. There are particular responsibilities on governments to protect those who are least able to protect themselves: the poor, children, aboriginal people, poor rural communities, those who lack education, knowledge and are at risk. Those people need to be protected against the wrong kind of tourism development, disease and exploitation. 'Child prostitution is booming in countries like Thailand, and the lure of foreign cash is one reason why officials are ignoring it' (*The Australian* 26 October 1992: 7).

Government must apply the constitution and law of the land, and international law on human rights and on such matters as child labour and prostitution based on slavery. In practice the national and socio-economic responsibilities of governments are also those of senior public managers. These managers have the capacity and commitment to formulate tourism policy in terms of national and international good, or national public interest. They should be able to evaluate the policy not just in terms of short-term economic or political gain but in a wider and longer perspective and using social and moral criteria. Tourism is not just about economic activity and profit making, it is also about human development and international understanding.

Ideologies

Managers operate within the ideological beliefs and political philosophy of the government. The ideology of a government is important, for it can determine whether tourism development will be supported and how much financial support, if any, will be available; it can set the style of tourism, and the nature and extent of government involvement. Normally the ideology reflects the national political culture and political parties.

While the ideology of the government will affect the role of management, governments in their policy making will take into account the national administrative culture. In the United States, historically, ideology and culture have given a minimal role to the public sector compared to that of the private sector or the individual citizen. The role, for example, of the government US Travel and Tourism Administration (USTTA) was very limited compared to that of comparable organisations in other countries. In practice, the application of political philosophies of the right or left can be similar, as seen by the *interventionist* role played by different governments. For example, the right-wing government in the Australian state of Queensland until 1989 played a highly interventionist role in tourism development, as did the Communist government of Cuba. For both these governments, at opposite ends of the political spectrum, their intervention had economic objectives.

All governments ultimately have to recognise the economies of the market. Governments of the right, however, such as Mrs Thatcher's, made market economies a basic political ideology, which became known as Thatcherism. Following this ideology governments withdraw as much as possible from tourism and leave it to the industry and market forces. President Reagan, for example, was eager to withdraw support from and abolish the USTTA. The user-pay principle enforces the market ideas. Examples of this ideology in practice include the termination in 1992, by the right-wing Swedish government, of the government national Swedish Tourist Board, and the US Congress cutting of funds for the USTTA in 1995.

Governments of the left have been more interventionist, with a concern for social equity, like the British Labour governments since the Second World War with their stress on using tourism to assist poorer regions. In 1972 the Australian Labor government authorised the Australian Tourist Commission to engage in domestic tourism to improve the quality of life of the Australian people.

Marxist governments such as those of China, North Korea, Cuba and Vietnam are all involved in tourism. Initially, tourism took place only with fellow socialist countries and friends of socialism, then it was extended to tourists from capitalist countries. In earlier years the tourists were on strictly controlled tours and only shown sites and monuments which the government wished them to see, such as collective farms, model schools, war museums or significant national monuments. There was anxiety among some Communist party leaders that Western-style tourism might introduce moral pollution, such as a black market in currency dealings or prostitution, and introduce young people to what the party saw as wrong ideas and values. Tourism has been used as a propaganda tool not only by Marxist governments but also by governments such as South Korea and the former West Berlin city government against former Communist East Germany.

Tourism can also be used to support nationalism, national ideology, culture and religion. Several of these features can also add to the exotic nature of the country and add to its attraction as a tourism destination. Ancient Christian churches, Islamic mosques or Buddhist temples can be popular tourist attractions. Managers, particularly those in the public sector, must work within the ideology of the regime but should also be able to use national cultural features to attract tourists.

Objectives

The objectives of a government and its tourism policy will reflect its perceptions of its responsibilities and its ideology. These objectives can be either formal or informal, stated or unstated. *Formal* objectives are normally consistent with the aims laid down in the national constitution or in the party policy documents or manifesto. The dominant *informal* objectives will normally be to hold on to or to increase power, and to stay in office. Tourism can be used to achieve these political objectives as it was by the Marcos regime, which aimed to stay in power in the Philippines in the 1970s and 1980s (Richter 1989). When the British government increased the authority of the Scottish and Welsh tourist boards it was also trying to influence the voters in those countries to support the Conservative party. Efforts to boost the number of incoming foreign tourists by governments have been used to improve the image of government, but government has given little attention to other tourism considerations. Managers cannot achieve formal objectives without the support of political leaders and a recognition of informal objectives and needs. Ideally, formal and informal objectives should be complementary, for if they get too much out of line, management cannot work effectively.

The general macro-economic objectives of governments are more important for tourism than micro-objectives or administrative changes. For example, the emphasis given to economic development and the earning of foreign currency will establish a positive climate for tourism and affect the thinking and behaviour of managers. On the other hand, micro-objectives for the tourism industry will have little impact if the government is not committed to development. If the major objective of government is privatisation and small government and to leave as much as possible to the private sector, this will affect the public management of tourism, as it has in Britain.

The main tourism objective of governments has been to increase the number of tourists visiting the country, consequently increasing the amount of foreign exchange entering the country and thereby strengthening the balance of payments position.

The formal objectives of the United States in 1981 were laid out in the National Tourism Policy Act 1981 (see Box 4.1).

WHO: LEADERS, MINISTRIES AND ORGANISATIONS

It is necessary to recognise who is involved in management from the centre, who has the power in the formulation process. Various organisations from the public and private sectors make up the *policy community* and contribute towards the formulation of tourism policy. The extent of the involvement will vary according to whether it is a federal or unitary system of government, the power of the organisations and the policy area.

Box 4.1 US National Tourism Policy Act 1981

A national tourism policy is established to

1 optimise the contribution of the tourism and recreation industries to economic prosperity, full employment, and the international balance of payments of the United States;
2 make the opportunity for and benefits of tourism and recreation in the United States universally accessible to residents of the United States and foreign countries and ensure that present and future generations are afforded adequate tourism and recreation resources;
3 contribute to personal growth, health, education, and inter-cultural appreciation of the geography, history and ethnicity of the United States;
4 encourage the free and welcome entry of individuals travelling to the United States, in order to enhance international under-standing and goodwill, consistent with immigration laws, the laws protecting public health, and laws governing the importation of goods into the United States;
5 eliminate unnecessary trade barriers to the US tourism industry operating throughout the world;
6 encourage competition in the tourism industry and maximum consumer choice through the continued viability of the retail travel agent industry and the independent tour operator industry;
7 promote the continued development and availability of alter-native personal payment mechanisms which facilitate national and international travel;
8 promote quality, integrity and reliability in all tourism and tourism-related services offered to visitors to the United States;
9 preserve the historical and cultural foundations of the nation as a living part of community life and development, and ensure to future generations an opportunity to appreciate and enjoy the rich heritage of the nation;
10 ensure the compatibility of tourism and recreation with other national interests in energy development and conservation, environmental protection and the judicious use of natural resources;
11 assist in the collection, analysis and dissemination of data which accurately measure the economic and social impact of tourism to and within the United States, in order to facilitate planning in the public and private sectors; and
12 harmonise, to the maximum extent possible, all federal activities in support of tourism and recreation with the need of the general public and the states, territories, local governments, and the tourism and recreation industry, and to give leadership to all concerned with tourism, recreation and national heritage preservation in the United States.

Leaders

The president, prime minister and cabinet are especially important in establishing the priorities of government, the climate and the broad ideological framework which will guide the government and its managers in policy formulation management. There can be no policy or progress in tourism unless there is at least passive support at this level. In Cuba, for example, tourism would not have been possible without the support of Fidel Castro.

In the United Kingdom a Conservative government supported tourism on the basis of a market ideology.

> The main thrust of the Government's economic policy is to make markets work better. Restrictions have been lifted. Business and individuals have been given new freedoms. It is no coincidence that the tourism industry has grown so rapidly. Many simplifications in taxation VAT, Social Security, employment, health and safety, company law, licensing, extension of opening hours have greatly benefited tourism.
>
> (UK, Department of Employment and Central Office of Information, *Tourism in the UK* 1992: 5)

A strong political leader can be crucial in getting a policy on to the agenda and putting it into effect. This was the case with Field Marshal Sarit in the late 1960s in Thailand. He was considered to be dictatorial and corrupt, but his strong support gave the necessary boost to business and tourism development. Tourism minister John Brown in the Australian Labor government of 1983 is given credit for getting Australian tourism moving into the major league.

The political leaders might have the power to decide policy, force decisions through and provide finance, but they lack time to formulate policy. There are so many issues coming before the cabinet that it can be difficult to get an item such as tourism on to the agenda and to debate the issues. The pressure can also make the cabinet a rubber-stamp body. A faction-ridden cabinet also creates problems for managers, for it is difficult to get decisions from such a cabinet, especially on controversial issues, such as new airport development. Decisions can be based on a consensus, which can also produce unsatisfactory results. It is normal for most decisions to be taken in some kind of inner cabinet or special committee. In Thailand this takes the form of an Economic Council, consisting of a small group of the most important ministers. Decisions are later formally ratified by the full cabinet.

Tourism minister

Most countries in recent years have accepted that there needs to be a specific minister who will play a leadership role in tourism. This can include the initiation and formulation of policy. Ministers, however, can have other responsibilities, which reduces the time they have for tourism. In order to have influence, the tourism minister needs to be a member of the cabinet, otherwise tourism is dependent upon a senior minister to present and fight for their case in cabinet. That senior minister may not have a strong commitment to tourism and may follow their own priorities. Junior, non-cabinet ministers lack the influence to obtain sufficient attention and resources for tourism. Ministers can move portfolios frequently and are often not in the tourism position long enough to acquire sufficient knowledge to make a significant contribution. In Britain until 1992, five different ministers held the position in five years. Managers can also have problems with incompetent and lazy ministers.

Management can also be made more difficult because often the minister will be responsible for a whole range of activities as well as tourism, and therefore is only able to devote a limited amount of time to the ever-growing tourism sector. In the British Department of National Heritage, established in 1992, the Secretary of State was responsible for a range of functions, including historic royal palaces, broadcasting policy, films, sport, museums, libraries, the National Lottery and tourism (see Figure 4.1). In 1992 the Australian government established a Department of Tourism (abolished in 1996) with a minister in the cabinet, but the minister was still not able to give his whole attention to tourism for he was also responsible for resources and energy. It is the minister who is the key player, especially in terms of policy formulation and gaining central government finance. Yet the limited amount of time which the minister has available for tourism places great responsibility into the hands of managers.

> Through unco-ordination there has been confusion in an industry that is essentially voluntary. We need to co-ordinate and to recognise the potential of tourism. We need a Minister whose sole responsibility is tourism and who will ensure that the industry goes from strength to strength.
> (UK, House of Commons, 7 December 1984: col. 670,
> Session, 1984–85)

This same conclusion was reached by an all-party committee after a thorough review of the public management of tourism in the United

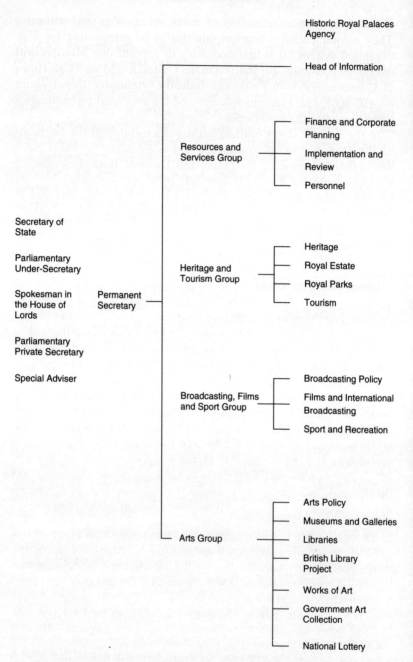

Secretary of
State

Parliamentary
Under-Secretary

Spokesman in
the House of
Lords

Parliamentary
Private Secretary

Special Adviser

Permanent
Secretary

Resources and
Services Group
- Finance and Corporate
  Planning
- Implementation and
  Review
- Personnel

Heritage and
Tourism Group
- Heritage
- Royal Estate
- Royal Parks
- Tourism

Broadcasting, Films
and Sport Group
- Broadcasting Policy
- Films and International
  Broadcasting
- Sport and Recreation

Arts Group
- Arts Policy
- Museums and Galleries
- Libraries
- British Library
  Project
- Works of Art
- Government Art
  Collection
- National Lottery

Historic Royal Palaces
Agency

Head of Information

Figure 4.1   Britain: The Department of National Heritage

Kingdom and an examination of many submissions and witnesses. They recommended a tourism minister to be responsible for a re-organised system. 'It is first necessary to appoint one Minister with overall responsibility for tourism in the United Kingdom' (UK, House of Commons 1985–86 Trade and Industry Committee Report, para. 84, HC 106). This recommendation and the proposed reorganisation was rejected by the government.

In the United States tourism is the responsibility of the Secretary of the Department of Commerce and is managed by the Under-Secretary of Commerce for Travel and Tourism. Both these officials are appointed by the President, but they are appointed 'by and with the advice and consent of the Senate'. Under the 1981 Act an Assistant Secretary for Commerce for Tourism Marketing is also appointed. Compared to other countries tourism has not been given the recognition or support its economic importance requires.

Ministries or departments

There are two main types of government ministries or departments. One is those ministries which play a central *service* role in areas such as finance or personnel; the other type is the *sector* ministry covering one particular activity such as transport, health, education or tourism. Ministry officials are important in the detailed formulation of policy.

Ministries of tourism

The lack of a separate, independent ministry of tourism has been a problem not least in the formulation and implementation of policy. It is argued that because tourism includes such a wide, diverse range of functions, touching on those of so many other ministries, it is impossible to group all these functions into one ministry. Further-more, the tourism industry does not present a united front or a strong case for a tourism ministry to governments, nor does it have the financial or political power to persuade governments to establish a tourism ministry. Those in favour of small government believe that a small tourism policy unit in a large economic department is adequate. Marketing functions would be carried out by a national tourism office and tourism development by the private sector. This pattern was followed by the new Australian government of 1996 when it abolished the separate Departments of Tourism and placed tourism in a new Department of Industry, Science and Tourism.

A tourism ministry can be opposed on ideological grounds if a government is against public intervention into industry. In the United States, for example, there has been strong opposition from the political right to a federal tourism department or agency. President Reagan repeatedly called for the elimination of the United States Travel and Tourism Administration (USTTA). 'Administration officials believed that the private sector can better safeguard America's share of the world tourism market than can a bureaucratic agency' (Ronkainen and Farano 1987: 3). The USTTA was cut back in staff, and in 1996 numbered 85 officers compared to 150 in the early 1980s. The USSTA was not a department as such but an agency of the Department of Commerce. It ceased to exist in 1996 with the withdrawal of its funding by Congress.

Tourism can be put in any kind of ministry but the most common is either in an economic or trade ministry, or in a sport, recreation and culture ministry. The political decision often comes down to what is convenient, what functions can reasonably be linked together or what is left over from the more traditional ministries. Other considerations are: what is politically desirable, what policy area the senior minister wishes to take, and what the prime minister wishes to give.

Independent ministries

Whether tourism should be a separate, independent ministry has been a matter of debate over the years. A single function ministry can allow for a greater concentration of managerial talent and effort. Specialist staff and expertise can be attracted and allowed to pursue their speciality. There can be a greater *esprit de corps*, for officials can have a much greater sense of belonging and be more aware of departmental activities and achievements. Problems can be identified and tackled more directly and swiftly, especially the coordination of so many diverse public and private organisations. Yet at the same time national tourism objectives and the public interest could be better protected against the special interests of other ministries or the industry. As a growing priority sector, tourism could find it easier to get managerial resources and finance from central sources, for it could be seen clearly where resources were going, into a single function tourism ministry, unlike resources going into massive multi-functional ministries or departments. In multifunctional ministries the position of tourism can be weakened as it has to compete with other sectors for attention.

In Britain in 1972 an attempt was made to establish a ministry oı tourism through a Private Member's Bill presented to the House of Commons. It was argued that a ministry should have been formed under the 1969 Tourism Act, and was necessary because tourism was one of the fastest-growing industries in the world and able to provide jobs in areas which needed work, but it was also an industry which needed to be controlled. The Bill did not get the support of the government, so it was lost (UK, House of Commons, 1971/72, col. 1454).

Service ministries

There are four main service ministries performing vital management functions, which have an overview and control position over the whole public sector. They have important formulation and coordination responsibilities – their support is necessary for successful policy formulation and implementation.

1 *Executive ministries.* These include presidential, prime-ministerial and chief executive ministries. This type of ministry will influence *policy* and *priorities* at both the formulation and implementation stages. This ministry acts as the eyes and ears of the chief executive and will convey information in both directions. What issues and how they come before the chief executive and cabinet will be influenced by this ministry.
2 *Finance ministries.* These can be some of the most powerful ministries, deciding what finance should be available for infrastructure or administration, what taxes should be levied, and what grants should be given. Infrastructure such as airports or roads essential to tourism, or budgets for tourism marketing, will all be affected by the management of these ministries. Connected to the finance ministry there can be a sub-ministry or agency concerned with investment generally or maybe foreign investment, such as the Australian Foreign Investment Review Board reporting to the Treasurer.
3 Another ministry can be that organisation which directs or controls civil service personnel and public sector management and processes. The policies and decisions of the ministry will affect the number and the grades of personnel allowed in the public tourism agencies and the processes which control them.
4 A planning or development ministry can take the form of an agency. This type of ministry is more common in developing countries and is not found in Australia, Britain or the United

he ministry is responsible for the long-term planning and
ient of the country. It will be the organisation which for-
he five-year national economic and social development
maybe the implementation of the plan will be left to a
development ministry or corporation. Countries which have such
a planning organisation will also include a tourism plan within the
national economic plan, as does the National Economic and Social
Development Board of Thailand.

Many of these ministries are of long standing and have powerful
and legitimate positions in the bureaucratic system. They have their
own responsibilities and objectives, and they have to be convinced
that tourism policy objectives are not contrary to their own objectives.
There can therefore be contradictions and opposition which can
be overcome by political leadership and competent and sensitive
management. This same leadership will help to overcome other
problems between ministries and tourism such as overlapping juris-
dictions, poor coordination and cooperation, poor communication
and lack of implementation of policy.

Sector ministries

Sector ministries control one activity, such as transport or education,
and their activities can be crucial for the survival of the tourism
industry. Aviation in particular has been important for the growth
of overseas tourism. Many nations have, or have had, national
government-owned airlines which they have endeavoured to protect
by restricting the activities of foreign airlines. This can also restrict
the number of tourists coming into the country.

The ministry responsible for immigration and the issue of visas is
also important. This function can be under a justice, interior, home
affairs, foreign affairs or immigration ministry. Policy decisions taken
by the ministers and managers of these ministries liberalising entry
have greatly helped the growth of tourism in recent years. Tourism to
the United States has been boosted since 1988 by the easing of visa
requirements for Britain, Japan and several European countries.

With the increasing public concern about the environment and
conservation, ministries have been established and have become
interested in the problems caused by tourism and tourists. In
Queensland, the state government's Department of Environment and
Heritage supported ecotourism and was responsible not only for the
Great Barrier Reef, tropical islands, rain forests, World Heritage and
wilderness areas and beach conservation, but also for flora and fauna,

caves, Aboriginal paintings and historical buildings from the period of European settlement.

These organisations and their activities are continually changing and with the dynamic nature of tourism a heavy burden of communication, negotiation and coordination is placed upon managers, and tourism managers in particular. This is one reason why consideration needs to be given to the appointment of a tourism minister and to the establishment of a tourism ministry.

Generalists and specialists

Public sector managers can be generalists or specialists – sometimes called professionals. In the British Civil Service and to a certain extent in the Australian Public Service, the most senior positions are mainly occupied by *generalist* civil servants who, while they have no specific technical qualification or experience have had considerable experience of how the bureaucratic system works. They can move their positions frequently and in Britain they normally move after three years. This group of bureaucrats is responsible for managing policy formulation at the centre; they are highly intelligent, experienced and hard working. However, they lack the specific professional knowledge and experience of the tourism sector and are not in position long enough to be innovative or acquire such knowledge and experience. Their contribution therefore to policy formulation is not in the introduction of technical policies but in the management of the inputs into the system so efficiently as to produce acceptable policy decisions. They have the management skills, for example, to negotiate, and to reach policy agreements involving a wide and diverse range of government ministries, agencies and private organisations. While tourism may not be as highly technical as some other sectors, knowledge and experience of the industry is still needed.

This knowledge is given by the *specialists, professionals* or *technocrats* in the tourism community, mainly from the national tourism offices, where officials have the specialist qualifications, skills and knowledge needed. These officials should have the opportunity to contribute to policy formulation but their main function is day-to-day management. They are more concerned with the implementation of policy, with practice and performance.

The number of civil servants working on tourism matters in central government ministries is relatively small. In Britain, for example, in 1996 the Department of National Heritage had a staff of about 300, of whom twenty were in the tourism division. In Australia, the

Department of Tourism established in 1992 had a staff of about 120, but of these, six were in the Senior Executive Service, which is the highest grading in the public service, a significant increase on past gradings. Numbers, rankings and budgets are important indicators of power and status in any bureaucratic system. There is no Department of Tourism in the United States, and the Department of Commerce, which is responsible for tourism in 1996, relied upon eighty-five specialist officials of the USTTA to manage those responsibilities. The influence of civil service managers, however, can be limited by factors such as overwork, low calibre ministers and weak tourism commitment from ministers and governments.

Statutory and other organisations: research, development and coordination

There are many public organisations which play a significant role in the formulation of tourism policy and these can take various forms, including statutory or non-statutory. Some are called quangos, 'quasi autonomous non-governmental organisations'. Organisations can be jointly funded by governments and the industry. They can be important – for example, if they undertake research and provide specialised information needed for policy formulation. The national tourism boards are the main managers of tourism marketing but with other organisations they make a contribution to policy formulation, research, development and coordination. An example of a research organisation is the Australian Bureau of Tourism Research which has as its mission 'To enhance (measure) the contribution of tourism to the well-being of the Australian community, through the provision of accurate, timely and strategically relevant statistics and analysis to the tourism industry, government and the community at large.

Tourism development is particularly important in Third World countries and requires special management skills and a flexibility and freedom not normally found in the traditional civil services. Countries such as Costa Rica, Cuba and Mexico have established autonomous corporations to manage the development. Fonatur (National Tourism Fund) established by the Mexican government has been very successful in managing the rapid development of tourist resorts. In Cuba a similar corporation has also been successful and has been able to escape the rigidities of the centralised planning system.

One of the main problems facing the tourism sector is the *coordination* of the many diverse governments and public and private agencies so as to reach agreement on how to tackle problems and take policy decisions. This problem is exacerbated by a federal system of government and the power struggles between organisations. Organisations have been established to help solve this management problem. In Australia, for example, they include the Tourist Minister's Council, the Australian Standing Committee on Tourism made up of public managers, and the Tourism Advisory Council. The latter institution includes industry and trade-union representatives. In the United States there is the Tourism Policy Council made up of public managers, and the Travel and Tourism Advisory Board of industry representatives. Britain has the Tourism Consultative Council which meets about twice a year, it is made up of about thirteen ministers and their advisers whose portfolios affect tourism. Coordination and integration of tourism policy in Japan is carried out by the Inter-ministerial Conference on tourism. This consists of twenty-one ministers and agencies chaired by the Director-General of the Prime Minister's Office.

Parliament and Congress

The legislative branch of the government is responsible for the enactment of legislation and it can allow the opposition parties and interest groups to have an input into the policy process. Members of Parliament can speak for interest groups in Parliament by means of debates and question time. Particular opportunities are given for an input during debates on specific tourism Acts, annual reports, budgetary proposals and committee investigations. 'Although generally supportive, Congressional activity on travel–tourism matters has been slow and isolated' (Ronkainen and Farano 1987). This experience in the United States has been the norm in most other legislative bodies. Parliamentary committees can examine legislation and investigate the public management of tourism and maybe influence policy. US Congressional committees have extensive power compared to the authority of a UK Commons committee. An example of a UK committee is the 'Trade and Industry committee appointed under SO No. 99 to examine the expenditure, administration and policy of the Department of Trade and Industry and associated public bodies, and similar matters within the responsibilities of the Secretary of State for Northern Ireland'.

The Committee consists of a maximum of eleven members, of whom the quorum is three.

Box 4.2 Committee powers

The Committee has power:

(a) to send for persons, papers and records, to sit notwithstanding any adjournment of the House, to adjourn from place to place, and to report from time to time;
(b) to appoint specialist advisers either to supply information which is not readily available, to elucidate matters of complexity within the Committee's orders of reference;
(c) to communicate to any other such committee its evidence and any other documents relating to matter of common interest; and
(d) to meet concurrently with any other such committee for the purpose of deliberating, taking evidence, or considering draft reports.
    (UK, House of Commons, 1985/86, Trade and Industry Committee)

Power or influence comes as much from the authority to question and examine those who manage tourism, and to gain information and publicity as it does from these examinations and subsequent reports and debates. Committees can encourage the policy makers to justify and rethink their decisions but rarely to change policy.

Examples of committees which have examined tourism include:

• United Kingdom: Parliament, House of Commons, 1983. Trade and Industry Committee. Tourism in the UK.
• Australia: Parliament, House of Representatives, 1978. Select Committee on Tourism.
• United States: Congress, Senate, 1978. Committee on Commerce, Science and Transportation. National Tourism Policy Study.

Political parties

In recent years, as tourism has become more important economically, political parties have been paying greater attention to it. References to tourism have appeared in party platforms, policies and general statements. Tourism has been used by political parties to boost support, as with the British Conservative government, which established the Department of National Heritage, which includes tourism in its remit, in order to counter nationalist fears about the danger to Britain from the party's pro-Europe stance. Managers need to be aware of party policies and to be prepared to implement them if the party gains power. For example, in the 1993 federal electoral campaign the Australian Labor party promised that tax write-off provisions for tourism-related building would be doubled. Tourism operators would be able to write off certain tourism site works, such as pools, tennis courts and landscaping. Extra funds of A$15 million were promised for the Australian Tourist Commission and A$6 million extra for the newly created Department of Tourism. Aviation laws would be relaxed to boost competition. The opposition Liberal party proposals included a comprehensive but controversial 15 per cent goods and services tax, which they said would be imposed on all Australian travel products and services. Travel to and from Australia would be exempt, but foreign visitors would have to pay consumption tax on all goods and services consumed in Australia, except at duty-free stores. The Tourism Department would be abolished and its functions transferred to the Australian Tourist Commission (ATC). In 1996 the Liberal Coalition government abolished the department.

Policy community

The actual policy making of the organisations proceeds through a policy community. This includes the key organisations and actors who participate in policy and who are continually in touch with and talking to each other about tourism issues. In the case of the Australian Department of Tourism this is necessary 'To meet the requirements of the Government, Parliament and the public for timely and co-ordinated advice and information' (Australia, Department of Tourism, Program Performance Statements 1992–93: 61). Some organisations will be involved in almost all issues while others will only participate if an issue is of interest to them. Organisations which are responsible for the public management of tourism, like the sponsoring government ministry or the national tourism body, will be concerned with all tourism issues. The development of the national tourism plan or strategy will involve all members of the policy community, but the development of a theme park in a locality will normally only involve those directly affected. Power in the community will determine who gets what, when and how. Tourism is typified by great diversity and a great number of organisations and issues, so policy making will pull into the policy community diverse institutions with diverse interests. This can involve a process of great complexity and at times of slowness (see Wilks and Wright 1987: chap. 12). Tourism policy communities are recognised formally, as seen in the membership of the boards of the national tourism bodies and advisory bodies (see Box 4.3).

Box 4.3   British Tourist Authority board members and BTA management

Office of Chairman

ADELE BISS became BTA Chairman for three years from 1 June 1993.

After a degree in economics at London University, Adele Biss joined Unilever in 1968 as a graduate trainee in consumer marketing. She then joined Thomson Holidays, where she headed their winter holiday division, before becoming head of the company's marketing communications and public relations. She set up her own PR company. Biss Lancaster, in 1978, which became a leading consultancy. She has been a non-executive member of the British Railways Board and is currently a non-executive director of Bowthorpe plc. European Passenger Services Ltd and Harry Ramsden's plc. She is a council Member of the Girls' Public School Trust. She is also Chairman of the English Tourist Board.

SIR JOHN EGAN was appointed to the Board in February 1994. He is Chief Executive of BAA plc, Chairman of the London Tourist Board, a non-executive director of Legal & General plc and Foreign & Colonial Investment Trust plc. He was knighted in the Queen's Birthday Honours List in June 1986.

THE HON. SIR ROCCO FORTE MA PCA has been on the Board since 1986. He has held various posts with Forte plc and became Chairman in October 1992. He is a Board member of the Savoy Group of Hotels and Restaurants, President of the British Hospitality Association and a member of the Executive Committee of the World Travel and Tourism Council. He was knighted for services to tourism in the New Year Honours List 1995.

IAN GRANT CBE has been an ex-officio Board member since his appointment as Chairman of the Scottish Tourist Board in March 1990. Until then, he had been president of the National Farmers' Union of Scotland for six years and a member of the Scottish Tourist Board for two years. He is a non-executive director of Clydesdale Bank, Scottish Hydro Electric, National Farmers' Union Mutual Insurance Society and a member of the CBI Scottish Council.

JOHN H. J. LEWIS LLB has been a Board member since July 1989. He is a solicitor, Chairman of Cliveden plc and Principal Hotels, Vice-Chairman of John D. Wood & Co plc and a director of Grayshott Hall Heath Retreat and a number of other hotel-based companies. He chaired BTA's British Heritage Advisory Committee. He is Chairman of the Attringham Trust for the study of the British Country House, a Member of the Council of the Historic Houses Association and a trustee of The Wallace Collection and The Watts Gallery.

TONY LEWIS DL MA (Cantab) is Chairman of the Wales Tourist Board and has been an ex-officio Board member since 1 October 1992. He was formerly England cricket captain and is a writer and television broadcaster. He was Chairman of the Association for Business Sponsorship of the Arts (Wales).

IVOR MANLEY CB was appointed to the Board in 1991 on retirement from a 40-year career in the Civil Service. He was formerly Deputy Secretary at the Department of Employment, a non-executive director of Business in the Community plc and Chairman of the Task Force on Tourism and the Environment. He chaired the BTA Marketing and Development Committees and working parties on VAT Harmonisation and the Channel Tunnel.

THE LORD RATHCAVAN, Chairman of the Northern Ireland Tourist Board since 1988, attended Board meetings by invitation, standing arrangement which continues to strengthen understanding and co-operation between BTA and NITB. He is also chairman of FRX International and a director of Lamont Holdings plc, Northern Bank Ltd, Old Bushmills Distillery Company and Savoy Management Ltd.

Gordon Dunlop resigned at 30 November 1994.

The Board is sorry to lose the services of *Ivor Manley* whose term of office was completed on 30 June 1995. Mr Manley has kindly agreed to continue as Chairman of the British Tourism Development Committee and of the VAT Working Party for the time being.

The Board welcomes the appointment of:

JOHN JARVIS CBE, Chairman and Chief Executive of Jarvis Hotels Ltd was appointed to the Board on 1 July 1995. He was previously Chairman and Chief Executive of Hilton International, and Ladbroke Hotels, Holidays and Entertainments. Before joining the Ladbroke Group in 1975 as Managing Director of Ladbroke Holidays, he held management positions within the Rank Organisation. He is Chairman of the Prince's Trust, a member of the English Tourist Board and was awarded the CBE for services to tourism.

PATRICK MCKENNA, Chairman and Chief Executive of The Really Useful Group was appointed to the Board on 1 September 1995. Formerly a Partner in Touche Ross, he specialised in providing international tax advice to clients in the entertainment and leisure industry and was head of their world-wide Media and Entertainment Group. He has written and lectured extensively on taxation matters around the world and has served on the Examination Board of the Chartered Institute of Taxation.

BTA management

Anthony Sell, appointed Chief Executive in November 1993, joined BTA from the Thomas Cook Group, where he was based in Paris as Managing Director, Continental Europe. Before Thomas Cook, he was a main board executive director of Boosey and Hawkes plc and president of its French clarinet manufacturing company.

Tim Bartlett is General Manager Europe, based in London, and was formerly General Manager Asia/Pacific and General Manager Southern Europe.

Gerry Carter is General Manager International and was formerly Assistant Director of International Marketing.

Sundie Dawe is Head of Press and PR and was formerly head of PR for the London Tourist Board.

Robert Franklin is General Manager Asia/Pacific, based in Singapore, and was previously Marketing Director, The Americas.

Jonathan Griffin joined BTA on 31 July as Director Commercial Services. He was formerly Marketing Director of English Heritage.

Sue Garland is Secretary to the Board and heads the Policy and Legal Departments.

Jeff Hamblin is General Manager The Americas, based in New York, and was previously General Manager Europe.

Chris Howard joined BTA on 18 April as Director Corporate Services. He is a management accountant and was formerly a management consultant with KPMG.

Colin Clark retired as Director Management Services and Secretary to the Board on 31 December 1994. We are most grateful to his for his contribution over 23 years of loyal service to BTA and to the English Tourist Board.

Due to restructuring, *Robin Bell* ceased to be Finance Director on 7 April 1995 and *Kevin Johnson*, who was Director Marketing Services, left on 30 April 1995.

BTA *Annual Report 1995*

HOW: PROCESS AND INITIATIVES, FORMAL AND INFORMAL

In the management or bureaucratic system there are principles which should be followed, but how these principles will be put into practice will be affected by the management system. This same system with its characteristics will also reflect and respond to the principles and to the needs of the tourism sector. Public sector managers are responsible for managing the process of policy formulation, for 'a purposive course of action . . . dealing with a problem or matter of concern'. This includes managing the various inputs coming into the system, collecting the information needed, and giving advice or making recommendations. Managers are responsible for managing their organisation, its finances and personnel, and for achieving its objectives. The management of tourism is crucial if the escalation and progress of the market is to be made methodical and permanent and in order to make a successful contribution economically, politically and socially. Richter (1989: 11) points out the importance of management as well as political action, saying 'that where tourism succeeds or fails is largely a function of political and administrative action and is not a function of economic or business expertise'.

Process

The process of managing from the centre is normally very complex, operating on both a formal and an informal level. There is the formal process which can be a legal requirement but there can be an informal accepted process which will be followed in practice. In the United States there is the legal concept of 'due process' which may or may not be a requirement in tourism policy making. *Consultation* is one of the key parts of the process and can be carried out by asking for inputs from the public through the publication of an issues paper which may be referred to as a 'Green Paper'. This is a discussion paper requesting submissions which will be taken into account during the policy-making process. A 'White Paper' will normally follow, stating the government's views and policy intentions before it moves towards the drafting of legislation or the making of a decision. The formal consultation will involve all public bodies and recognised private bodies and may or may not be a legal requirement.

Participation should be an integral part of the consultation process, where those affected are allowed to have an effective input into the process, including other public bodies, industry organisations (normally the peak organisations), trade unions, local and regional bodies and especially the local people. In democratic systems there may be an expectation that there will be participation, consultation and representation of affected groups and that the process will be legitimate and open and that all information will be available. The application of principles by management, however, is not always so clear cut. In north Queensland, for example, the Royal Reef Resort development attracted negative responses during the tendering process from environmentalists, the fisheries board, the Aboriginal community and residents of Cairns. To soften these concerns the government made a lengthy Impact Assessment Study of the project, prepared by an independent party, available for public review, and with increased reviewing time advertised and publicised through the local media. All this was to create an open image. The process, however, should be more than about creating images. It should be legitimate, democratic and rational and allow for genuine participation.

Australia

An example of this type of process was followed in the formulation of the national tourism strategy for Australia. In September 1988 a discussion paper, 'Directions for Tourism', was issued containing various possible goals and options for future development and this generated useful public and industry comment and debate. Following this input in September 1991 a background paper was released, and a series of public consultative meetings was held around Australia conducted by the Minister of Tourism. More than 1,000 people participated, representing community and industry interests. Written submissions were also received. *Tourism: Australia's Passport to Growth: A National Tourism Strategy* was released in June 1992. As the introduction states: 'This strategy is the result of extensive consultation between Commonwealth and State/Territory governments, the tourism industry and other relevant interest groups.' The difficulty in this kind of process is the need to reach agreement among such a wide range of diverse interests, so that the final agreement and document are too vague and too full of pious hopes and therefore of little practical use to management.

Negotiations

In practice, however, the process within the management system is more limited in its scope and participation. It is more mundane, bureaucratic, informal, less open and more concerned with special interests. Managers are continually concerned with negotiations with members of the policy community. Those not directly within the community and those without power can be left out of the negotiations. Such was the case for the subsistence-level sea gypsies of south Thailand, who were not involved in the island and coastal tourism development which took away much of their livelihood.

Negotiations require a great deal of communication, coordination, cooperation and consensus decision making. The process can be very slow because of the complexity of the issues, the fragmentation of the system and the diversity of the participants. All this makes great demands upon the coordinative ability of the management system. This is achieved through a system of advisory bodies, consultative committees and interdepartmental committees. What is most important is the close relationships, formal and informal, which link together the top decision makers. There is ongoing daily contact between the top public managers especially during the concluding stages of a policy determination, and if necessary private sector managers will be involved. There will be internal memos and minutes, daily and regular informal telephone conversations, periodic meetings and more formal gatherings, especially if the annual budget is being considered. Because public managers are at the centre of the system they have the knowledge and opportunity to wield considerable influence and power.

In practice, the process can be of a *disjointed incremental* nature; that is, where decisions are made without being connected to other decisions or to any long-term strategy or plan (Lindblom 1959). The decisions make minor amendments to policies, at the margins of the policy; they are not major changes to policy. There tends to be reactive, *ad hoc* management, responding to the demands and needs of the moment. In this process there are no strong, clear or long-term objectives or plans, and policy appears to drift or react to market or other forces. This process, in practice, is common in countries such as Britain and the United States, and in Australia even with its national tourism strategy.

Managers have tried to make the system and process more rational and predictable by the introduction of a planning system where policies will be determined or guided by a national *plan* or *strategy*. National economic plans can be found in Japan, Thailand and many developing countries. Even in countries which do not have national planning, such as Britain, most organisations will have departmental plans and objectives. In the case of the British Tourist Authority

(1992–93: 5), 'The Corporate Plan shows how the BTA plans to take forward its mandate to release the potential of an industry that can play an ever more important part in the country's future prosperity.' In practice, however, planning systems are not always so rational and implementation of the plan and objectives is more difficult than the formulation.

Advisory committees or agencies are used extensively in the PSM system in the formulation of policy. They can be permanent or *ad hoc* and only established when needed. Their value is their independent expert input from industry, employees and employers, and from the public sector. Committees can contain other representatives; for example, from conservation and other concerned groups. The chair of the committee is normally an eminent expert with experience in public life and, in the case of tourism, often with experience in the industry. Committees can investigate and they can take an in-depth look at potential future development, they can commission research, call for official papers, and collect evidence and interview witnesses. Committees can avoid political conflict and involve industry and the community in their work, so helping to make the policy process more open and democratic. Advisory committees can be useful to the minister, ministry and the industry, but they can also be used for political purposes rather than for policy advice. Their main value is in the independent, expert nature of their work, reports and recommendations and as a source of fresh insights and new policy initiatives. A permanent body of this type is the Industries Assistance Committee of Australia established in 1973. A temporary committee was the Australian Government Committee of Inquiry into Tourism 1986–87. Private consultants have been used extensively by governments in recent years, as, for example, by British governments since 1979 inquiring into the public management of tourism in Britain. Japan has the Council for Tourism Policy, which consists of twenty-seven advisers from the universities and other private organisations. The Council was established in 1963 under the Tourism Basic Law.

Initiatives and inputs

With a dynamic industry such as tourism, management must be responsive to new initiatives and be prepared to undertake and to be open to inputs. Policy initiatives often arise because of pressure from those holding power, or from forces which are powerful, such as economic movements. Governments have taken policy initiatives in tourism because of a shortage of foreign exchange and a need to improve their balance of payments position. This pressure has led governments in recent years to relax visa restrictions on tourists. In the 1960s it led the British government to impose a foreign currency allowance on their citizens travelling overseas as tourists. For similar reasons the government of South Korea did not allow its citizens to travel overseas as tourists until 1989. Economic needs and rising unemployment have forced many governments, like the Australian government in 1983, to boost tourism as one of the few growth industries. Economic pressure can be brought about because of political inputs into the system, such as the military violence and political unrest in Thailand in 1992. This forced the Thai government and its tourism managers to take the initiative and to launch a massive tourism marketing campaign to compensate for the disastrous fall in the number of foreign tourists and the threat to the balance of payments.

An important initiative of recent years which is effecting PSM and tourism in many countries is deregulation.

> Deregulation in the USA (especially airlines) has created competition among institutions such as transportation, banking, energy and telecommunications and has had an effect on tourism. It has resulted in an improvement in the standards of marketing skills, organisational aspects and negotiations between institutions at a federal and state level.
>
> (Matthews 1978: 21)

Any manager can deal with the normal situation but the good manager will be able to deal with a crisis. A crisis will always create policy initiatives, and political leaders and managers will always respond to forces of power. Governments will endeavour to help poorer regions through tourism initiatives, but they will give greater attention to those regions where their political support lies and where there are political inputs putting pressure on them to take action. This was the case with the British Labour governments in the 1960s, and resulted in the policy to emphasise tourism in the regions, as against London. The reactive behaviour of politicians and managers supports the disjointed nature of the policy process.

Positive leadership is needed from politicians and managers but this is not always easy to find and that is why managers with this quality are so eagerly sought after and so highly paid, at least in the private sector. Leadership is particularly needed when major initiatives are required in an organisation. In the Australian Department of Tourism the executive strategies were to 'Provide strategic direction for the Department. Work to reinforce the cultural values of the organisation and in particular, the adoption of leadership as a primary focus of management' (Australia, Program Performance Statements 1992–93: 57).

The input from the political leader or the manager can be the key factor gaining acceptance of the policy changes in the system. In Britain in 1985 the input from Lord Young on his appointment as Employment Secretary led to his initiative to transfer tourism responsibilities to his new department from the Department of Trade and Industry, and to the publication of the report *Pleasure, Leisure and Jobs – the Business of Tourism* (UK, Cabinet Office 1985). To get an item on the policy agenda of the cabinet the initiative must come from a senior cabinet minister. Inputs into the policy process will come from various sources, the tourism industry, public tourism agencies, public sector managers and groups established to provide advice.

Planning systems are also integral parts of the policy system and will also have an input in policy formulation. In the case of Thailand this input can be definite and specific and can be written into the National Economic and Social Development Plan. With Australia the input can be non-specific and in the form of a strategy, *Tourism: Australia's Passport to Growth* (1992).

Formal and informal factors

Managers work in formal institutions, are governed by formal rules and perform formal functions but there are many informal factors which affect their formal and informal behaviour. The British television series *Yes, Minister* was a satirical example of public management practice, but a more serious insight is given by a former Cabinet Minister (Crossman 1977). The formal position of top public sector managers in policy formulation is not easy because of the pressure of conflicting responsibilities and demands.

Restrictions, efficiency and effectiveness

Managers in the public sector find that their freedom to manage is limited for various reasons. They can be limited because there is no definite sectoral policy, so all they can do is to react to pressure from the policy community and the market.

> The criticism to which reference has been made elsewhere in this report sometimes centres on the lack of policy for tourism in Britain. This merits examination certainly. . . . Those responsible

for the marketing and development of tourism generally find themselves in agreement. But frequently Britain does not seem to know what she wants from tourism.

(BTA, *Annual Report 1974*: 5)

Box 4.4 Formal responsibilities of senior public sector management

1 Formulation and implementation of legislation, laws and regulations
2 Management of their department or agency
3 Advice and support for the minister in the formulation of policy
4 Support and advice for the minister in his daily functions; preparation of policy briefs, letters and information generally
5 Coordination of the tourism agencies, reception of policy inputs, ensuring that the agencies supply the necessary policy information, and ensuring value for money in agency operations
6 Acting as the focal point for tourism policy formulation for the rest of the public sector system, and being prepared to have an input into policy formulation in other ministries where that policy affects tourism
7 Communication with, and awareness of, policy and other requirements of the industry.

The tourism lobby can bypass managers and communicate directly with the minister. Another restriction on managers, formal or informal, is the continual pressure to conserve resources and to justify expenditure and requests to the finance ministry. The same ministry can also oppose the introduction of long-term planning if the ministry believes it will restrict their freedom and ability to control. An informal restriction can be the organisational culture of the ministry, in which the tourism branch is placed. Some cultures can impose a very rigid bureaucratic process on policy formulation and others are not attuned to the dynamic needs of an industry such as tourism.

The frequent changing of tourism responsibilities from one ministry to another does not improve the efficiency of managers or their relationships with the industry or policy community. Internal decisions by higher management changing the status or position of tourism within the ministry can also have adverse effects. The tourism industry contains a very high proportion of managers who have been in the industry for many years, and they do not appreciate frequent changes, which make their input into policy more difficult. Short-term postings, maybe of three years, of public sector managers are not necessarily conducive to efficient policy making. This is particularly so when these managers are generalists and they have to deal with specialist tourism managers of many years' experience. Tourism has not always had a high status in the public sector or in individual ministries, which means it does not always attract the most outstanding managers, or get the support a more powerful industry would receive. Despite this, however, because of its increased economic importance in recent years, it has improved its position and financial budget, and tourism officials are listened to more often.

Public service managers not only manage the formulation of public policy but also financial and personnel resources, which place considerable demands upon their time and skill. There are regular procedures to deal with these and other matters in the bureaucratic system but the managers must be very clear about their priorities. One priority with an industry like tourism is the necessity of close communications, particularly in policy formulation. In the 1980s the Australian government introduced an Arrival Tax on incoming tourists; it could not be implemented and created bad feeling among the tourism community. The tax was withdrawn. Finance managers, in their eagerness to raise revenue, had failed to communicate and keep in touch with the tourism community. In 1996 a similar situation occurred when the government decided to increase six-fold the Great Barrier Reef tourist levy. Again there was no prior communication. Managers must enter into dialogue and negotiate with the community so as to achieve cooperation, coordination of effort and the right policy. The head of the tourism ministry or branch must spend a considerable amount of time liaising, visiting and talking with the tourism community. This contact and awareness is crucial for the efficient management of policy formulation, and particularly so in tourism because of the diversity of both the industry and the public sector. Formal committees of ministers or bureaucratic heads of ministries can be used for deciding major policy issues and solving major differences between ministries and agencies, such as whether tourist taxes should be imposed or whether foreign airlines can fly into particular airports. The great majority of problems and issues, however, are decided at a lower level by managers being regularly in touch with one another and deciding issues in an *ad hoc* fashion. This procedure is essential if business is to be conducted quickly and reasonably efficiently, and it is typical of a disjointed incremental approach to management.

Informal factors

The informal factors in the operation of a bureaucratic system are important and they are not covered by the Weberian system. These can include organisational culture values, objectives and behaviour and they need to be recognised, understood and utilised by managers in their formulation and implementation of policy. They can assist in the attainment of the formal objectives of the organisation or the opposite. It is easy in such a dynamic and diverse sector as tourism, with its stress on growth, numbers and financial objectives, for private informal factors to become dominant. In theory, managers should resist these influences and enforce the formal principles of public service, efficiency, effectiveness and accountability.

Public sector managers can be suspicious of tourism, as being against public sector values, or on nationalistic grounds. Tourism can be seen as not being a real industry but a candy-floss activity, unreliable, menial, destructive, and sometimes tainted with the seediness and corruption of sex tourism. Values can include the values of the individual such as integrity, commitment and self-interest, while those of the organisation will be concerned with protecting the interests of the organisation. The objectives of the individual can include personal gain and promotion and can lead to hard work or to corrupt practices for financial gain. The first informal objective of the organisation will be survival and the second will normally be growth, or at least to retain the status of the organisation. This is reflected in the efforts of government airlines resisting the entrance of foreign airlines into their markets even when this entry would achieve the formal government objective of an increase in tourist visitors. The airlines have been supported by their sponsoring ministry in this informal objective. Informal behaviour can take many forms and can be conducive to, or militate against the efficiency of the organisation.

The informal abuse of official power for personal gain is a form of corruption, as is bribery and nepotism. This behaviour can be found in the formulation of tourism policy where it is the intention of the policy to benefit individuals as against the public. Corruption can be found in tourism development in developing countries such as Thailand but also in developed countries such as Australia. In ministries the policy process can become more important than the policy objectives. Ministries can spend more time fighting internally and with other ministries than they do on formal, legitimate management. Consensus decision making can become more important than the best decision. In policy formulation, as in other areas, power contacts are important; whom you know can be more significant than what you know. Objective inputs from technocrats can be neglected because it is not in the personal interests of the policy maker. There can be an unseen informal agenda as well as the visible formal agenda. Formally governments can be committed to environmental protection, but covertly their priority is growth before anything else. There can be informal exchange understandings, as when a private manager receives favourable treatment from a public official he will be very willing to give something in return, informally and surreptitiously. This is not to say that all informal behaviour is detrimental to formal organisation: it can in fact be the opposite. Organisations could not survive and achieve objectives without the informal contribution, such as communications and networks, the loyalty and integrity of managers and their staff. Senior officials working for NTOs – for example, in Britain, Thailand and Japan – have impressive records of long service to their organisations.

WHAT RESULTS? PRACTICE AND PERFORMANCE, UNITED KINGDOM

This section considers the PSM of tourism in the United Kingdom, particularly since 1979. The formulation of public policy is only one of several responsibilities. In principle, PSM should be concerned with tourism for the United Kingdom as a whole. The practice, however, has been more concerned with the individual countries that make up the United Kingdom. Northern Ireland, for example, has its own Act of Parliament, and tourism management in Scotland and Wales has in recent years become more autonomous.

Why the government is involved in tourism: practice

The UK government became involved in tourism for economic reasons, because of the need to redress the adverse balance of payments position and to increase the amount of foreign currency coming into Britain. Economic need was the driving factor for government intervention in the 1920s and this was still true for the 1990s. Until 1969 government management of tourism was minimal and it was left to the private sector to manage as they desired. Governments became more directly involved because of their acceptance of their responsibility for the management of the economy and because tourism was becoming an increasingly important part of that economy. There was also a limit as to how effective the private sector could be in managing the multifaceted tourism sector. Officials were also responsible for accounting for public funds given to the industry.

The political culture of Britain has meant that governments have been slow to get involved in the management of tourism. Labour party ideology, however, has been willing to accept government intervention in the public interest. Hence it was a Labour government which introduced the crucially important 1969 Tourism Act which established a PSM system for tourism. Tourism in Northern Ireland is managed under a separate Act of 1948. The ideological difference with the Conservative party was reflected in a Conservative MP's objection to the term 'authority' being used in the British Tourist Authority title. He suggested that this was typical of the Socialists' control attitude towards the private sector. On the other hand, the Conservative ideology under Prime Minister Thatcher came through when the 1969 Act's Clause Four government grants to tourism were withdrawn. The ideology stressed that industry should stand on its own feet in the market place and not rely upon government handouts, while government involvement should be kept to a minimum.

Who is involved in tourism management?

Historically the private sector has led the way in the development of tourism and it still dominates in the Britain of the 1990s. The British Travel Association was established in 1929 and the private sector continued its lead role until the inauguration of the new management system of the 1969 Act. Government ministries and their departments have tried to help the tourism sector, as with the Come to Britain Movement supported by the Minister, the Chancellor of the Exchequer and the Department of Overseas Trade in 1928. One of the weaknesses of the public management of tourism has been the movement of tourism from one department to another and the rapid succession of different ministers responsible for tourism. In 1985 Lord Young, Minister for Trade and Industry, became Minister for Employment, reflecting government concerns about unemployment, and he moved tourism responsibilities from the Department of Trade and Industry to the Department of Employment. In 1992 after the general election tourism was moved again to the new Department of National Heritage. Opposition to the appointment of a single minister for tourism or the establishment of a tourism ministry has continued. As the senior civil servant responsible for tourism said:

> I have been a civil servant for many years and I have very often heard similar arguments from those with a particular interest

at a particular time. Government is all about balancing interests of various kinds on various fronts. There is never an ideal way of organising government. I am satisfied that we within the Department of Employment have the mechanism for influencing other departments. We have, for example, the Tourism Coordinating Committee chaired by the Secretary of State which has all the ministers on it . . . it meets . . . about twice a year I believe.

(UK, House of Commons, HC 18, Employment Committee 1989/90: para. 389)

The Coordinating Committee is not very effective or efficient. It cannot perform all the functions required or fill the gaps in the policy system. The tourism boards are not represented on it. It is not a systematic coordinating device, and ministers and senior PSM are not always sure what its functions are, when it meets or whether they want it.

Tourism is considered to be a minor portfolio so it is given to junior ministers as perhaps their first ministerial responsibility. Ministers are therefore keen to win promotion and so they pursue vigorously the ideology and policies favoured by the prime minister, perhaps without fully understanding the needs, or having a strong commitment to the industry. Conservative ministers from 1979 followed market ideology and initiated policies to curtail the expenditure and activities of the BTA and the English Tourist Board (ETB). Policy formulation is made difficult because the tourism industry is highly fragmented. 'English tourism (for example) involves many companies, hundreds of authorities, scores of related agencies and organisations, twelve regional tourist boards, and numerous local tourism organisations, as well as some fifteen government departments' (ETB, *Annual Report 1990/91*: 2).

How managers manage

Tourism has continued to grow and develop in Britain through a partnership of the public and private sectors. Governments have given limited financial assistance to the industry compared with other industries. They have been supportive of the industry in a general sense and this has helped to create a positive climate for tourism within the public sector and in the society. There has been some criticism, however, of the government's contribution to, and its management of, the industry, as from the House of Commons Trade and Industry Committee Report (UK 1985: para. 73).

The Government minimises the appearance of involvement by reducing policy aims to statements of the obvious but maintains the face of involvement in the tourism boards and the grants provided through them. The trouble is that this actual financial commitment is then left without there being any clear specific strategy to guide its use. More important still, the present legislative framework, creating as it does three independent and separately funded tourist boards in Great Britain, means that there is no overall policy applied to developing tourism in the UK as a whole. There is no coordination of funding, so relative priorities are not assessed, nor is there any cohesion between strategies pursued by the boards.

PSM has reacted to pressure from the industry and to economic and employment needs without the help of clear government objectives. The management has been reactive, disjointed and incremental with no overall strategy or policy except with the general objective of increasing tourism numbers and foreign currency earnings.

Government has made its contribution through the financing of the tourism boards especially for marketing but also through grants for tourism development. Such development grants, although no longer available in England, can be obtained in Scotland and Wales. The central department responsible for tourism has liaised and coordinated tourism issues with other departments. For example, the Department's Tourism Division negotiated with the Home Office to cut the television licence fees for hotel rooms, and with the Education Department on the introduction of a four-term school year to help the industry. The Division monitors the activities of the tourism boards and their finances. Most issues are dealt with on an *ad hoc* basis, which civil servants believe works well.

Practice and performance

Practice

Public interest: historically governments have given little attention to the public management of tourism and to the formulation of tourism policy. Tourism has not been rated highly by governments and even in more recent times it has been given lip-service, rather than the position of high public interest which its economic contribution merited.

The industry has been neglected because it does not have the political weight required, it is not powerful or well organised as an industry or through its workers. It is not important ideologically, like education or health. Its public importance was recognised for economic reasons with the 1969 Tourism Act establishing a public management system through the tourism boards. Under both Labour and Conservative governments the public interest was seen as being best served by leaving tourism management to the boards. Governments stated that it wanted to see an increase in tourist numbers but in practice gave little attention to tourism policy.

Under the Conservative governments since 1979 the emphasis has been away from the boards to the industry, the market, regional tourism boards and local government. Conservative political ideology held that public interest was best served by allowing industry and private individuals to formulate their own policy and pursue their own interests. It was the responsibility of government only to try and provide the best possible environment, so allowing a vigorous industry to develop in response to the demands of the market.

> The government, quite rightly, insists that the taxpayer must get value for money. It accepts that there is a need for continued public support of tourism, because there is clear evidence of 'market failure' in this highly fragmented industry, but it feels that the future direction should be shaped by the private sector, the regions, and the English Tourist Board working in the closest possible partnership.
>
> (ETB, *Annual Report 1990/91*)

In practice the stress has been on the avoidance of government responsibility for tourism, and for cuts in public expenditure, which is not the same as 'value for money'.

Whether this is the most efficient management system to protect the public interest and to formulate public policy for tourism has been questioned by the all-party House of Commons Trade and Industry Committee (1985/86) and by sections of the industry. In practice a clear idea of what the public interest was for tourism in the United Kingdom as a whole has been lacking. Guidance, policy and objectives given by government have been vague. The joint chair of the BTA/ETB said: 'I personally do not think we have a policy. I think there are certain strategic proposals which emerge from time to time, but cannot be substantiated when funds are not there' (House of Commons, Trade and Industry Committee, 1985/86, para. 627). The government has not been sure what its role should be and therefore has not provided the necessary authoritative voice to guide the industry and 'policy community' in policy formulation and action. There has been a high degree of generality in government statements made by the many government ministers since 1979. In practice, this has not been in the public interest and has been unhelpful in the formulation of specific policies and long-term and overall strategies for the industry.

This state of affairs arose partly because of the ideological stance of the government but also because there is not one minister or ministry responsible for tourism in the United Kingdom as a whole. It is therefore difficult to formulate clear overall policy guidelines or to decide what is the public interest. Boards are not in a position to make national policy, for they only meet periodically and have many other pressing matters to attend to. In their truncated form the management of the BTA and ETB are also under great pressure, but it is also difficult for them, and the boards, to make a substantial contribution to policy without more specific and authoritative guidance from government.

Public service: the government established the 1969 tourism management system to provide a public service to the industry and to assist the foreign exchange situation. Clause Four of the Act allowed grants to be given as a public service to establish or pump prime new tourism projects. These were also seen as providing public assistance to poorer regions of Britain. In 1989 these grants were withdrawn for England but continued for Scotland and Wales. This introduced an element of inequity into this public service, for some regions in England were just as deprived as those in Scotland and Wales. England also received less per capita for tourism than Scotland and Wales.

Governments have been willing to use tourism to help poorer regions and unemployment, as in 1974 when the Minister Peter Shore requested the boards to assist the underdeveloped parts of the country. In the 1970s tourism was used as an instrument of regional policy all over Europe. British Conservative governments, while cutting back on tourism expenditure, have been keen to use tourism as a public service to help decaying urban areas, inner cities and areas of high unemployment.

Effectiveness: the main objective of British governments has been to increase the number of foreign tourists to help the foreign exchange balances. This objective has been achieved, with receipts going from US$7,120 million to US$13,449 between 1985 and 1992. Yet during this period the UK share of tourism receipts world-wide declined from 6.13 to 4.40 per cent, and its decline in the share of the international market was steeper than the rest of Europe. In numbers its share of world tourists fell from 5.6 per cent to 4.3 per cent between 1980 and 1993. The total number of visitors were up, but the UK share was down because its rate of growth was so low in a booming world market. Governments and PSM have failed to get British people to take their holidays in Britain – 23.5 million travelled overseas in 1993. The travel account which shows the income from and the expenditure on tourism was last in surplus in 1985.

Until 1969 British governments did not even provide a framework of PSM for tourism and were unaware of its importance. This was shown in Montreal in 1969, when the Chancellor of the Exchequer, Roy Jenkins, was negotiating with the International Monetary Fund (IMF) to get assistance for the UK balance of payments problems. He was unaware of the state of the British travel account and had not been briefed by his civil servants. This was similar to the position in 1933 (see Ogilvie); there was no real interest in tourism, and public information and statistics were defective.

For policy formulation to be effective there need to be clear directions coming from governments and management. There has, however, been insufficient guidance given for overall tourism development; reviews of tourism PSM have concentrated on cutting expenditure and neglected the system for formulation of policy and national objectives. Neither the campaigns for rationalisation or new managerialism have made for more effective formulation of tourism policy.

The British government ministerial coordination committee, which is supposed to solve UK-wide problems and recommend policies if necessary, rarely meets and at the most does so twice a year. Civil servants responsible for tourism are few in number and only meet colleagues from other ministries if there are major problems. This system helps to explain the lack of overall direction and coordination, and sometimes confusion, in tourism management. While there was much discussion by the BTA and ETB about the challenge posed to British tourism by the opening of the Channel Tunnel, actual policy formulation proved to be ineffective due to the lack of government and senior management input and the unwillingness to take tough decisions on matters such as public investment and rail routes.

The boards of the BTA and ETB have little power and only meet occasionally. They have to formulate policy or take policy decisions without clear direction or any overall strategy from the government. The joint chair is only part-time and lacks information as to how the actual system works in Whitehall. This can extend to not knowing how, and on what basis, funds are allocated among the various boards. It could be argued that the organisations could be more effective if the chair, board members and senior managers were active politically, explaining the value of board activities to the government. Managers in a sense tend to be almost too professional, and do not lobby the policy community as to the value of their work. On the other hand, many tourism ministers are more interested in furthering their own career than in formulating tourism policy.

Efficiency: Conservative governments, particularly since 1979, have been giving overwhelming priority to efficiency – efficiency, however, defined as the curtailment of government activity and public expenditure. The actual efficiency of management and efficient formulation of policy were not considered. Several reviews were carried out by ministers, their ministries and consultants.

The main unstated objective, however, for all the reviews was simply to cut government expenditure and leave the tourism industry to manage and finance its own affairs. In practice, the easiest way to do this was to cut the tourism board's expenditure and activities and to place them on a 'tight leash'. Government objectives therefore were very limited, with no broader vision or longer-term strategy for the industry. The policy process was for the minister to institute a review managed by the Tourism Division of his department and use consultants to investigate and report on specific topics. Consultation was carried out with the tourism boards, government departments, and various sectors of the industry such as hotel and catering, transport and travel, attractions and facilities, and local governments. The House of Commons committees, Trade and Industry, and Employment, however, took a wider perspective of the tourism industry, its public management and its efficiency.

The 1982–83 review led to substantial cuts and changes to the BTA and ETB by merging several of their services, including the establishment of joint headquarters in West London with 60 per cent of activities operated as joint common services. Included were publishing and information, corporate public relations, research, finance, training, administration and personnel. A new chair, Duncan Bluck, was appointed to both the BTA and ETB boards. In the summer of 1984 the tourism information office in St James's was closed. What was claimed to be a more fundamental review in 1988–89 led to further staff cuts, so by January 1990 it was claimed that BTA and ETB staff had been cut by one-third. This latter review also led to the phasing out of Clause Four grants. It was influenced by an article in the *Spectator* magazine in 1987 which was very critical of the performance of the BTA and its efficiency. It argued that the BTA was essentially concerned with building up its own power with its 'considerable network of offices overseas – 26 at the last count, costing some £10 million year'. The BTA, it was said, by its 'very nature' could not act with any speed or decisiveness to solve problems (Trend 1987). There is no doubt that organisations can become slack and reviews can be helpful in improving their efficiency. Government claims that in total no less money is being spent on the BTA, but much more of it is being spent on the actual marketing of Britain overseas and much less on London office activities.

The cost of these 'efficiency' drives has been high. For example, the closure of the St James's office was costly in terms of redundancies and then a similar office was opened in Regent Street which re-employed some of the same people. The relocation costs of the offices to Hammersmith were also costly; just as damaging were the series of reviews and changes on the morale and efficiency of management and staff. The damage continued and the 1994 ETB *Annual Report* stated, 'Continuing uncertainty about the Board's future resulted in very low staff morale.' Strong language for an official report (1994: 33). The reviews were time-consuming as staff had to provide all the information needed, especially for the private consultancy firms which were employed by the ministerial departments. Demands were particularly heavy on senior managers, for they also had to answer to House of Commons committees and introduce the new changes. Government reviews were said to take too long, placing the boards in limbo until they were published. They were also too short in content and of poor quality. The Commons Trade and Industry Committee said of the Young Review, 'even given its limited scope, it is a superficial analysis; its recommendations, though specific, on the whole are weak' (Report UK, 1985/86, HC 106, para. 71).

The 1985 House of Commons Committee Report to improve the efficiency of the PSM of tourism was rejected by the government. In 1990 the House of Commons Employment Committee suggested that too many reviews into tourism could well prove more disruptive than productive. Government ministers in 1985 were keen to emphasise that after recent reviews the new system needed time to settle down, yet in 1988 another review was instigated.

The efficiency of UK PSM of tourism is not helped by the lack of cohesion in public management and the duplication of BTA efforts by the Scottish and Welsh boards. This duplication leads to extra costs and confusion among tourists. There is no efficient, rational disbursement and coordination of public funds for the development of tourism in the United Kingdom overall, and there is a wasteful and inefficient fragmentation of effort.

Accountability: since 1979 there has been a continual series of investigations forcing tourism PSM to account for their activities. While these reviews have been mainly aimed at the tourism boards, House of Commons committees have examined the government's contribution to tourism management. Widespread use was made of outside consultants by those responsible for the reviews, to gain greater depth, expertise and objectivity. There was a tendency, however, for the consultants to be mainly concerned with the results of cost-cutting management to the neglect of wider public service and industry requirements. They neglected the accountability of the senior ministers for such crucial decisions, or non-decisions, in policy initiation, formulation and implementation, the creation of new ministries, and the switching of sectional responsibility from one ministry to another. As a succession of ministers, senior and junior, has been responsible for tourism since 1979 and their decisions have impacted on their successors decisions, so it is difficult to allocate individual accountability for any specific impact, especially when the impact occurs after the minister responsible for the decision has moved on from tourism.

Included in the reviews were:

1982–83	Tourism Review by Department of Trade. Ministers, Sproat/Lamont
1984–85	Inquiry into tourism by Lord Young, Minister for Employment, by the Enterprise Unit of the Cabinet Office to remove 'obstacles and burdens' to tourism
1984–85	House of Commons, Committee of Trade and Industry inquiry into tourism
1990	House of Commons: Committee on Employment inquiry into tourism
1988–89	Major review of tourism by Department of Employment. Ministers, Fowler/Strathclyde.
1994–95	McKinsey & Co., analysis and strategic overview of tourism. Ministers, Dorrell/Inglewood.

Terms of reference for the tourism review, 1988–89

First, to consider the role of Government in relation to the industry;

Secondly, to consider the level, and distribution of funding provided by the Department of Employment;

Thirdly, to consider the mechanisms by which these funds

are applied; and their cost-effectiveness in relation to the Government's objectives;

Fourthly, to consider the implications for the BTA and the ETB of any changes that might be recommended.

(UK, Department of Employment 1988)

Terms of reference such as these are good, but not when they are used selectively with an almost exclusive concentration on funding. The accountability, effectiveness, efficiency and public responsibilities of management can be improved by an effective system of accountability. Since the 1980s the public management of tourism was subject to an intense form of accountability but this overconcentrated on efficiency in terms of cutting the activity and expenditure of the tourism boards. Improvements were made but the policy formulation system was not made more effective or efficient. More responsibility has moved to the industry, regional tourism boards and local government, but the public management of tourism policy formulation and implementation for the United Kingdom as a whole has not been improved.

Performance

The practice of the public management of UK tourism has declined since 1979 due to cuts in budgets and organisations, although there has been some growth in overseas offices. There has been a decline in the performance of tourism despite the rhetoric of the new government which took power in 1979. In 1995, in its major report on tourism, *Tourism: Competing with the Best*, the government said that if it could restore the world market share to its 1980 level it would increase earnings by £3 billion. It also stated that between 1980 and 1992 'Almost all destinations offering comparable attractions to Britain had been able to increase their international tourism receipts faster than Britain' (1995: 8). Too many overseas visitors were dissatisfied with accommodation and high prices, while British people found it easier to book holidays abroad. The senior minister stated:

This programme is not a comprehensive strategy for the tourism industry. It is the beginning of a process of identifying some of the key issues for the industry with some practical actions to address them. I hope it will be the start of an evolving programme of policy development.

(Rt. Hon. Stephen Dorrell, MP, Secretary of State for National Heritage, UK, Department of National Heritage 1995: 5)

After sixteen years in power to be putting forward a programme which is only a 'beginning', a 'start', and which 'is not a comprehensive strategy' suggests a failure of policy formulation and management on the part of the government. The fall in the UK market share also indicates poor performance.

SUMMARY

Governments at the centre are involved in policy formulation because it is their responsibility to formulate national objectives and make the major decisions. They have the power, the information on the total situation and the legitimacy to define public interest and public need. The top policy makers, politicians and public sector managers formulate policy, strategies and guidelines within the national political culture with inputs from party ideology and the policy community. Lower-tier managers need these policy guidelines and a supportive environment in their management of tourism. Governments are involved in tourism management for reasons of economics, politics, power and principle.

A considerable number of organisations and other participants are involved in the policy community which formulates policy. Among the most significant can be the tourism minister and ministry, the national tourism office and powerful political and industry leaders.

The management process can be complicated, disjoined, incremental, slow and too reactive to industry. More difficulties can be created by an environment of uncertainty and vagueness. An effective and efficient system requires managers to be experts in the policy process, skilled in communication and coordination and in consensus building. Informal factors can be important, helpful or detrimental. It is in the public interest, however, that the process should be democratic and open with maximum participation even though this could delay formulation.

The basic ideology of the government can be crucial, especially if principles are vigorously pursued by tourism ministers, as shown in the UK case study. Government power can affect the formulation process and the practice of managers with consequent results. Policies can be narrowly formulated with a limited perspective and neglect the wider considerations of public interest and public need. The UK study suggests there is a danger that the real needs of the industry and its development can be overlooked, especially if there is an excessive concentration on the economic aspects of effectiveness and efficiency. Public expenditure cuts may be achieved in the short term but may prove to be more costly to tourism in the longer term. Plans, strategies and policies can be unrealistic and fail to give sufficient attention as to how policies will be implemented, and the management mechanism and resources required.

In the formulation of policy the objectives should be not only to utilise national resources for tourism development but also to maintain their sustainability. To achieve the best results formulation needs to achieve a balance between public interest and public service principles, and the drive for a more dynamic, effective and efficient tourism. The ultimate test of successful formulation is the actual implementation of the policy. This will be discussed in the following three chapters.

SUGGESTED READING

Adams, I. (1990) *Leisure and Government*, Sunderland, England: Business Education Publishers. Chapters on the British system of government, local government, the countryside, tourism – history, government, issues.

Anderson, C.W. (1984) 3rd edn, *Public Policy Making*, New York: CBS College Publishing.

Callaghan, P. (ed.) (1959) *Travel and Tourism*, Sunderland, England: Business Education Publishers. Chapter on government and tourism in Britain.

Dye, T. (1995) 8th edn, *Understanding Public Policy*, Englewood Cliffs, NJ: Prentice-Hall.

Hall, C.M. and Jenkins, J.M. (1995) *Tourism and Public Policy*, London: Routledge.

Hogwood, B. and Gunn, L. (1984) *Policy Analysis for the Real World*, Oxford: Oxford University Press.

Holloway, J.C. (1994) 4th edn, *The Business of Tourism*, London: Pitman. Explains how public sector tourism is organised in Britain.

Parsons, W. (1995) *Public Policy: An Introduction to the Theory and Practice of Policy Analysis*, London: Edward Elgar.

Pearce, D. (1992) *Tourist Organizations*, Harlow, Essex: Longman.

Williams, A.M. and Shaw, G. (1991) 2nd edn, *Tourism and Economic Development*. London: Belhaven Press. Chapters on the United Kingdom, development and tourism policies.

5 Management from the centre
Implementation

This chapter explains:

- why implementation is so important and so difficult
- who are the actors involved, especially the statutory organisations
- how public sector managemnt (PSM) manages implementation and the instruments used
- what the implementation has been in one country: Thailand.

It is relatively easy for PSM to formulate policies, strategies and plans but it is much more difficult to implement them. Managers can negotiate in their offices, form committees, write reports and policy programmes, draft legislation and make decisions, but these all still have to be implemented. Since the end of the Second World War there has been a tremendous outpouring from PSM of publications, programmes and plans for many sectors, including tourism. Developed industrialised countries and international organisations have been very productive in producing plans for developing countries which could have been of tremendous benefit, but they were never implemented. In some ways the essence of the Weberian bureaucracy is the formulation and production of paper documents. Management documents are not worth the paper they are written on unless the policies and decisions are implemented. Implementation is not easy and requires many kinds of resources, including commitment from political leaders and managers, personnel, finance, leadership, power, knowledge, skill and experience.

WHY: IMPLEMENTATION AND DIFFICULTIES

Implementation

The implementation of policy is one of the most important tasks of public sector managers. It is a basic responsibility but it is one of the most difficult to achieve. This is particularly so if there have been deficiencies at the formulation stage. Non-implementation of policy means there has been a wastage of resources, time and expertise spent in formulating policy, expectations have been raised and not realised, and the standing of managers as well as political leaders has been damaged. Members of the policy community and those affected can lose faith in the public sector, and the problems which the policy was designed to solve may become more acute. Policies, decisions and objectives formulated through the legitimate process should be implemented by public sector managers even though they may not agree with them. Much will depend upon the nature of the policy. Some policies are relatively straightforward involving few institutions and resources, or power transfer. Overseas tourism marketing can be such an area. It is relatively simple, involves few organisations, has specific funds and is not an area of political controversy, so policy has been implemented successfully. Furthermore, professional marketing managers have competently managed the resources granted to them.

A major test of any manager is how successfully policy objectives can be achieved, but the successful implementation of tourism development plans is a test of the PSM system, not just the individual manager. In these cases it is not just a question of marketing and increasing tourist numbers in a growth market but it includes a whole series of other policy objectives and power groups in the society. Such policy proposals are also a test of how sensitively and democratically public managers and political leaders use their power in the implementation of policy. Singapore, which has been one of the most successful countries in tourism, has not always been sensitive in development and has destroyed many of its old but attractive buildings and the charm of old Chinese neighbourhoods. Yet when tourism started to decline, competent managers changed these policies and started to restore historic areas and add new attractions, so allowing objectives still to be implemented.

Point of application

The specific application of policy, what happens at the actual point of application, is the most important. Has the situation or service actually improved? Managers can plan and take decisions and start the process of implementation but, especially in tourism, it is not easy to implement fully, or as planned, at the point of application. For example, it might be decided to improve tourist arrival procedures at an international airport. Poor management communication and supervision, however, can result in no improvement in immigration and customs procedures. This is a failure at the point of application; it is a failure to deliver the improved service.

Managers must be able to bring together the various resources available to them into a cohesive organisational system and to motivate personnel to implement the organisation's stated formal objectives, and deliver the required service. While implementation of policy is the primary function of managers, they are also responsible for the total operation of the organisation and the maintenance of the administrative system. The actual managing of the organisation, such as the Weberian bureaucratic system, can take up the whole time of management and can lead to a lack of implementation at the point of application. There can also be a failure of implementation because of displacement of goals. For example, the survival instinct is strong in organisations and this can displace the goals ordered by the government. National airlines have often been more concerned with their survival and their dominant position than with supporting national goals of attracting more international tourists.

An example of success at the point of application is in the English Tourist Board (ETB) Chairman's foreword to the 1990/91 *Annual Report*, with management applying a programme and funds directly for a crisis situation:

> The regional boards have told me that they recognise and welcome the national leadership role of the English Tourist Board. There are many issues which have to be tackled at the national level, with the co-operation of our partners. A good example was the Britain's Great! campaign which we launched when the Gulf War led to a crisis in the industry. The Government agreed to make extra funds available on condition that they would be matched by the private sector and we were naturally pleased that, despite the recession, the industry swiftly responded to the challenge and that our colleagues in the regions gave strong support to our initiative.
>
> (ETB *Annual Report 1990/91*)

Difficulties of implementation

There are numerous difficulties which may arise, including the meaning of a policy especially when it is not clear or even appears to be contradictory. Policy can range from formal government statements to whatever the political leaders or senior managers say. A major difficulty for managers, however, has been the lack of any strong policy direction despite the assurances of support for the industry from government. In Britain, for example, there have been continual complaints about the lack of government guidance to the industry, such as by Ogilvie in 1933, and in 1985 a Commons committee complained that 'there is no overall policy applied to developing tourism in the UK as a whole' (UK, Parliament, HC 106, Trade and Industry Committee 1985). For such a vital industry it is surprising that there is no government strategy to cover threats to British tourism, whether coming from a successful Euro Disneyland, the Channel Tunnel or security dangers such as IRA attacks on London airports. Managers also do not always give sufficient attention to the possible obstacles to implementation. 'Too often costly investment encouraged by central government has been prejudiced after the event by differences of views locally or regionally, by no means a good way of achieving prudent investment in a national sense' (BTA *Annual Report 1975*).

The tourism sector is a great producer of glossy brochures and paper plans, proposals and objectives but public sector managers have found it difficult to implement these. This situation can occur in any country but it is particularly apparent in developing countries where development plans are rarely, or inadequately, implemented, partly caused by lack of resources and infrastructure. If the resources of finance, personnel and management skills are not available and if there is not the commitment from the political and administrative leaders little can be achieved. There can be opposition to the new policies, directly by vested interests who may lose some of their power or privileges, or by public organisations which are not committed or are under pressure to implement the policy. It can be difficult to implement policies because the policies are unrealistic, like some tourism development plans which can express more the ideals of professional planners than actual possibilities. Development implementation is always more difficult and controversial for it involves so many organisations and the transfer of considerable resources, including the possibility of local communities losing their livelihood and life style. Local people can also suffer if the implementation is only for the benefit of powerful economic and political interests.

There is also the problem of management control of implementation, when there are over-runs on time and costs and poor monitoring of the achievement of objective. In Britain, for example, during 1971 and 1973 the government gave a grant of £1,000 per room to encourage the building of new hotels (the Hotel Development Incentive Scheme). The estimated total cost was £8.5 million but the actual cost was over £50 million, covering 2,500 projects. Too many hotels were built in London, over half the total, and too many were in the higher price range. There were conflicts and delays between two ministries over planning permission. In 1974 the Minister said, 'There is a good reason to believe that most of the hotels built in recent years would have been built without assistance' (UK, House of Commons Debate 1974).

WHO: FEDERAL, STATE AND STATUTORY ORGANISATIONS

Who, or what organisations are involved in the management of policy implementation is subject to change, especially if there is a stress on small government and market forces leading to political pressure to transfer responsibility from national government management to other agencies, or to the private sector. It is possible to have policy formulated by a small policy unit at the centre of government which makes recommendations to political leaders while the implementation is managed by another organisation. In most public management systems the tourism agency or the tourism division in a ministry is involved in both policy formulation and implementation, but in practice may do little of either, leaving most of the functions to private sector management and the public marketing to the national tourism office. In practice it is not possible to make clear distinctions. Most good policy formulation requires considerable research and inputs from those who are implementing policy at the grass roots or impact level. Tourism is one sector in particular, where actual experience and a deep knowledge of the industry and the sector are required. In practice therefore no clear distinction can be drawn between the management involved in formulation and implementation.

National tourist administration (NTA) normally refers to all those public organisations responsible for the management of tourism at the national level.

Federal and state governments

The management of implementation includes national or federal, state, provincial and regional governments. Their tourism responsibilities will reflect the constitutional and political position of the various governments in their respective country. Many of the tourism activities and institutions of state governments are similar to those of federal and national governments. In Australia, both the federal and state governments are equally active in tourism, but in the United States most state governments are much more active in the management of tourism than the federal government. There is an excellent discussion of the role of American state governments in tourism by Richter (1985). Successful tourism in any country requires good communication, cooperation and coordination between management at all levels of government and with the industry.

Canada has a successful tourism industry, which is in the world's top forty tourism earners and makes a major contribution to the Canadian economy. Tourism management is carried out by federal, provincial and local government organisations. At the federal level the public management of tourism started in 1934 with the creation of the Canadian Travel Bureau. It is now the responsibility of the federal Department of Industry Canada, which operates Tourism Canada. There is also the Canadian Tourism Commission comprised of public and private sector members which advises the minister. It is the federal Department of Foreign Affairs and International Trade which is responsible for delivering the tourism programme overseas through its commercial officers in Canadian embassies.

Statutory organisations: national tourist organisations

The statutory organisation is seen as one of the most efficient and effective form of public management and is widely used by governments throughout the world. They are particularly important in the implementation of tourism policy and marketing. Even when a country has a ministry solely responsible for tourism it will normally use a statutory organisation also, as in Australia between 1992 and 1996. Statutory organisations are established by statute or law, to manage functions which are difficult for the ministries or departments within the traditional bureaucratic system to perform. They have the freedom which the ministries lack and therefore can respond with speed and flexibility to the demands of the industry and market.

In theory, statutory organisation management should have the same freedom as management in the private sector but it has public interest and accountability requirements. Formal and informal political intervention and ideological beliefs, however, can restrict the freedom of management. Statutory bodies are used in many ways and in many sectors, including the following:

• marketing, as with a national tourism office
• regulatory, as with environment protection, foreign investment control

- development, as with tourism development and investment
- government business enterprises, as with airlines and railways (these can take the form of a normal private company rather than that of a statutory body).

Box 5.1 Advantages of the statutory organisations

1 They are autonomous and independent of the minister and central bureaucratic system compared with the normal ministry, and are an independent legal entity.
2 Independence, objectives and powers established by Act of Parliament.
3 The board and chair of the organisation are independent of the minister and ministry.
4 The board will include representatives of the tourism industry thereby increasing its management capability. Other relevant persons can be members from the civil service, trade unions and environmental interests.
5 Have their own independently managed finances from the ministry of finance, industry and own sources.
6 Personnel independent of the civil service in terms of appointments, salaries, dismissal, terms of appointment.
7 Independent, expert staff with experience of tourism and the public sector. This expertise is not normally found in the traditional civil service.
8 The chief executive or managing director is better appointed by the board rather than by the minister.
9 The board decides major policy, mission statements, major objectives and priorities, and monitors performance and community and public interest obligations.
10 Can work closely with industry and have efficient partnership arrangements. Aware of market supply and demand situation.
11 They have experience and knowledge and are part of the public sector and work in relationship with the public sector.

In tourism, organisations such as the Australian Tourist Commission, the Tourism Authority of Thailand and the Japan National Tourist Organisation have evolved because the ministerial departments and the private organisations were found to be incapable of providing the management which the tourism sector needed. Although they have several functions they have concentrated on marketing. In Britain, four statutory bodies were established by legislation in 1969, the British Tourist Authority (BTA), the English Tourist Board (ETB), the Scottish Tourist Board and the Wales Tourist Board.

1 It shall be the function of the British Tourist Authority
   (a) to encourage people to visit Great Britain and people living in Great Britain to take their holidays there; and
   (b) to encourage the provision and improvement of tourist amenities and facilities in Great Britain.

2 Each Tourism Board shall have power to do anything for the purpose of discharging the functions conferred on it.
                                     (Development of Tourism Act 1969)

The BTA had several functions but concentrated on marketing Britain overseas. Similarly, the other three boards have several functions but concentrate primarily on marketing their region within Britain. Political pressure from Scotland and Wales has won those two boards the right to market their regions directly overseas rather than going through the BTA. In a similar situation in Australia, because of the growing importance of the tourism sector and its management needs, the Australian government established the Australian Tourist Commission in 1967. As in Britain, it replaced an existing private organisation which had been heavily subsidised by government. In the United States there is not a statutory authority as such, but the US Travel and Tourism Administration (USTTA), established by the National Tourism Act of 1981, had similar characteristics and played a similar management role in marketing, advice and coordination. The USTTA replaced the US Travel Service (1961 Act) as the federal government's tourism organisation. In 1996 the US Congress cut the funds of the USTTA and expected its functions to be performed by the industry.

Development

The statutory organisation has been useful in implementing tourism development, especially large-scale or regional development. It has been used in developing countries to channel government investment into tourism projects when no private investment has been available, or it has been a joint public–private venture. The advantage of such a body is its independence from the central bureaucracy but with control of public finance and objectives. Managers are experts in their area and have the freedom to achieve the specific development objectives more speedily and effectively than the traditional management processes. This type of institution was used successfully in Mexico, Cuba and Indonesia (Bali) in developing large beach resort areas. In Mexico, the agency has since been disbanded after successfully achieving its objectives and in the political move towards privatisation. Limited development and investment can also be managed through a national or state tourism office, sometimes providing public land as a form of investment.

Management by the board

Management at the board level can make a substantial contribution to the success of these statutory organisations, especially if there is a dynamic and committed chairperson. The chair is normally a political appointment for a set term and is normally part-time. A successful chair has the experience and the confidence of the industry. Political support is required from the minister to obtain resources from, and to implement policy through, the bureaucratic system. The chair obviously must have a close relationship with the rest of the board but particularly with the chief executive officer (CEO). Ideally the chair, with the board, should decide major policy and leave the management of the organisation to the CEO.

Boards are normally part-time and independent and serve for a set period to allow new ideas to be brought into the organisation. They can be representative of the industry, related sectors and regions of the country. Members may be drawn from trade unions, environmental groups and the civil service. Ideally they should not be appointed for party political reasons. A civil servant can either be seen as a useful link with the bureaucracy or as a threat to the independence of the board. In Australia, a public servant from the responsible ministry is a member to 'facilitate an understanding of public administration and statutory accountability requirements, and government policy' (Australian Government Inquiry into Tourism (AGIIT) 1986:79). The board is responsible for the appointment of the CEO and should approve senior staff appointments and establish priorities, corporate policies and strategic plans for the organisation. It is common for board members to meet monthly and receive reports from the CEO. The USTTA did not use the management board but came directly under the Secretary for Commerce, who chaired the Tourism Policy Council.

Management by the chief executive officer

The CEO is the key person in the organisation responsible for the management of resources, personnel and the implementation of policy. Management responsibilities are wholly in the hands of the

CEO, who will work closely with and keep the chair fully informed about major developments. The minister will also be informed. The CEO should have a proven track record of successful management and leadership of a large organisation. The personal management qualities of the CEO may be more important than experience in the tourism or government sector but such experience would enhance the performance of the CEO. Success can depend upon maintaining a balance between specialist tourism management and general management competence. It requires caution in sensitive political and public areas. Yet the CEO position also requires personal initiative and a positive contribution towards new areas of service. It is important that the CEO keeps closely in touch with and has the confidence of the industry, but there should also be a close relationship with the public sector.

The personnel of the tourism management agency will include many specialists in the tourism sector or in specialisms needed by the sector, especially marketing skills. These will be outside the normal civil service personnel system and will operate under their own independent system of salaries and conditions. This is essential if the agency is to have the flexibility to operate within and to be able to respond to market demands. It is possible that some of the staff, including managers, were recruited by the agency at an early age and therefore have considerable experience, but they must be responsive to the continual challenges posed by tourism and not become complacent or too bureaucratic.

Other organisations

Many organisations are important for the implementation of policy and the delivery of services in tourism. For example, without the support of central agencies such as finance, personnel, management, planning and chief executive offices and the resources of finance and power which they can give, implementation is impossible. In the United States the Tourism Policy Council is responsible for co-ordination but the organisations of its members are essential for implementation of policy. These include the Office of Management and Budget, Departments of Commerce, Energy, Interior, Labor, Transportation, and the State Department, which is responsible for foreign affairs. The Department of the Interior covers national parks and heritage conservation. Congressional support is also essential in the United States.

Gaining the support of other organisations poses a challenge to the skills of tourism managers. There are a great number of organisations with their own objectives and political and policy agendas yet all touching upon tourism, so that great demands are placed upon tourism managers to gain their cooperation. These organisations are powerful in their own right and often have high status and influence in the political and administrative system and they can be disdainful of low-status sectors or agencies such as tourism. They can sometimes agree to tourism proposals but can fail to implement them in a meaningful way. The cooperation of transport and airport organisations and airlines is necessary if the number of tourists visiting the country is to increase, and immigration agencies also have to agree to minimise entry requirements. Financial requirements of various kinds, including taxes and foreign investment regulations, have to be at least equitable for the industry to succeed, and several agencies can be involved. A multiplicity of organisations are involved in the management of tourism development at all levels of government and this is one of the most difficult policy areas to implement. Other organisations involved in tourism include police, health, education, marine and environment.

HOW: POWER, FINANCE, FUNCTIONS, PROBLEMS AND PLANNING

Power and its use

Managers have power because of their position and leadership ability but they also have power from various sources which they can use to implement policy. They can enforce or not enforce laws and regulations, financial measures, the granting or refusal of permissions, rights of consultation and participation. A direct control on tourists can be to restrict their right to travel, or to foreign currency – as, for example, in Britain in 1966 where an annual limit per person was imposed for overseas travel. This was to protect the value of the British pound. A more informal mechanism would be the use of bureaucratic methods to speed or slow the implementation process either to favour or penalise other parties in the process. Managers also have the power to interpret guidelines or wishes expressed by ministers. In Britain, as in many countries, the capital city is the main gateway for tourists into the country. Labour party government guidelines have tried to counter-balance this dominance by asking the BTA to emphasise the other regions. In 1984 the Conservative government asked the BTA to recognise the importance of London as a gateway because the previous guidelines did not adequately acknowledge that. Managers often have discretion as to how they implement policy.

The highest level of formal power lies in the national constitution. It is normal, as in the United States and Australia, for the constitution not to mention tourism, and this can lead to difficulties of implementation. In Australia under Section 51 there can be indirect implementation of tourism policy by the federal Commonwealth government through control and management of quarantine, aviation, customs and excise and, more recently, World Heritage areas. The residuary power is left with state governments, and consequently they are responsible for domestic tourism. This lack of constitutional specificity can lead to conflict, duplication and problems of policy implementation. A formal agreement was made in 1976 to try and overcome the problem. The Tourism Ministers Council Agreement defines the value of tourism to Commonwealth and state governments and outlines their respective responsibilities. In this, the Commonwealth was to play the role of overall facilitation and coordination. Other governments were to be responsible for domestic tourism, infrastructure, planning, regulation and the development and promotion of state facilities and attractions.

In the United States, organisations are involved in the implementation and formulation of tourism through national councils. One of the most important is the National Council of State Travel Directors, which is the main coordinating and information organisation for the states. All state and territory travel directors can meet and exchange information and agree on a united approach to the federal government. They have more influence than direct power. Other national councils cover areas such as regional tourism, urban tourism and travel attractions.

Finance

Public finance is crucial for the development of tourism. It is almost impossible for the private sector to provide the infrastructure needed for tourism, such as roads, railways, airports, power, water and refuse disposal. This is seen quite clearly when a new resort is being developed in an untouched coastal or rural area. The private organisation is dependent upon the public sector to provide the expensive infrastructure. Governments, however, can demand a contribution towards these costs. In Britain, Lord Young claimed:

Even excluding transport and infrastructure spending, which is undertaken for a far broader objective, central government's involvement in tourism and leisure accounts for a very significant annual expenditure. Expenditure on support for tourism and for tourism projects, on conserving the countryside and the natural environment, maintaining the heritage and encouraging sport totalled almost £300 million in 1984/85.

But the government believes its first priority for action should be to deal with administrative or other obstacles which may have been placed in the way of the industry's development over the years.

(UK, Cabinet Office 1985)

In practice the first priority has been to cut expenditure and not to back tourism implementation with finance. Following a review of tourism, the British government in January 1989 announced that it would terminate its assistance to tourism schemes under Clause Four of the 1969 Act.

One of the most difficult and controversial areas for governments and management has been in policy implementation and the financing of new or the extension of existing international airports. Airports are accepted as a key factor in increasing the number of incoming overseas tourists. Britain is having similar problems with the railway development needed for the Channel Tunnel. France, however, has been prepared to provide the enormous public funding necessary for the super express railway system links for the tunnel.

Public money has also been provided in most countries for the provision of a national tourism office whose main function has been to market the national tourism product overseas. That marketing has been mainly financed and managed by the public sector. In Australia, for example, funding for it has increased in recent years. In 1993–94 the Australian Tourist Commission (ATC) was granted A$77.817 millions, an increase of over 150 per cent since 1986–87. There is pressure on management for more efficient and effective management of finance. Government taxes can be used to support the industry when a hotel room tax is paid over to the national tourism office for marketing purposes, as in Singapore. The Australian government doubled its airport departure tax from A$10 to A$20 from July 1991, and the sum raised, while not directly related, was similar to that given to the ATC. Many countries, such as the United Kingdom, Japan and Thailand, have a departure tax, but taxes added to the cost of tourists' expenditure can make a country less competitive.

Management functions

Tourist managers acquire power not only from legal and financial resources and management skills but also from their knowledge. There can be generalist knowledge of the administration system, and its operation, legally and in practice. The good manager will know the system intimately and how to utilise it to achieve objectives and implementation. Management will also possess the more specific technical expert knowledge about the tourism sector and how it operates. This knowledge will be possessed more by managers with experience who may also be professionally qualified in tourism. Both types of knowledge enable managers to advise political and industrial leaders on the implementation of tourism policy. Continuity in office should add to the experience, knowledge and skill of the manager. Because of its volatility and diversity the tourism sector requires managers who can operate effectively in competitive and maybe hostile external and internal environments. Continuity can be important especially when policy implementation takes place over a long period of time, as in airport and regional development. Good relationships between the various sections of the tourism policy community need to be established and developed by managers. This is a key element in successful management and policy implementation.

Efficient communication is essential, particularly because of the swift-moving changes in tourism demand and supply. To ensure positive cooperation managers must be prepared to engage in negotiations and conciliation and this can often be achieved by consultation with, and participation by, those involved in and affected by implementation. These management roles are particularly important when the government system tends to be disjointed and incremental. The easiest changes to implement and those which meet with the least opposition are those which are incremental.

Interdependency is the basis for management in the tourism sector, for none of the tourism community can survive without the others. Each has something to exchange with the other and ideally, it is a relationship of partnership. There are obviously strong elements of self-interest involved, and public sector managers should try to ensure that the public interest is protected.

Managers may play a passive sponsorship role but the needs of the industry may require an active leadership role in taking the initiative and pushing for action and implementation of policy. Coordination is also a key function – of policy initiatives, programmes and the many participating agencies and actors.

Box 5.2 Essential functions of a CEO

1 Strategic planning leadership
2 Initiating policy plans and papers for discussion by the Board
3 Ensuring effective management of human resources
4 Maintaining regular contact with all key external and internal publics
5 Decision making on important, non-routine matters
6 Maintaining accountability for total results and resource use
7 Ensuring consistency of operating procedures.

(AGIIT 1986: 94)

In Australia, under the influence of new managerialism, the CEO of the ATC has the title of Managing Director, but his functions are similar to other tourism CEOs.

Some idea of the range of activities and positions needed to implement tourism policy are given by the management chart of the English Tourist Board of 1990–91. These can be contrasted with the organisational structure of the Canadian Tourism Commission of 1996.

Criteria and problems

Many criteria can be used to test the success of managers, including the performance of essential functions as listed for the ATC Managing Director. General principles of public interest, public service, effectiveness, efficiency and accountability should also be applied.

Effectiveness is the achievement of formal objectives; it is the most widely recognised test of tourism management. For example, success in tourism development includes growth in number of visitors, foreign investment, length of visitor stay and money spent, new hotels and number of hotel rooms and regional tourism development. It is more difficult to evaluate the contribution of management to the long-term viability of the industry or to ecological sustainable development. What appeared to be successful coastal development in Spain in the 1960s has not been able to survive the 1980s and 1990s.

Efficiency is the achievement of tourism objectives at the lowest possible cost; that is, getting the best possible return from the resources available. Under new managerialism governments have tried to encourage efficiency by curtailing the funds available. There are formal policy objectives which must be achieved and there are informal objectives, but there are also the other responsibilities of a senior public sector manager.

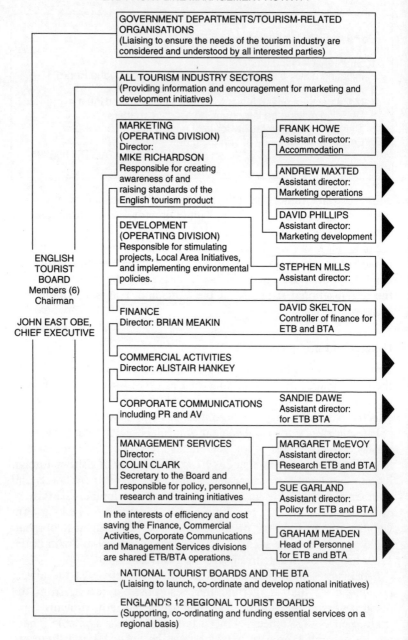

ETB FRONT LINE MANAGEMENT ACTIVITY

GOVERNMENT DEPARTMENTS/TOURISM-RELATED ORGANISATIONS
(Liaising to ensure the needs of the tourism industry are considered and understood by all interested parties)

ALL TOURISM INDUSTRY SECTORS
(Providing information and encouragement for marketing and development initiatives)

MARKETING (OPERATING DIVISION)
Director:
MIKE RICHARDSON
Responsible for creating awareness of and raising standards of the English tourism product

FRANK HOWE
Assistant director:
Accommodation

ANDREW MAXTED
Assistant director:
Marketing operations

DAVID PHILLIPS
Assistant director:
Marketing development

DEVELOPMENT (OPERATING DIVISION)
Responsible for stimulating projects, Local Area Initiatives, and implementing environmental policies.

STEPHEN MILLS
Assistant director:

ENGLISH TOURIST BOARD
Members (6)
Chairman

JOHN EAST OBE, CHIEF EXECUTIVE

FINANCE
Director: BRIAN MEAKIN

DAVID SKELTON
Controller of finance for ETB and BTA

COMMERCIAL ACTIVITIES
Director: ALISTAIR HANKEY

CORPORATE COMMUNICATIONS
including PR and AV

SANDIE DAWE
Assistant director:
for ETB BTA

MANAGEMENT SERVICES
Director:
COLIN CLARK
Secretary to the Board and responsible for policy, personnel, research and training initiatives

MARGARET McEVOY
Assistant director:
Research ETB and BTA

SUE GARLAND
Assistant director:
Policy for ETB and BTA

In the interests of efficiency and cost saving the Finance, Commercial Activities, Corporate Communications and Management Services divisions are shared ETB/BTA operations.

GRAHAM MEADEN
Head of Personnel for ETB and BTA

NATIONAL TOURIST BOARDS AND THE BTA
(Liaising to launch, co-ordinate and develop national initiatives)

ENGLAND'S 12 REGIONAL TOURIST BOARDS
(Supporting, co-ordinating and funding essential services on a regional basis)

Figure 5.1 English Tourist Board management structure
Source: ETB *Annual Report 1990/91*

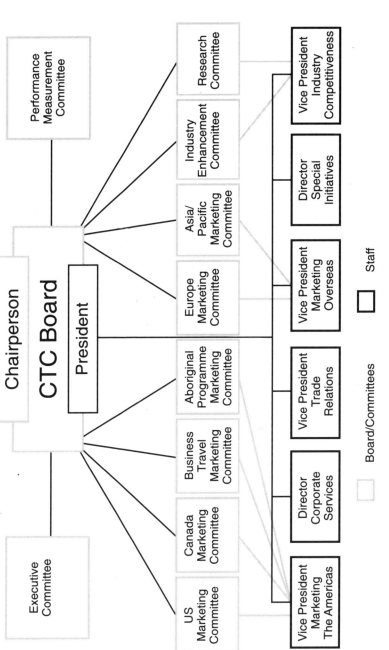

Chairperson

CTC Board

President

Executive Committee

Performance Measurement Committee

US Marketing Committee

Canada Marketing Committee

Business Travel Marketing Committee

Aboriginal Programme Marketing Committee

Europe Marketing Committee

Asia/ Pacific Marketing Committee

Industry Enhancement Committee

Research Committee

Vice President Marketing The Americas

Director Corporate Services

Vice President Trade Relations

Vice President Marketing Overseas

Director Special Initiatives

Vice President Industry Competitiveness

Board/Committees

Staff

Figure 5.2   Organisational structure of the Canadian Tourism Commission (May 1996)

Evaluation is difficult because there can be conflicts and contradictions between the various objectives and responsibilities, such as between effectiveness and public interest. Management can be effective in achieving the objective of increasing tourist numbers yet fail to support the public interest by not protecting the environment. Successful managers will be as good as if not better than their competitors. They will be responsive to, and in front of or will actually create demand. Yet they are also aware of and responsive to the needs of the domestic sector and the local communities. Successful managers not only utilise the national tourism product but they also improve it.

Problems in tourism management

Problems in the management of tourism can occur because of the conflict of objectives and conflict between different agencies. Objectives can be too narrow or too economically focused leading to an over-use of the environment or a neglect of non-economic factors. Wider public interests can be displaced by narrow economic interests promoted by the tourism industry. There have also been major problems caused by the non-implementation of policies by inefficient or corrupt managers. There are problems because of the diverse nature of the industry and the fragmentation and rivalry within the public sector. Public management systems can be slow, cumbersome and out of touch with the needs of the industry. Implementation at the lowest level, the street level, can be ineffective (see Lipsky 1980).

Informal factors can also pose problems. Hidden power groups and links, private and vested interests in the management system and policy community, can prevent the effective implementation of public objectives. Secret agendas can be followed by politicians and by managers, with self-seeking and greed leading to corruption and the misuse of public resources including the PSM system. The PSM system is a public resource which should be used to benefit the public, not private, interest. A management system with its own self-serving culture, which is closed and secretive and is driven by informal interests and officer and agency rivalry, can be very destructive of tourism development based on the national interest. National tourism offices are mainly concerned with marketing and increasing tourist numbers and managers rarely go beyond these objectives. These managers can become too specialised or too technocratic and so develop a tunnel-like vision.

Ministers can use the national tourism organisations (NTOs) politically and the board members can place their own political and personal objectives before those of the organisation. Sponsoring ministries of NTOs may have no real interest or commitment to tourism, which can be a very minor category in a large ministry. Ministries can also use NTOs for the purposes of, and as a device to protect the ministry and avoid accountability. In this kind of environment managers can become politically partisan, and fail to implement formal objectives. NTOs can also become tools of the tourism industry and fail to carry out community service obligations. When an industry such as tourism is in a growth period and tourist products are in great demand it is difficult to isolate the management qualities involved in the success of tourism from the success brought about by natural market demand. This is particularly so when the private sector plays such a prominent role in the development and marketing of tourism. In marketing, for example, it is normally the lower price which is the most important factor in attracting tourists, and other factors such as management skills are secondary. It is therefore sometimes difficult to evaluate management. One test of management is how well it operates in a crisis situation, if the industry is threatened by civil war, terrorism or labour withdrawal by workers.

In implementation one of the problems is the different marketing and promotion programmes pursued by different governments, such as state governments in Australia and the United States, or in the four tourism organisations in the United Kingdom actively marketing overseas. This can also be a problem with local governments from the same region competing against one another. Competition can stimulate managers to improve their performance. It can also be a waste of resources, it can confuse the potential tourist and their images of areas, and lessen the impact of the marketing efforts. This is unsatisfactory for management and is against the five principles but is supported by political and economic power groups. The UK government allowed Scotland and Wales to market overseas so as to gain political support from these two countries. To try and solve the problem in Australia the federal Commonwealth government in 1993 provided supplementary funds of A\$2 million for the new 'Partnership Australia' marketing scheme to coordinate better and channel the combined resources of Commonwealth, state and territory governments.

In the United States there can be problems between the federal and state tourist organisations, leading to a failure to tackle national needs and priorities in tourism. These difficulties were recognised by the holding of a tourism conference at the White House, Washington, DC, in 1995. This was a partial recognition that the federal government had some responsibility for one of America's most important industries, and that there was a need for stronger organisational, management and other links between different governments, and with the industry.

Management and planning

Planning is a very important part of the process by which tourism is managed by governments at the national, local and organisational levels. It can be used to implement policy and to achieve objectives but it can also be used to help formulate policy. There are several definitions of planning, but one that is useful for the management of tourism is: 'Planning is the process of preparing a set of decisions for action in the future, directed at achieving goals by preferable means' (Faludi 1973: 330). Planning is used extensively in government, as in national economic planning; sectoral planning, as with tourism or national parks; land-use planning, which is often applied to city, urban and rural development; and corporate planning, as found within public and private organisations. While planning is used in this study as a process it is also seen as an instrument of management to achieve objectives, not least economic development. From a management perspective, and reflecting the Weberian ideal, planning is seen as rational and objective, based on professional expertise and experience, administered by competent, qualified permanent officials as compared with the irrational, impermanent, amateur politicians.

How much a government will utilise planning and the nature of that planning will reflect the political culture of the country. This culture also helps to determine the role of governments, and how much they intervene in the society. In the United States the culture limits national economic planning but allows other types of planning. In some political cultures politicians and members of the tourism industry may regard planning as an unacceptable and dangerous government intervention into the affairs of the industry. They see it as socialistic and going against the free movement of the market and the vigorous private response to market movements. Those who support this position can follow a disjointed incremental or *ad hoc* policy approach to tourism development, the United States being the best example of this. Yet the USTTA was required to collect and disseminate data 'in order to facilitate planning in the public and private sectors'. The Communist states of China, Cuba and Vietnam have moved from the rigid central planning of the past, with much more freedom given to sectors including tourism.

The United Kingdom and planning

There has been no long-term, comprehensive planning for tourism in the United Kingdom. In the mid-1960s when there was a form of national economic planning, insufficient attention was given to tourism in that planning. Since that period no national planning system has been in existence, but according to the ETB CEO in 1990:

> One of the key outcomes of the Government Review was that the ETB should have a keener look at tourism, planning and thinking for the future. To compete with other countries and encourage Britons to holiday at home, we need a strategy before setting objectives and raising standards.
>
> (*Travel GBI* 1990)

While the government or the ministry has produced no plan or strategy for the future of tourism, the BTA and regional boards have produced documents after consultation with the industry and government. For example, in 1987 the ETB had the *Vision for England* strategy and after the Review it produced *Planning for Success 1991–95*. This was produced after research and 'lengthy consultation with public bodies and the industry'. Four major challenges were identified, as shown in Box 5.3.

Box 5.3 Tourism challenges, England

1 Mounting international competition – especially from Europe – for increasingly sophisticated travellers
2 Pressure to balance the needs of tourism with those of the environment
3 The urgent need to improve transport and communications
4 Recruiting, training and motivating a skilled workforce in a competitive labour market.

(ETB *Annual Report 1990/91*)

Implementation of the 1991–95 strategy required commitment and finance from governments as well as carefully coordinated marketing and development at national, regional and local levels. The BTA produced *Guidelines for Tourism to Britain, 1991–95*. The chairman said it was 'to provide a framework for planning and decision taking by public and private sector organisations involved in tourism' (BTA *Annual Report 1991*).

WHAT RESULTS? THAILAND

Tourism planning in Thailand

This section considers the management of the implementation of tourism policy in Thailand within the context of national economic planning. The political culture of Thailand is a mixture of strong central government in theory, but in practice considerable freedom can be enjoyed by public organisations and the private sector. Thailand is a mixed economy, with government providing the infrastructure and the private sector making up most of the rest of the economic system. The tourism industry, for example, is mainly made up of private organisations within the infrastructure provided by PSM. Part of that infrastructure is a national economic planning system. This does not provide a mandatory comprehensive blueprint plan which must be followed but a five-year indicative plan laying down guidelines and objectives agreed after consultation with the public and private sectors. Because of the nature of the political culture and system, the Thai government is not in a position to enforce the plan. It can only indicate what are its preferences.

Why tourism planning?

As is common with developing countries, the main objective was economic development, but as with developed countries, tourist development was seen more specifically as a means of raising foreign exchange earnings and improving the balance of payments position. While economic motives were the predominant reasons for government involvement in tourism, these were joined by other objectives reflecting wider responsibilities to the society. Tourism was seen as a growth industry where Thailand had the assets to make it an attractive tourism destination. Domestic tourism had been established for many years, as at Hua Hin with its famous grand railway hotel and residences of the upper classes. The early major international development came with the Rest and Recreation (R and R) programmes of the American servicemen engaged in the Vietnam conflict in the 1960s and 1970s. Thailand, like many developing countries, was also encouraged by international agencies such as the World Bank and the International Monetary Fund (IMF) to establish planning systems.

The formal objectives of the government for tourism were expressed in the objectives given to the Tourism Organisation of Thailand (TOT), later the Tourism Authority of Thailand (TAT), when it was established. The TAT was required to do the following, as shown in Box 5.4.

Box 5.4 Tourism management objectives, Thailand

- To seek for optimum growth for tourism
- To establish tourism plans for all Thailand
- To seek economic development of Thailand through tourism
- To accomplish these objectives in a manner which will preserve and enhance the social, cultural and historical aspects of Thailand.

These objectives were the basis of the National Plan for Tourism Development published in May 1976. They are similar to those of the 6th National Economic and Social Development Plan (1987–91) which, according to the Governor of the TAT, 'may be considered the master plan for Thailand's tourism development and promotion' (TAT *Annual Report 1985*).

Box 5.5 Main tourism objectives of the sixth plan, Thailand

1 Development of domestic tourism
2 Encouragement of international tourism
3 Provision of incentives to the private sector towards the establish-ment of tourism facilities in accordance with a proper development plan
4 Encouragement of public investment in the development of infra-structure and superstructure for tourism in specific areas
5 Preservation of the tourism environment
6 Maintenance of a high standard of tourism business and services
7 Enforcement of the safety measures provided for tourists.

While these formal objectives are fairly wide, there is no specific mention of responsibility for the people's welfare in them. Yet it is expected that there should be optimum growth for tourism and the plan and development should be for *all* Thailand.

Who is responsible?

Ultimate responsibility for establishing objectives and prioritisation, for policy formulation and implementation lies with government. In Thailand this is the Prime Minister and Cabinet and central agencies such as the Ministry of Finance, the National Economic and Social Development Board (NESDB), the Board of Investment (BOI) and the Budget Bureau. Other ministries with some responsibility for tourism include the Ministries of the Interior, Transport and

Communication, Agriculture and Cooperatives, and Science. The National Environment Board, National Parks Agency and Forestry Department act as regulatory bodies. Thai Airways International and the Airport Authority of Thailand (AAT) are other important government agencies. A great deal of responsibility for policy implementation lies with provincial governors and local governments. Direct responsibility for tourism lies with a Cabinet Minister attached to the Prime Minister's Department. The Minister is the Chairman of the TAT, which is the key body for tourism policy formulation and implementation. The TAT was established as the Tourism Organisation of Thailand (TOT) but with the growing economic importance of tourism was raised in status to the Tourism Authority of Thailand (TAT).

The majority of officials staffing these organisations are generalists with general qualifications and general experience such as in the Ministry of the Interior. In the central agencies, however, there are a significant proportion of technocrats who have specialist qualifications and experience, such as economists and planners. The top position is normally occupied by a generalist but in some agencies such as the NESDB the top official, the Secretary-General, will be a specialist. In the TAT the Governor has a generalist qualification but long experience of tourism, and hence is a specialist in tourism. The PSM of tourism needs all types of expertise and experience, and a good manager will recognise this and be able to utilise these personnel resources in achieving organisational objectives. In the management of tourism it is no longer applicable to use the simple old adage 'The generalist on top and the expert on tap.'

The ministries all have provincial and sometimes regional officials to assist with the implementation of policies and plans. The TAT has regional offices in Thailand, such as Pattaya and Phuket, and also international offices. The role of the private sector is crucial to tourism development and the implementation of the government's tourism plans, especially in a mixed but predominantly capitalist economy as in Thailand. Then the question is how well PSM manages its relations with the private sector. This is discussed in Chapter 7. One organisational device used by the Thai government has been Joint Public–Private Consultative Committees.

How managers manage the planning for tourism development

The Thai government accepts the responsibility for long-term planning for the economic and social development of Thailand. The National

Economic and Social Development Board (NESDB) is the agency responsible for drafting the national five-year plans and tourism is included in the plans. The NESDB Secretary-General is one of the TAT Board of Directors. In 1973, the NESDB Sub-committee on Tourism Industry Development functioned as a Steering Committee to draw up a National Plan for Tourism Development. The plan was to serve as the basis for detailed plans after an investigation of the demand for tourism in each region of Thailand. The potential of all regions was evaluated and an examination was made of the need for infrastructure. A broad outline for development was put forward based on an assessment of relative rather than absolute priorities. The TOT was a key body in formulating the policy and the plan, and the Deputy Director-General, Colonel Somchai, chaired the Steering Committee, which included four TOT members. The TOT provided much of the primary data, such as the identification of 510 primary tourism attractions in Thailand. A Dutch firm of tourism consultants was employed to draw up the plan based on the Committee's terms of reference, guidance and data provided by the TOT. There was a Dutch Study Team of five which started work in December 1974 and conducted field studies.

The consultants encouraged local participation and claimed that the cooperation received was very effective. The plan was published in May 1976 and was a well-balanced, comprehensive document, but it lacked detail because of various constraints, such as time and finance. It not only acknowledged the importance of tourism to the economy, but also the dangers, including the risk of commercialisation of tourism and the deterioration of socio-cultural values. It acknowledged that particular care therefore should be taken to protect remote areas with a vulnerable culture, and that strict regulations should be enforced to protect the environment. The plan recommended that there should be optimum growth, with tourism plant and development being planned for all Thailand and that objectives should be accomplished 'in a manner which will preserve and enhance the social, cultural and historical aspects of Thailand' (TAT Plan 1976: 61). Although social and cultural effects are difficult to quantify, they should still be taken into consideration. It was suggested that international tourism should not be allowed to develop unrestrictedly and that the intake could be stopped at a maximum level at some time in the future. The carrying capacity of an area should not be exceeded.

Planning proposals and management

The Development Plan and the Programmes recommended for the five years from 1 January 1975 covered all the important regions. For Pattaya, a long-term development plan was to be prepared and a development agency established. Environmental standards were to be set and measures taken to combat beach and sea-water pollution. Similar pollution measures were recommended for Phuket with a controlled use of the Phang-nga Bay islands. Samui Island was to be developed for local and domestic tourists only and the development plan was only to allow the construction of modest and moderately priced hotels. Various management changes were recommended and it was strongly recommended that the TOT be converted into a ministry with sufficient power to ensure an integral development of international and domestic tourism. It was recommended that the TOT managers should be able to coordinate the public sector and guide and control the activities of the private sector. Two departments were recommended, marketing and promotion, and product and service development supported by research and planning sections. Major projects would be undertaken by special agencies while co-operation between the private and public sectors would be under the supervision of a Tourism Development Authority. All these activities would be directly under a government minister. Any tourism development had to be balanced with those of other interests such as regional development policies and priorities. The plan acknowledged the importance of the private sector and how its initiative had created the industry, 'indicating a striving, clear business mind'. It was, however, also noted that the industry could get out of hand and that its interests did not always coincide with the national or public interests and it was largely guided by *laissez-faire* principles. Development required strong management and a government agency with knowledge to handle and control implementation, and the TOT was inadequately equipped to perform this.

What results? practice and performance

Non-implementation

Since the plan was published in 1976 tourism has developed to a massive extent and without real restriction. Most of the perceived dangers and deficits have come to pass and become increasingly worse, if not out of hand. There has been no balanced development for the benefit of the whole of Thailand. No attention has been given to the carrying capacity of areas. The sea off Pattaya became so highly polluted as to be unsafe for swimming. There have been expensive developments in Samui for international tourists. Other areas, such as Chiang Mai and Hua Hin, have been overdeveloped.

There has been no neglect of formal planning in Thailand. The NESDB has regularly introduced five-year plans which recommended tourism development. Below the level of the 1976 tourism plan there have been several regional or resort plans for areas such as Pattaya and Phuket. The problem has been that these plans were not implemented. New plans have been proposed.

The TAT and the Japan International Cooperation Agency (JICA) undertook a study on Potential Tourism Area Development for the Southern Region of Thailand in 1988–89. This study assumed, however, that tourism would increase and that this was desirable. The same assumption was made in an important guideline study into the carrying capacity of an area on Samui Island in 1988 which was carried out by the Thailand Institute of Scientific and Technical Research. The JICA study, like other studies, also avoided the difficult question of the real beneficiaries from the development. It was assumed that there would be a trickle-down effect to local people, but there were no hard data on this, nor was any study made of various social, environmental and other costs. JICA predicted that 1.6 million visitors would visit the three southern provinces of Phuket, Phang-nga and Krabi by 1991, 2.2 million by 1996 and 3 million by the year 2001. By 2001, 32,000 hotel rooms would be needed, which would create land shortages in Phuket so developments would have to proceed along the coast. JICA proposed that its plans be implemented over the next twelve years. It is, however, relatively easy to formulate plans. The major problem is to implement them, as the Thai experience shows.

Constraints on PSM

One reason why managers fail to implement policies or development plans is because they are not in complete control of the implementation process and factors affecting that process. They are constrained by the international and national environment in which they have to operate. Tourism industries must operate within a highly competitive world market. Nations are dependent upon other nations for capital, aid, markets, tourism and general cooperation. In this respect Japan was the most important country for Thailand. Japan was under pressure to cut its enormous trade surplus. One government answer to this was to boost Japanese tourism overseas, including to Thailand. The Thai government has to be careful it does not damage its tourism product, industry or image overseas. Considerable effort therefore is given to marketing and public relations and projecting a favourable image overseas including the curtailment of bad publicity on pollution or on AIDS.

National political culture

Governments are constrained by their national environment, including geography, climate, history, culture, economics and politics. The values, characteristics and behaviour of the political and administrative system will reflect these factors. For example, the tolerance and easy-going nature of Thai society is reflected in the lax administration of law and the relaxed attitude to policy implementation. Government and power is highly centralised in Bangkok but localities continue to do their own thing. Thailand is a strongly Buddhist society, which also explains the tradition of tolerance. This tolerance extends to the freedom given to foreigners, ethnic groups and business to pursue their particular interests and to economic development, but it can also allow corruption in the public sector. Another factor is the desire for economic gain which can determine objectives and attitudes in the tourism industry as well as elsewhere in the society. Formal status, a strong hierarchy and a highly centralised governmental system in Bangkok is part of Thai society. Yet so also is a well-developed informal network of contacts and obligations operating under the rules of the game. Managers must operate within, or with, the given factors but this is not to say that the factors will always remain constant. Factors will change and the situation is fluid and dynamic. One test of management is not only how it utilises the given factors but its ability to respond to a demanding and changing environment.

One reason for the apparent ineffectiveness of management is that the responsibility and role of the Thai government is seen as being limited. In the economic field it tends to be passive, takes minimal action and is reactive rather than active. Governments are committed to economic development in general and will support policy areas such as rural development. Yet often the commitment to a policy will only be verbal so there is no policy implementation. Governments give top priority to survival and self-interest and then to security and defence. They are constrained by and react to the demands of powerful groups in the society, such as the army and large interest groups, and secondarily to public opinion. Policies can also be contradictory, such as increasing the number of tourists, which can prevent the preservation of the natural environment.

Politics

In any country, management is dependent upon politics at both the national and local levels. In Thailand political parties are weak and have no strong political philosophy. Management in Thailand is made difficult because the Cabinet is made up of a coalition of political parties, which, if it is to maintain unity, must recognise the interests of various groups. This makes it difficult to agree on national objectives and more difficult to implement them. Policy formulation and implementation is secondary to unity. Decisive action and major new initiatives will only be taken if there is strong support, or a ground-swell of public opinion in favour. Powerful tourism groups will get their development implemented, unless there is opposition to it which could threaten the government. Local politicians can be paid to support the development. Because of its increasing economic importance political parties are now taking an interest in tourism policy but their input is limited.

Policy initiatives and implementation can fail because of the diverse and wide range of public organisations involved each with its own political agenda and seeking to increase its power. Organisations can have considerable independence and their own values, and follow their own objectives and self-interest. They can be supported by coalitions of vested interests each backing an increase in its own influence or in maintaining the *status quo*. There is often no strong leadership or control from the Prime Minister or Cabinet. This is one reason why the NESDB five-year plans have limited effect and the National Tourism Plan of 1973 was never implemented. The nature of the government and its priorities means that in many areas there is management inertia or inaction. The government does not implement its policies in a rigorous way, as, for example, protecting weaker groups in the community. This approach by government can encourage anti-social behaviour by public and private organisations. Industry can be encouraged to cut corners and engage in corrupt practices and managers to listen to, and protect only influential groups. There is little or no popular participation or consultation of the small or local interests affected, and the process is hidden, thus encouraging corruption and helping particular interests to get privileged attention and benefits from the public sector. Politicians and managers can be rewarded by private economic interests when they give these interests preferential treatment in the application of public policy.

National objectives are outlined by the government, such as economic development and the earning of foreign exchange. Tourism is an ideal industry to achieve these objectives and is in an excellent position for further expansion and development. Priority, however, is given to swift development, and PSM and the industry tend to neglect long-term economic consequences and the social and environmental costs. This approach makes it very difficult for public agencies, even if they wished, to follow the policy of public interest. Thai public organisations, as with most organisations, are more concerned with protecting and increasing their own influence rather than with pursuing actively public policy matters. Organisations are keen to keep their own interest groups and community satisfied; they rarely take the initiative and see their main responsibility as keeping the system going. There is therefore a major problem at the policy-making centre of Thailand. Because of politics and power conflicts it is difficult to formulate policy especially on controversial issues, and even more difficult for management to get policies and plans implemented against strong economic interests and in the prevailing political and administrative culture.

Public organisations

Plans have not been implemented, law and policies not enforced and tourism development not controlled partly because of the failure of the government's administrative organisations. The internal politics between and within the organisations are made more complicated by their great diversity in terms of legal position, status, responsibilities, formal and informal roles, power, size and expertise. Formal and informal objectives of the organisations can be in conflict and legal compliance can hide the informal reality. There can be problems of competition, communication, coordination and cooperation within and between organisations. 'There are too many hierarchical levels and too great an emphasis on top-down supervision' (Amara 1983).

In comparison with employees in the private sector civil servants in Thailand are poorly paid. The disparity has increased in the economic boom of recent years. As a consequence some officials may 'aspire for positions from which they can reap additional income even though it is against the law . . . ' [and] 'for their survival these people spread their network throughout the system and work in teams to gain wealth' (Amara 1983: 168). Tourism development can involve large amounts of money and so is not immune to this kind of problem. Having the appropriate qualifications for a position can be secondary to having the right connections with a senior official who has influence over appointments and promotions. These various factors make it difficult to come to efficient decisions, reach agreements and implement plans and enforce policies effectively.

Central government organisations

The central organisations such as the Ministry of Finance, the Budget Bureau and the Bank of Thailand were only concerned about the foreign income which tourism could bring into the country and the budget required by the TAT. Because of the foreign currency earnings they supported the development and growth of tourism. They were involved and concerned about high cost infrastructure development related to tourism such as airport construction. This kind of expenditure only became acceptable when tourism replaced rice exports as the chief foreign currency earner. The Board of Investment (BOI) was interested in the development of tourism only in terms of investment grants of privileges, but in recent years many developers have preferred to find their own investment because of the limited privileges given and the long-drawn-out terms and conditions set by the BOI. The BOI has not always been correct with their forecasts regarding tourism nor have they been concerned with tourism impacts. They have only two or three officials who specialise in tourism projects. The BOI did not evaluate foreign investment in tourism as to its actual benefit to Thailand taking into account all the costs involved. Investment can be speculative, and it is not always clear how much of the local investment actually comes from overseas. Furthermore, 'investment in luxury hotels represents a continuation of the speculative real estate orientated investments which are characteristic of the ruling classes of many underdeveloped societies' ('Tourism-selling Southeast Asia' 1981:7–8).

The central organisation with the direct responsibility for assessing the importance of tourism development, especially in the long term, in both the social and economic spheres, was the NESDB. Under Prime Minister Prem (1980–88) NESDB was extremely influential and vetted all big projects before they went to the Cabinet. Under Prime Minister Chatichai however, projects, including tourism projects, went directly to the Cabinet. NESDB has direct knowledge and experience of tourism development, for its Assistant Secretary-General is a member of the TAT board. Yet there are only about five officials with some responsibility for tourism planning. There are many demands upon the resources of the NESDB so there is a tendency for the forecasts and plans of the TAT to be accepted as they are and placed within the National Plan. Little consideration has been given to the long-term costs of development and to who actually benefits from the development or to the strains placed upon local communities and infrastructure by too rapid development.

Central organisations are responsible for formulating policy based on an overall balanced assessment of the economy and needs of the society. They are responsible for advising on priorities, development and short- and long-term planning. The organisations, however, are conditioned by the growth mentality and give insufficient attention to the real benefits to the people and adverse effects of such growth. Another defect is the weakness of the machinery of implementation.

> At the governmental level the office of National Economic and Social Development Board (NESDB) and the Budget Bureau help to make policy and to plan, including allocation of resources, follow-up and evaluation. There is, however, no organization specifically responsible for supervisors and acceleration of the work at this level
>
> (Xuto *et al.* 1983: 144)

The main organisation responsible for the PSM of tourism, including implementation and planning, is the TAT.

A PSM organisation: the Tourism Authority of Thailand

Why the TAT, and who are involved in its management?

The TAT is necessary, for the traditional Thai government department cannot perform the functions essential for successful tourism for Thailand. It is only this type of organisation that can manage tourism in the public and private sectors, domestically and internationally, on behalf of the government.

Such an organisation should have the expertise and freedom and dynamism required to operate in the highly competitive tourism market. There was no ministry of tourism in Thailand so the TAT has to try and fill the power vacuum and perform ministerial functions. In 1994 the TAT had a workforce of 937 based in the head office in Bangkok, and provincial and international offices including London, New York, Sydney and Tokyo. The chief executive officers have been highly experienced in tourism public management. Colonel Somchai retired in 1987 after twenty-five years with the TAT and eleven years as chief executive. His successor, until his transfer in 1994, had been with the TAT for about thirty years. The new Governor has served with the TAT almost as long. There are three deputy-governors, responsible for administration, marketing, and planning and development respectively (see the TAT Organisation Chart, below). The CEO is responsible to a board of governors, which includes a minister who acts as the chairperson. The minister has other responsibilities, which in 1994 were investment and energy. Of the eleven members, seven are there by law and represent government organisations, the others represent the tourism industry. Although major decisions are taken by the board, which performs valuable communication and coordination functions, its input into policy initiation and implementation is not normally strong. The TAT was founded in 1960 and raised in status to an Authority (TAT) in 1979 with a governor as its head, but there was little, if any, increase in its authority.

How managers manage

The TAT board is ultimately responsible for management, it sets the policies, directions and guidelines. The governor and the TAT managers are responsible for implementing board policy, for ensuring delivery at the point of application. To do this they must know the tourism market, and be active in it, and they have to cooperate closely with the industry and other government organisations. It is normally these other organisations and the industry which are directly responsible for policy implementation. The priority in the TAT, however, has always been towards the promotion and marketing of Thailand overseas. This emphasis is reflected in the selection of the governors from the marketing side of the organisation. In this the TAT does not differ from most other national tourism offices (NTOs) around the world with the stress on raising the number of foreign visitors. This side of the work is more glamorous, less demanding and less dangerous politically than development control.

What results? practice and performance

In practice the performance of the TAT can be affected by the minister responsible for tourism who chairs the board. The minister is appointed by the Prime Minister and based in the Prime Minister's Office but this does not necessarily increase the influence of the TAT.

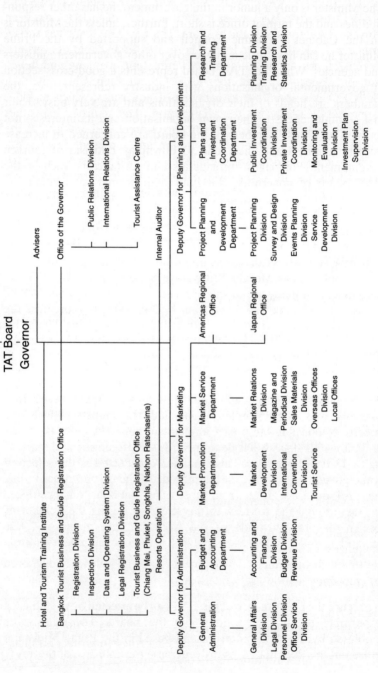

Figure 5.3 Tourism Authority of Thailand organisation chart
Source: TAT *Annual Report 1994*

The Minister is only a junior in the government, he has other responsibilities and the term of office is short. Further, unless the Minister is on the Cabinet Economic Council and supported by the Prime Minister he can have little influence over other government ministers and agencies. While the TAT board represents a good cross-section of governmental organisations with industry representatives, the members are heads of their organisations and are very busy. Their first commitment is to their own organisation and its interests, not to the TAT. Most members of the board are concerned to increase tourism numbers and they tend to downplay criticism of tourism development. Politicians, bureaucrats and technocrats, such as the TAT board of governors, can fulfil their formal role within the administrative system but, in practice, informal influences upon them and management can curtail the implementation of policies and plans. Politicians and managers can also be misled by their own public relations and rhetoric.

Tourism ministers can play an important role if they have the ability and the policy ideas. Meechai Viravaidya helped to make the TAT and the industry more aware of the problems of sex tourism and AIDS. Dr Savit Bhotivihok was active from 1993 in trying to reorganise the TAT, to make it more effective, efficient and accountable. Under his chairmanship in 1994 the board transferred, or removed, the governor. The Minister said that tourism management was slow to respond to initiatives and policies.

> The hardest part with which I have met fairly stiff resistance and which has to be worked up is the re-organisation and re-engineering. But I think we are moving on this line, once the structural change has taken place, we will see a new breed at the TAT.
>
> (Bhotivihok 1994: 4)

The TAT governor and the organisation are responsible for implementing the policies and plans approved by the board. They also 'have a responsibility to the overall country and industry that this organisation [TAT] is efficiently run and capable of meeting the challenges' (Bhotivihok 1994: 15). It is suggested that the TAT did not follow through on its development plans and policies and ignored the recommendations contained in them. The board felt that the governor was not performing as required and was not producing results. So his services were dispensed with despite the opposition of the eight tourism industry associations. There was also the possibility of a hidden agenda, with the governor concerned to protect his financial position after retirement. It could be argued that the TAT has had a narrow view of its role. There was an over-concentration on total numbers and insufficient attention given to the quality of the tourists and to the effects of mass tourism on Thai society and the environment. Despite increased funding, insufficient resources were given to tourism research and analysis of net economic and social returns. The TAT has been slow to give sufficient attention to the long-term impact and the problems arising from development. It is involved in planning, as with the JICA plan for southern Thailand, but it has in the past made little attempt to have tourism plans implemented, and attempts made have failed. The TAT has not been so successful either in terms of meeting public need or providing the public service required. It did not control development and was itself not subject to a rigorous accountability system.

Performance problems

The TAT in its management of planning and development has been severely restricted by lack of power and resources and by opposition. There has only been limited success in development control, plan implementation, environmental protection and the solution of long-standing problems. Plans have been criticised for being ill conceived, too expensive with unreliable statistics and targets, and so unimplementable. There has been no development corporation for tourism, and development has been haphazard and piecemeal with too much building and excessive exploitation of natural resources. It is easier to produce paper plans than to implement them against vested interests and developers. There are also problems which can affect any organisation, such as empire building, nepotism, paternalism, over-concentration on paper work and regulation, poorly qualified or motivated staff especially at the lower levels. A limited perception of and a cautious bureaucratic approach to its functions can also curtail the contribution of the TAT. It should promote talented people internally, but also recruit talent from outside to foster a 'new breed' of managers.

Government policies can be contradictory, such as priority given to increasing tourist numbers and development running contrary to the policy of protecting the natural environment. This is one reason for the destruction of Pattaya's environment and the massive pollution there. The TAT has tried to raise its status and increase its powers by becoming a ministry but has failed. Its position is also weakened by insufficient political support and direction from the government and its central organisations. The organisation has no power and limited funds with which to influence developers or local government to enforce plans or policies. Managers at the regional level have no authority, all they can do is advise. The TAT has always blamed the lack of implementation of policies and plans and the deterioration of the environment on its lack of power. In practice, however, the preservation of the tourism environment has never been given any priority by managers.

Tourism planning in Thailand in practice has mainly been concerned with land-use development and has been dominated by market forces. Major policy areas of public interest and public service such as the community, environmental protection and sex tourism have been neglected. In March 1994, former Thai Tourism Minister Meechai, in a speech in Cambodia, warned them not to follow the Thai model for tourism. He suggested that some governments had lied and were still lying about the extent of AIDS for fear of damaging tourism.

Performance and success

The Thai tourism model, despite its failures and problems, including military *coups*, has still been one of the phenomenal success stories since the 1970s in terms of growth and investment. Public objectives, including market targets, have been achieved and the public interest as defined by the government has been followed. The quality of the public tourism product has been improved, such as immigration, customs and airport services. Various forms of necessary infrastructure have been provided. The TAT management and PSM have made a substantial contribution to the successful performance of tourism. The expertise, intelligence, dedication and hard work of many have resulted in efficient, effective public service management in the public interest and with accountability for successful tourism. In 1976 the establishment of a Ministry of Tourism was recommended; in 1996 a powerful ministry is still needed to make successful tourism sustainable.

SUMMARY

Implementation is vital if policy objectives are to be achieved, the public interest is to be protected and tourism development is to be successful. In practice, implementation is one of the most difficult management tasks because of politics, power struggles, vested interests and irrationality. There are also many different organisations, public and private, within the policy community, that can be in conflict with one another and internally about policy implementation. Changes, in the power structure, policy perceptions and practices, over time can also affect implementation and results.

Tourism implementation, especially development, requires a strong, active and experienced national tourist organisation (NTO) or ministry which has power. The Thai case study suggests that while the TAT was an organisation of long experience it was ineffective in development control because it lacked power. The minister, chair of an NTO or chief executive officer can be the key participants because of their power positions. Implementation to achieve the required results should be pursued vigorously and consistently over time, which requires stable organisations and long-serving managers committed to policy objectives. Managers can, however, concentrate too much on marketing effectiveness to the neglect of wider issues of public interest and social need.

Managers are dependent upon others for successful implementation, therefore the formal and informal system and factors should provide the necessary mutual information, respect, trust and support. Resources of power and finance and formal processes such as planning are useful for implementation but may fail over time due to a lack of commitment or corruption at the point of application.

In terms of results, in Thailand the practice of tourism management has been satisfactory within the constraints of the political and administrative system. There was efficient formal planning but ineffective implementation, leading to the degradation of several tourist resorts and the environment. The formal system accepted the five principles but failed to implement them in practice. In any system the formal practice of management may be satisfactory but the performance in terms of results and impact may be highly unsatisfactory.

The management of implementation is particularly important at the local level and this will be discussed in the next chapter.

SUGGESTED READING

Elliott, J. (1983) 'Politics, power and tourism in Thailand', *Annals of Tourism Research* 10(3).
—— (1987) 'Government management of tourism: a Thai case study', *Tourism Management* 8(3). Material on tourism management in Thailand is limited but the basic system has not changed since these two articles were written.

Gunn, C.A. (1994) 3rd edn, *Tourism Planning*, Washington, DC: Taylor & Francis.

Hall, C.M. (1994) *Tourism in the Pacific Rim: Development, Impacts and Markets*, Melbourne: Longman Cheshire. A chapter on ASEAN including a section on Thailand.

—— (1995) 2nd edn, *Introduction to Tourism in Australia: Impacts, Planning and Development*, Melbourne: Longman Cheshire.

Inskeep, E. (1991) *Tourism Planning: An Integrated and Sustainable Approach*, New York: Van Nostrand Reinhold.

Pearce, D.G. (1989) *Tourism Development*, Harlow: Longman.

Richter, L.K. (1989) *The Politics of Tourism in Asia*, Honolulu: University of Hawaii Press. Chapter on Thailand.

Selin, S. and Beason, K. (1991) 'Interorganisational relations in tourism', *Annals of Tourism Research* 18(4): 639–52.

6 Management at the local level

This chapter explains:

- why local government is important, and its responsibilities
- who are the important participants
- how public sector management (PSM) manages tourism at the local level
- what are the results of PSM at the local level.

Public sector management at the local level is mainly carried out by local government, but it also includes management representatives of national and state government departments, and public agencies such as tourism boards and transportation agencies. To be effective the various managers and their organisations should cooperate with one another and the private sector. Local politicians as elected representatives can be much more involved in detailed management than at the national or state level. This can improve, or impair, the application of the five principles of public interest, public service, effectiveness, efficiency and accountability.

WHY: REPRESENTATION, RESPONSIBILITIES, IDEOLOGY AND OBJECTIVES

Representation

Local government, or local management, is found in all political systems and is necessary to enable local people to appoint representatives and managers to administer the local area on behalf of the residents. It is better that decisions which affect local people directly are taken by local representatives at the local level. Democracy means that politicians are elected to look after the local people, they are responsible for their welfare and they are there to represent their interests before all others. Local areas belong to the local people and they pay local taxes, for which they are entitled to the services of the local politicians, and managers. Local government may have to protect the rights of local people against upper-tier governments and private interests. Management has many responsibilities at the local level and tourism may be low on the list of priorities, yet in a resort such as Blackpool in England or Reno in Nevada, United States, it may be top of the list.

Public sector managers are concerned about two main issues in tourism at the local level. One comes from the responsibility to look after the local people, and is related to the impact of tourism on the community. Managers should try to manage tourism so that the impact is beneficial and not detrimental. Second, there is the responsibility for the development of the area economically and socially.

Box 6.1 Local government/authority roles

Local authorities in Britain also play a vital role in helping to promote and develop tourism in their areas. Beside their marketing and information activities, they provide many facilities and amenities enjoyed by visitors and local residents alike. Their role in land-use planning process gives them an important influence over tourism development. They play a major part in supporting the work of local Tourist Boards.

(UK, Department of Employment 1992)

In recent years more and more local governments have taken decisions to encourage tourism development as a means of boosting the local economy and government income. This development, however, can have adverse effects on the local people, and to be successful and beneficial it should be sensitive to their feelings and the environment. It is relatively easy for management locally and at the centre to formulate policy but to implement policy is not so easy unless it is supported by the local people.

In practice local managers must be close to the people to understand their needs and they should be able to communicate these needs and local information effectively and efficiently to the managers at national level. Economic forces are very strong, and managers at the local level especially should ensure that tourism development is in the best interest of the local people in the short and long term. Management has considerable power legally but also, because they can speak for the local people, they have a legitimate standing of influence and can be in a position to protect their localities from economic forces and national and state decision makers. Local managers also have a duty to explain and to educate local politicians and people about the plans and wishes of the national government and tourism interests, including the advantages and disadvantages of tourism development.

Local managers do not and cannot act in a vacuum. They work within and are influenced by society, and the political and administrative system. As Weber suggests in his ideal type system, individual managers, to fulfil their responsibilities, need the support and control of a system and organisation. Ideally, the system should be efficient, effective and moral. A system is moral when it is honest and based on the public interest and manages for the benefit of the people.

Local government responsibilities

Local governments are as important as national governments, for they represent the people, but in particular they are important because they deal with, and can affect, people directly where they are. They are also important, for decisions and plans formulated by officials at the centre are useless, unless they are implemented efficiently and effectively by management at the local level. At the local level there are many examples of the failure of implementation to match policy initiatives and objectives which failed to gain the support of the local people.

Management at the local level should follow the same five normative principles as national management. Managers have a responsibility to place the public interest as their first priority in their management activities – they should serve the needs of the local people. The interests of national and state governments or of tourism developers must be placed within the context of benefits and costs to the local people. It is the local people who experience the tourism impact directly and have to live with it permanently. Managers can have difficulty if their official duties lead them into conflict with elected representatives whose main objectives are private financial gain at the expense of the public interest.

Local governments and their managers have responsibilities to their national and state political system and they are given power to administer laws and services by these governments. The UK government in the Local Government Act of 1948 gave local governments the power to provide information and publicity for tourism. In a federal system like that of the United States, with a non-interventionist federal and state government, it is possible for a local government to have considerable freedom to decide its own responsibilities. This is particularly true of the larger cities. In the United Kingdom, which is a unitary state, local government is required by law to provide a wide range of services. Generally in local government much of the effort of management goes into providing basic services such as rubbish collection, and infrastructure, such as roads and sewage systems. Security can be another responsibility, as for the 1996 Olympics in the United States, the local government of Atlanta, Georgia, increased the police presence to protect the tourists. Tourism is only rated highly as a management activity when it is economically important to the local area. In periods of recession, however, all local governments are eager to stimulate their economies and attract tourists to their area.

Local government responsibilities go beyond the legal and economic and include the welfare of the poor and needy, the morale of the citizens, good visitor relations, cultural matters and the conservation of the natural and built environment. Good managers try to solve problems and prevent the alienation of local people brought about by tourism whether in capital cities like Washington, DC, or London, scenic areas such as the Great Barrier Reef in Australia or historic cities such as Cambridge, England. The problems mentioned by Cambridge in its Visitor Management Plan are common to other local governments.

Box 6.2 The main problems caused by tourism, Cambridge, England

1 Congestion, disturbance and damage in the colleges and on the river
2 Congestion in the streets
3 Unsatisfactory coach parking and setting-down points
4 Inadequate car parking
5 The difficulty visitors have in finding their way about in a strange city and
6 Restrictions on the operation of the tourist information centre.

(Cambridge City Council 1985: 45)

Political ideology

Tourism has not normally been a matter of dispute between political parties. Local government managers, however, work within a political environment which can be determined by political party beliefs, as for example the British Labour party giving priority to social welfare before the regeneration of seaside holiday areas. Likewise in

alia, the Labor-controlled Waverley Council in Sydney followed
rking-class traditions and gave priority to affordable housing
before the redevelopment of Bondi, which contained the most famous
surfing beach in Australia. More persuasive in local government than
political party beliefs are the beliefs about development, but these can
be extremely political for they affect power – about who get what, how
and when.

There is general agreement among the political parties, except
green parties, in favour of tourism development. Yet there can be
those in the community who are strongly opposed to development for
ideological and empirical reasons. These can include those dedicated
to protecting the environment and community life style and those
opposed to high-rise development in tourist resorts. Local government can allow or stop development, but its views can be disregarded
and overridden by upper-tier governments. In Australia in July 1993
the Queensland government decided not to extend the electricity
grid north of the Daintree River, so limiting the possibilities of local
government attracting more tourism development into the very
isolated northern sections of the Far North region. This was a political
decision based partly on ideological grounds, anxiety about the
World Heritage tropical rain forests and the Great Barrier Reef, but
it was also a response to the power of the environmental lobby.
Local governments ignore at their peril the power of environment
and conservation groups with their criticism, publicity and effect on
the electorate.

The political ideology can determine how far local governments will
intervene into tourism, and what kind of private organisation or
tourism activity will be supported. Does the ideology look favourably
on large tourism resorts, or backpacker hostels, eco-tourism or
casinos? Local governments can strictly control development or allow
a lot of freedom to the private sector. They can impose taxes and
charges but also give grants, land and permission for development.
Local governments, however, can only act within the law and policy as
established by upper-tier governments, and this varies considerably
between political systems and countries. Within local governments
the ideological stance will decide how open the policy system will
be, how much participation will be allowed and what priority will be
given to conservation and ecologically sustainable development.
Religious views can also influence local government policy, as in the
United States when local governments acting under religious pressure
curtailed homosexual rights, leading to a boycott by tourists of those
areas.

Politics is about power in its various forms, and local government managers try to reconcile the various conflicting power groups and forces within the local administrative system as well as in the local community. Managers' ability to bring about reconciliation are important for the success of local tourism development, for private developers also have power, the power to invest or not. Although upper-tier governments have almost all the power, financial and legal, that power has to be used with caution, for local governments have authority as the legitimate legal representatives of the local people.

Power is used by economic and conservation interests, and by rival local governments to achieve their objectives in local areas. A local government can use its power to ensure that local objectives and public interests are protected. Public sector managers within national or local government may use their position as a power resource against other managers or departments.

While party politics and ideology may not be dominant factors in local government tourism, broader philosophical positions can be important in determining how power is used and the policy priorities of those governments and their managers.

Objectives

There can be formal and informal objectives, which may be stated or unstated. There is the stated general objective to represent and serve the people. The informal objectives of managers may differ from and be more legitimate than those of the politicians, especially if politicians are involved in corruption.

Management, however, mainly concentrates its efforts on achieving service objectives, providing the legally required services efficiently and effectively, such as water supply and sewage, recreational facilities, car parking, health and welfare, inspection, licensing, regulation, land-use planning and economic development. With tourism there is not normally any legal requirement for local governments to be involved but services and facilities are provided for tourists as part of the broader leisure and cultural programmes managed by local governments for local people. Increasingly, however, in recent years tourism development has become one of the economic development objectives of local governments.

Declining industrial cities in Europe and the United States and small townships in outback Australia all have the same objective of attracting the tourist dollar and pound. Many traditional tourist resorts which are in decline because of changing tourist patterns need regeneration and new ideas helped by local governments. This decline was seen in 1984 when British tourists began spending as much overseas as they did at home. Governments are committed to the development and growth of their areas, and their objectives include an increase in the tax base and in the financial income or revenue, including taxes, rents and service charges. Included in these objectives can be the achievement of full or high employment which will also improve the economy of the area. Attracting tourist resorts to an area, or a casino, are major steps towards economic objectives.

> Pha Dua a village in Northern Thailand of 900 residents, may on a busy day receive 300 tourists. The Yao high priest says, 'Tourism has made life better. Before we could only survive by planting crops. Now we can also sell souvenirs to tourists. We are better off, and less dependent on agriculture.' The hill farmers have been encouraged to replace opium cultivation by tourism.
>
> (Forsyth 1993: 30)

Non-economic objectives can get less attention than economic objectives. Informal objectives can be important, such as those resulting from the rivalry common between different local governments, and between managers. One local government may be trying to have more tourism facilities or more visitors than the neighbouring local government.

Objectives are important to ensure that management concentrates on the priorities of the political leaders for the benefit of the people. They help to inject a sense of drive and of purpose into administrative organisations. They can be used to enable managers to obtain the resources they need and to gain the support of other organisations. Formal objectives give legitimacy to the behaviour of managers. Well-defined objectives are necessary to be able to evaluate the performance of managers, and care needs to be taken to avoid local objectives conflicting with national objectives.

Informal objectives can be used by management to assist in achieving or avoiding the formal objectives of the organisation. They can be used to boost the morale of the organisation, to help in its communication, cooperation and coordination. The morale of tourism organisations can be boosted by the possibility of attendance at overseas conferences and travel. Career planning and promotion based on performance can boost the efficiency and productivity of an organisation. Yet if promotion is based on connections or seniority alone and if managers have no objectives and are complacent time-servers, efficiency will be reduced. The most important informal objectives of politicians will be to retain or increase their power and re-election chances, and to be elected or re-elected as the chairperson in the local council, or on a committee, such as finance, planning, economic development or tourism.

The danger of informal objectives is that they can be used for personal power and gain, tourism projects can be approved by local government at the expense of the public interest and local objectives. They can lead to institutional and financial corruption. Short-term, private objectives can displace long-term public objectives in such areas as tourism development.

WHO: REPRESENTATIVES, MANAGERS AND INDUSTRY

Elected representatives, local managers and private stakeholders are among the most significant actors and participants in the tourism policy community. Included should be local citizens or minority groups liable to be affected by policy decisions. The normative principles require that managers accept the responsibility of gaining meaningful participation for citizens. Those who are involved will vary according to the policy issue, and with proposals such as for a new airport or new runways, local government managers must deal with a vast number of individuals and organisations, often with strong opinions for and against.

The legal entity responsible for management is the local authority entrusted with this task by law, and management has authority and manages in the name of the local government. There are different types and levels of local government, ranging from large cities such as New York and Bangkok to small village communities and huge rural areas like Cook Shire in north Queensland, Australia, covering 115,000 square kilometres. Some local governments are successfully developing tourism for the first time, such as declining industrial cities which have innovative managers. Other managers, as in some traditional domestic tourism resorts, have failed to meet the challenge of overseas competition and have lost their markets. The tourism market is always changing and so also is the tourism community. Local government managers gain influence, respect and power because of their success. This power is more effective than that which they get from the legal authority and legitimacy which goes with their official position in the public organisation, as described in the Weberian system.

Elected representatives

Elected representatives as the legitimate decision makers speak in theory for the people, establish policy and priorities and direct the managers, but in practice they may be deeply involved in day-to-day management as full-time representatives and in chairing committees in sectors such as planning and tourism development. Much of the work of public organisations is accomplished through committee systems. Local government committees are an essential part of the management system, making it more efficient and effective, but representatives can also be business people who can use their committee membership to push particular projects which will benefit their own interests. Managers must be able to respond to, but also be able to manage, the committee system.

Local government managers

Managers in local government cover a wide spectrum of disciplines and some are engaged in general policy and resource management – that is, the staff side of management – while others are on the line side, managing specific areas such as transportation or tourism marketing. Managers can be generalists or specialists but in practice there is often no clear-cut distinction between their activities. The chief executive officer may be technically qualified as a lawyer or engineer, but will be performing general managerial functions.

Local government tourism managers

As tourism has only recently been seen as an important industry, tourism officers normally do not have high status nor are they on the higher salary scales. Tourism is often a branch or section of the economic development department or the leisure and parks department. More recently in the larger cities and tourism areas, convention and visitor bureaux have been established. New managerialism, the continual rising importance of tourism and links with the private sector are raising the status and salary of tourism managers. With the increasing number of tourism courses at universities and colleges more graduates are available for positions in tourism management. In local government there has been a movement from a focus on leisure for social welfare among tourism and leisure managers to an economic development focus. Managers are now required to have had experience and a proven track record in tourism or marketing. The top managers will have first-class presentational and interpersonal skills, an ability to communicate, and above all leadership qualities. Tourism managers must have the ability to work closely with other managers within the local government system, including finance managers, planners and engineers. They must be able to deal with inter-departmental rivalry and the administrative culture.

The tourist industry

There can be no tourism without the industry. In countries where the private sector is weak or non-existent, it is the willingness of PSM to compete in the market place that becomes important. It is the industry which provides the investment and the entrepreneurial drive and skill that is essential. At the local level these can include lawyers, real-estate agents, landowners, sugar-cane farmers, developers and local merchants apart from those directly engaged in tourism. They can be prominent and wealthy people in the local or national community or local people hiring out donkeys for a ride along the holiday beach. The local chamber of commerce, with the local tourism association, often plays a leading role. Local tourist boards, as in Britain, can be managed by joint boards of the industry and local government. Some of the industry's leaders will also be active in the local political party or be elected members of the local government council. Trade unionists and tourism employees can also be important, participating in the policy process and pressing for tourism development. Many local people support the industry's demand for development because it provides employment and more income. Public managers have a responsibility, and a common interest, in working in partnership with private managers, for the mutual benefit of tourism and the local community.

In the United States it has long been common for local government to manage its tourism responsibilities in partnership with local industry through a separate legal entity. Localities also cooperate with state governments and there can be regional agreements. In New York City the legal entity is the New York Convention and Visitors Bureau of which New York's mayor is the honorary chairman. Houston, Texas, is covered by the Greater Houston Convention and Visitors Bureau. Similar management arrangements can be found in Britain, such as the Merseyside Tourism Board and the Leicester Tourism Development Ltd, which proclaims that it is 'more than just a Midlands city'.

Public managers must also take into account the objectives of the many interest groups both locally and nationally, *ad hoc* or permanent.

In recent years conservation and environment groups have been particularly active and often opposed to tourism development. Some groups have had support from local residents.

There are numerous national organisations operating at the local level, either through local offices or through visits, meetings and telephone contacts. Federal and state government departments such as finance, police, lands, marine and national parks are important participants in local level management. They can operate directly through departmental organisations, provincial governors, or through statutory authorities. They can provide infrastructure such as airports or make central government land available for development. Local governments can depend heavily upon upper-tier governments for financial grants and permissions, including foreign investment approval.

Whatever the administrative arrangements, officials at the local level must manage tourism in conjunction with numerous other participants and power brokers.

HOW: LEADERSHIP, COMMUNITY, POWER AND PRINCIPLES

How the local government system is managed will vary among systems, and among the types of managers, whether they are generalists responsible for general functions, or specialists responsible for sectors such as tourism. All types of managers, however, should be competent to manage within their own system and be able to use that system to achieve objectives. To do this they may have characteristics similar to the Weberian ideal. To be successful managers will have an excellent knowledge of and experience with dealing with other organisations both public and private, and they will be able to manage effectively within the policy community. Managers will have the technical skill and expertise needed, or they may be able to utilise consultants effectively to obtain the information needed.

Leadership

The power of managers comes from their official position and through their knowledge and expertise; it also comes from their leadership qualities. Local government managers tend to be reactive to events but successful tourism managers have the leadership ability to be proactive. It is easy to manage an organisation if all is going smoothly, but real leadership is needed to manage an ever-changing, dynamic sector like tourism, especially if the local tourist industry is in decline, as in the case of the British coastal resorts, or if there is a crisis, such as terrorist attacks in Egypt and Turkey, or paralysing industrial disputes, like the 1989 airline strike in Australia. Leaders should be legitimate, and have integrity, but if they have vision, initiative and determination they can sell what appears to be un-marketable. This was done in Bradford, a run-down, old industrial textile town in northern England with high unemployment and a working-class migrant population (Buckley and Witt 1985). Strong, innovative leaders can prefer the greater freedom to be found in local autonomous tourism organisations. These can be partly financed and directed by local governments. The low priority and status, however, given to tourism management by local governments and the shortage of resources does not normally attract outstanding leaders.

Policy community

Management operates within a policy community and a national legal system. It is constrained by laws and the availability of resources. Managers operate on the basis of their knowledge and experience, which is gained by good links and contacts with other members of the policy community. A good communication system is necessary, which will use formal mechanisms such as advisory committees, or co-opted members on government committees, but also informal contacts and consultation. Close links, however, should not allow management to become captured by the industry, or to be used as gatekeepers by private interests. Managers must maintain their integrity and serve the public interest. Often their role however, is to manage conflict, to reconcile opposing groups, to negotiate and consult in order to find an acceptable balanced solution to problems. Heated controversy, for example, can arise between tourist developers and local conser-vationists, with the former being perceived by opponents as only interested in financial gain. 'At the local level, the result is often one of conflict between the demands of private capital accumulation and the contingencies of the requirements of local authorities to discharge their statutory duties in environmental, social, and economic terms' (Shaw *et al.* 1991: 183).

Management therefore has to be clear about public objectives and priorities, with plans and strategies already formulated. Managers should have the skills to achieve the objectives in conflict situations. Management has to take care that not too much time is spent in meetings and consultation at the expense of efficient implementation.

There is no doubt that the formal bureaucratic process can be slow and time-consuming for public and private managers. Costs can escalate and increase rapidly especially in periods of inflation, and the proposed tourism project may even be put in jeopardy. This is one argument for the fast tracking of tourism development by managers.

Power

PSM has considerable power available to it both formally and informally. Informally, the way managers actually manage the process can confer or withhold benefits. As already stated, delays can be costly to those dependent upon local government decisions and actions. The law may leave the discretion to managers, so it is up to the manager whether the law is applied rigorously or laxly. Policy decisions and strategies have to be interpreted and applied by managers. Managers have the power to place issues on the policy agenda, to influence priorities, to push a tourism proposal or put it at the bottom of the pending file. They can recommend that permission or a financial grant be given, or refused. In these cases managers can act informally and apply their own values instead of following the principles of PSM. The paradoxical situation can arise when tourism developers have to bribe officials to behave as they formally should behave, efficiently, effectively and honestly. This is different from bribing a manager to do something for which the applicant is not legally entitled, like not enforcing the law against the construction of a road over a nature reserve, to a tourist resort.

The formal powers of managers come from statutes and from their official position. Specific laws can give PSM jurisdiction over a wide range of functions of significance to tourism, including infrastructure such as roads and transportation, planning, regulation, licensing, conservation, environment, marketing and public health. Under the terms of the 1972 Local Government Act, which came into force in England and Wales in 1974, the power of local governments in respect of promotion and development of tourism are firmly established. Depending upon the political system, it is possible that local governments may have a general competence to take action unless prohibited by law; for example, in the provision of car parks, tourist viewpoints and camping grounds. Some laws are mandatory; for example, the requirement that a development proposal include an Environmental Impact Statement, or as in Britain where local governments must prepare development plans for their areas. Local governments must take care to ensure they are not acting *ultra vires*, beyond their powers. Managers can use their planning powers to achieve tourism objectives, to control the industry and development and implement the five principles. Planning can vary between simple land use planning and zoning for use, to more elaborate, long-term planning strategies. The effectiveness of management will vary according to the resources available, including finance, expertise and leadership.

A local government system should have within its resources the power to protect the public interest and to control corruption internally and externally. Resources and assistance can come from upper-tier governments or specialised agencies such as the English Tourist Board.

> We also commissioned a detailed study of the problems faced by England's smaller seaside resorts, which we are following in the current year. Here again, it is easier to identify the problem, and to make appropriate recommendations, than to secure effective action. Many resorts suffer from a legacy of neglect and there are no simple solutions. The problem will have to be tackled mainly by local authorities and private developers, but we shall do all we can to help.
>
> (ETB *Annual Report 1990/91*: 2)

Financial powers

One of the most important powers held by local government is the power to levy taxes, or rates based on land values. The more local finance local governments can raise, the more they can provide in services and the more independence they can have from upper-tier government and the private sector, including the tourism industry. Wealthy local governments are in a much better position to resist or refuse tourism development. Governments and their managers are under pressure from citizens to raise more money from tourists to help to pay for the cost of services provided. There is resentment when expenditure is incurred because of tourism and residents believe that the tourists diminish the quality of life and disturb the normal comfortable community life style. At times political leaders supported by managers will push ahead with projects and investment without an efficient appraisal of the economic and social benefits to the local community. It is difficult to gauge the benefits from tourism investment, and often political leaders are more interested in gaining political kudos from projects rather than evaluating their efficiency.

This appraisal is particularly necessary in local governments where resources are scarce and unemployment is high.

The giant Seagaia resort complex on the Kyushu coast of Japan illustrates the dangers. Opened in 1994, it is the joint venture funded by the Miyazaki prefectural and municipal governments and local companies, costing ¥200 billion (over US$2 billion). It has a 753-room hotel, a convention centre for 5,000 people, an indoor water park, a Tom Watson golf course, tennis club and amusement park including a high-tech games zone. The question is whether the resort can attract sufficient visitors from Japan and overseas; can it compete with resorts which have beaches, better weather, lower costs and an international airport? Are local governments justified in the short and long term in investing public funds, personnel and other resources in such business ventures?

Under new managerialism, PSM is more willing to introduce user-pay schemes for tourists and there is a wide range of charges which can be levied, on hotel accommodation, food and beverages, rented accommodation, and taxes and levies for tourism promotion and environmental protection. The poor management of the financial powers of local government can be detrimental to the citizens and to the tourism industry. There have been financial schemes available over the years which at times local governments and the industry have been able to utilise for development purposes. In Britain, the national government made financial grants for tourism under Section Four of the 1969 Act.

Tourism and local government have benefited from schemes established to help the poorer regions, including funds from the European Union for Structural Assistance and Economic Regeneration. The British government has also given financial assistance through such schemes as the Inner City Partnership. It has been local government management which has played a key role in helping to initiate and implement these schemes. It has used its power and acted as a pressure group and catalyst.

Principles and problems

In assisting tourism, management needs to be conscious that its primary responsibility is to the local people – for example, in the provision of leisure and recreational facilities, which should first be of benefit to the local people. Expensive tourist resorts are eager to have exclusive access to or use of beaches in their locality, and at times management has too readily agreed to such demands at the cost of loss of access, or time-consuming difficult access to local beaches, which were easily accessible to the local residents before the development. Port Douglas in Queensland and Phuket in Thailand are two examples.

This underlies the importance of principles, of the public interest and service to the people being the basis on which PSM must operate. In practice, management is helped in keeping these principles by the political and control systems. A democratic open system, which encourages participation of the community in development proposals and changes, which is not elitist, closed and secretive, is more likely to keep to the five principles of PSM. Local areas belong to the local people, they live there and they pay in various ways for the cost of tourism, and they pay for the managers and give them power to act on their behalf. With certain ideologies, however, tourism development is left almost entirely to the private sector, or to regional tourism bodies with only token local government representation. Some political leaders and managers at the local level want a quiet life and only make the minimum contribution, sometimes because they want to maintain the *status quo* and their own comfortable power base. Others are not capable of managing the dynamic, powerful tourism organisations and forces.

Among the problems faced by local managers are difficulties in communicating with, and getting the cooperation of, the many small organisations and individuals which make up the industry. For example, in taking initiatives in marketing or other spheres, it is difficult to obtain the coordination needed or even agreement about objectives. The difficulties, however, start before this at the formulation and implementation stage, as in Australia: 'Local government, the level of government closest to many of the problems associated with tourism development and the one which is best suited to a community planning approach, is excluded from nearly all of the ministerial councils and consultative committees' (Hall 1991: 69). Local management may lack resources, personnel, finance, legal power and the necessary knowledge to manage large proposals. This is particularly so in smaller local governments and those in developing countries. Big developers can be in positions of considerable power in such situations, especially when managers are under local pressure to allow development, and to allow it quickly. There is always the pressure on management 'to do something', and especially in a recession, to allow development to provide employment. Some elected representatives, and managers, are very sceptical about the value of tourism, they want 'real jobs', as provided in the former manufacturing industries, which are now dead or declining. They see tourism as being about waiters and barmaids, and insubstantial, so they pressurise management to concentrate on non-tourism development. In a similar way, in developing countries, some politicians and civil servants are critical of efforts and resources going to a 'luxury industry for foreigners', when priority should be given to building up rural production and providing 'real jobs' for the people. They see local people only being employed in servile positions, not in management positions which are often filled by foreigners. Yet at times rural crops and basic industries, such as tin and rubber, can be in decline and uncompetitive, as with many manufacturing industries in the developed country. There is then the danger that decisions and policies may be made on grounds of expediency and for the short term, and not allow for sustainable development and the long-term future of the area. Management itself may be inflexible, inefficient and ineffective in achieving objectives. Tourism management in local government can be like those in leisure services. 'Leisure Services Departments are established, and their roles are being consolidated, but generally, personnel still act as in introverted, narrow and separate disciplines' (Travis 1983).

WHAT RESULTS? ENGLAND, AUSTRALIA, THAILAND

The effects of tourism development on local areas can be seen clearly in mass tourism and high-rise development in coastal areas of countries such as Spain and Thailand and in cities such as those of the Gold Coast, Australia, and Acapulco, Mexico. Economic and social costs and benefits, however, are not so easy to evaluate. Some areas have successful results because they are famous, others because they are comparatively unknown. Cooktown, in far north Queensland, for example, claimed to be 'the best kept tourism secret'; it had been able to restrain the impact of tourism and preserve its attractive qualities.

Newcastle upon Tyne, England

Newcastle upon Tyne is an industrial city in the North-east of England, famous for its historic coal trade from the River Tyne, shipbuilding and heavy engineering. All its traditional industries, however, are in decline or exist no more. The city, which lies 60 miles south of the Scottish border, has a population of almost 300,000, but is the commercial and financial centre for a region of 832,000 people. Historically, the city traces its origins back to Roman times and there are remnants of Hadrian's Roman Wall, and the 'new castle' still stands from the Norman period. The city is independent of the County Council and has its own elected City Council.

The city has not been a great tourist attraction. Most visitors travel through, without stopping, from London, York and Durham on the way to Edinburgh. Local tourism managers speak of the city and region being isolated from the rest of the country with long journey times. In the 1960s, there was an attempt to attract more Scandinavian visitors for duty-free and low-priced shopping, as most of these visitors from the five Nordic countries travelling by sea arrived in Tyneside. During this period, however, the overwhelming focus was on urban redevelopment, where the city was the leader in inner city redevelopment; but there was barely a mention of tourism. It was, however, planned to preserve as much as possible of the city's historic heritage, and to provide hotels for businessmen.

Why governments are involved

The main reason for Newcastle's growing interest in tourism was economic, with the decline in the British economy, in the traditional industries and with rising unemployment. Many older industrial cities in the developed countries, including the United States, were also suffering from the same economic decline. By the late 1970s, there was a growing concern for economic development and growth, and tourism was seen as one of the few growth industries.

Box 6.3 Advantages of tourism

At the local level, tourism can provide jobs and incomes in areas where it is difficult to generate alternative forms of employment. Apart from jobs, tourism spending helps to support a wide range of community facilities including shops, restaurants, theatres and other leisure facilities. Without tourism, the number and range of such facilities available for the local community would be reduced. Tourism can also provide new uses for old buildings, thus helping to maintain the historic fabric of towns and villages throughout the country.

(Newcastle City Council 1981, quoting the ETB)

Other local governments were moving into tourism. Newcastle's management was also aware that if the city was engaged in tourism, it could apply for financial grants under Section Four of the 1969 Tourism Act.

Who is involved in tourism management?

The main participants in tourism in Newcastle were the political leaders, the officers of the city, tourism leaders and the Northumbria Tourist Board (see Box 7.5). National bodies, like the English Tourist Board and international bodies, such as the European Commission in Brussels, were on the periphery of tourism policy making. As in most PSM systems, the city managed its affairs mainly through a committee system, with officers having specific responsibilities. In the case of tourism, responsibility lay with the Economic Development Committee under its chairman, a local businessman, a part-time councillor like all other members of the City Council. A Tourism Sub-committee had the responsibility to oversee the management of the tourism development strategy. Other committees, such as Finance, Planning, and Arts and Recreation, also touched on tourism issues. Full-time officers responsible were the Economic Development Officer, a senior officer of the city, and the Tourism, Conference and Convention Officer. The latter officer headed a unit of two or three officers responsible for tourism and conferences.

The tourism industry in Newcastle was not strong and included many small operators, a few larger hotels and the local airport. Peak bodies included the Tyne and Wear Chamber of Commerce and the Northumbria Tourist Board, and regional organisations such as the Tyne and Wear Development Company, Northern Development Company, and the North-east Region of the Confederation of British Industry. There were also several conservation and environmental groups concerned with the protection of heritage and the effects of tourism development.

How managers manage

The acceptance of tourism management and development in Newcastle has been slow and gradual, with the City Council's priorities being directed more at the provision of basic services, such as housing and education, and social welfare problems. Urban planning in the 1960s, under a dynamic City Council leader and strong active City Planning Offices, saw the acceptance of the historic heritage, but also the destruction of much of the inner city with often poor and mediocre replacements. Since that time the city has had more traditional leaders; but it has also suffered from industrial decline and the general economic recession.

The City Council has, however, accepted its responsibility for economic development and has established a committee with a senior chairman. It has appointed an economic development officer and tourism officer. Economic development has been one of the top priorities for action, and tourism development was listed as the seventh of the eight objectives of the Economic Development Committee, 1987–89. The Chairman stated that more than 3,000 jobs had been created over the previous two years, and that

> The growing mood of optimism and buoyancy that prevails in the city have been brought about by the close working relationships which have developed between public agencies and the private sector. There is now a genuinely community-wide approach to economic regeneration in Newcastle and a determination to succeed which, I believe, will bring about significant economic benefits to the City and surrounding Region in the forthcoming years.
>
> (Newcastle City Council 1989)

There has been no shortage of research and reports about Newcastle and its economic and tourism needs. In the 1960s the City Planning Department was accused of being the 'greatest publishers since Caxton'. The ETB in a report prepared for the organisation in 1973 on *The Marketing and Development of Tourism in Northumbria*, including Newcastle, stressed the potential revenue that could be raised. In Circular 13/79 in 1979, the Department of the Environment urged local authorities to recognise the social contribution that tourism could make in supporting a wide range of amenities and services, such as sport and recreational activities, restaurants, cinemas and theatres, and noted the importance of coordinating policies concerning tourism with policies in inner areas, employment, sport and recreation. Newcastle had many old inner city areas. In 1980 therefore, it was appropriate for the ETB to launch, in the Newcastle Civic Centre, their report on *Tourism and the Inner City*.

City politicians and managers slowly began to acknowledge the importance of tourism and to formulate policies. The City Council's Policy Service Department and the Recreation and Leisure Department in 1981 produced a joint policy report, *Tourist Development in Newcastle*. More specific policy was proposed in the 1982 report on Newcastle as a conference city. The City Planning Department placed leisure and tourism as Topic 5 in the 1983 City Centre Local Plan, and pointed out how tourism could provide new employment opportunities. Managers from the Policy Services Department and Recreation and Leisure Department started to meet regularly in a Tourism Officers' Working Group to guide the work of tourism development. They had regular contact with the Northumbria Tourist

Board and tried to have regular contact with the private sector, including hotel managers and other relevant organisations. A major step forward in the acceptance of tourism was the appointment of a Tourism and Conference Officer and the establishment of a Tourism Unit in 1986 with a staff of two and in 1988, of three. Its value was acknowledged in that its budget remained constant in money terms (but declining in real terms because of inflation), while other departments had their budgets cut in money terms and in real terms. Newcastle has been successful in building up its heritage tourism attractions, gaining development of Newcastle Airport as an international airport, attracting more conferences, gaining tourists through the 'Great English City Breaks' programme, and finance for projects from the ETB and the European Commission.

What results? practice and performance

Using the PSM basic normative principles and the check-list of the PSM of tourism, the record of Newcastle is mixed. The five principles have generally been followed in the city, especially public interest and public service, and management has operated well within the liberal democratic political and administrative system, showing efficiency and effectiveness. The number of tourists and their expenditure has increased and more tourist attractions and local employment have been provided. Yet has the performance of management been as efficient and as effective as it could have been?

In 1989 management acknowledged that 'for 15 years the facilities of the city had been relatively static – no new hotel and few developments to increase meeting facilities – the Eldon Square shopping and recreational centre are distinguished exceptions to this'. This same centre, however, was also a symbol of one of the great tourism failures on the part of the city managers and planners of the 1960s. Eldon Square, one of the finest historic squares in England, was destroyed as a square, against strong public opposition, on the justification that the site was needed for, and on the promise of, a five-star hotel designed by a world-famous architect. The hotel was never built, and the hole in the ground was filled by a recreational centre. In 1978 two cities, very comparable to Newcastle – Sheffield and Cardiff – had conference business valued at £6.5 and £6.2 million respectively; Newcastle in 1980 made a little over £1 million. Bradford, whose public image was much worse than that of Newcastle, successfully met the tourism challenge and overcame problems, raising its package holidays from 2,000 in 1981–82, to 25,000 in 1983–84. In Bradford, 'Private capital has been attracted into tourism development. New hotels have been built and one large abandoned hotel refurbished and reopened' (Buckley and Witt 1985).

Politics

Newcastle city government in the 1960s had strong political leadership and management with vision, ability, drive and the political authority to get things done. In more recent times leaders and managers have been good and adequate but have had to operate in a declining economy with internal party political disputes. The Labour party has controlled the City Council for many years but there has been little interest in, and little commitment to, tourism development. Many councillors, especially those with working-class or left-wing backgrounds, give limited support to tourism initiatives. Instead, they were in favour of manufacturing industry 'real work, real jobs'. City tourism managers therefore did not have full-scale political support, nor were they given the financial or personnel resources needed. Other city senior managers were sceptical about the value of tourism and gave it little or no priority. Often their interests were focused only on their own departments and they lacked the wider perspective and the ability to take the essential holistic view and make the necessary contribution to wider policy objectives. They were not interested in, or capable of stimulating, private sector participation or investment. Their view of the public interest was limited purely to the provision of services. Private sector tourism was weak in Newcastle in resources, investment and management talent, but public managers did little to utilise what was available, or seek to increase those resources. Employment in the service sector was over 80 per cent of Newcastle's total employment. In March 1981 a report on this sector, presented to the City's Economic Development Committee, recommended tourism as one of the key areas of activity by the City Council in its drive for new employment in the service sector. Management's success in following this recommendation, however, was limited.

The weakness of management in Newcastle reflected the weakness of management and political leadership at the regional and national level. National governments and management in practice did not give priority to tourism development or establish clear, consistent national objectives. Instead there were often conflicting objectives, programmes and organisations. Labour governments gave priority to tourism in the poorer regions, but allocated few resources. The Conservatives re-established London as a priority, 'the gateway to the country'. Neither under Labour nor Conservative governments did the regional offices of the national government departments make a significant contribution to regional, or Newcastle's, tourism development. After 1979 Conservative governments cut back severely on tourism expenditure, especially on management, with the objective of creating 'lean and hungry organisations' which would therefore go out desperately seeking business and finance. In Newcastle neither the finance nor the private business organisations were available.

Northumbria Tourist Board

Conservative governments moved the focus of responsibility and resources from the national tourism boards to the regional tourism boards. In the case of the Northumbria Tourist Board this was almost a retrograde step; the Board was completely dominated by the local governments of the region, especially the county councils. This dominance and the poor quality of the leadership and management proved to be inadequate to meet the tourism challenges of the region. The chair of the BTA/ETB, Adele Biss, claimed that the 'region was selling itself short'. Only 50 per cent of beds were taken up by visitors (*Evening Chronicle*, Newcastle, 25 March 1994). Policy initiatives were often lacking, or poorly funded and managed, and given no, or half-hearted, support by local government and the private sector. The essential spirit of voluntary cooperation was lacking. There was a lack of entrepreneurial skills and drive, thorough research, coordination and consistent strong management. For example, there was a history of the Chief Executive Officer (CEO) of the regional board staying in the post only for two or three years. In Northumbria also there was no long, close relationship between those occupying the chair position on the board and the CEO.

Newcastle's financial contribution to the board was about 10 per cent of the total local government contribution. Its influence, however, was limited, especially as its representation was only two in a very large board and only one when the board size was cut. Private sector representation was also small. One reason for the poor record of Newcastle in tourism must rest with the regional and national tourism boards, for failing to utilise the great potential of the city with its regional environment and access to Northern Europe. The city and region have failed to capitalise on its rich history and the growing popularity of heritage tourism. City managers, however, must also accept responsibility for the lack of initiative and failure to escape from the ghetto of the city's physical surroundings, political and

administrative system, culture and thought patterns. Manage
and tourism, though, are continually changing, and the Northui
Tourist Board's strategy, 'Partners in Tourism 1991–96', \
includes green tourism and control of visitor numbers, may bring about
a more effective partnership. The position may also improve by
the promotion of the four northern regions by BTA as 'England's
North Country' with its own 'brand' manager.

The Gold Coast, Queensland, Australia

The Gold Coast, which includes the famous Surfers Paradise surfing
beaches, is one of the most popular tourist resorts in the southern
hemisphere and has been one of the most successful in the world. It
has developed continually from holidays based on railways in the
1880s, to improved road transportation in the 1920s and domestic air
travel from the 1960s, and, particularly since the 1980s, international
air travel. Accommodation has moved from small cabins, to low-rise
flats of the 1950s to high luxury apartments and hotels of the 1980s
and 1990s.

Apart from ease of access and the availability of accommodation,
the main attractions are the long ocean beaches, the sea, surf and sun
and the mild winter climate. Its popularity has spread from local
Queenslanders to other Australians, and in more recent years it has
become very popular with Asian tourists, and many of the luxury
hotels, apartments and houses are owned by Japanese and other
Asians. The success of the Gold Coast reflects the success of
Queensland tourism, which by the early 1990s had provided 120,000
jobs and injected about A\$4.5 billion into the state's economy. Within
the same period half the Australian tourism infrastructure came
within the wider Gold Coast region. In 1995 Queensland had 6.9
million tourists and the city had 3.7 million. Unlike Newcastle, the
Gold Coast is a successful tourism product but one which still has to
be managed.

Why governments are involved

Governments in Australia – federal, state and local – have been
forced to get involved in tourism because of market pressure and the
increasing importance of the industry. Gold Coast local governments
and their successor, the Gold Coast City Council, were forced to
provide the basic services for the tourists, such as roads, sewerage,
water supply, rubbish clearance, public parks and toilets. They were

keen to attract the economic benefits of higher incomes, rates, taxes, private investment, more jobs and the boost to the local economy. Tourism was also attractive because there was little industrial development at the Gold Coast and returns from agriculture were low.

The City Council was also required to be involved in tourism because Queensland state government laws placed responsibilities upon local governments to prepare town plans and provide other services. For example, the 1994 Environmental Protection Act placed most of the responsibility on local governments. Requests also encouraged or forced the City Council to react to the tourism market. Another important factor was the Queensland political culture with its all persuasive development ethos coming from below and from above, from citizens, politicians, developers, and from federal and state government ministers. The City Council was part of this culture and could do little to resist it, even if individuals wished to do so.

Who is involved in tourism management?

The Gold Coast City Council is responsible for the local public management of tourism. A united Gold Coast city with its own council was proposed in 1928 but did not come into being until 1949 following a 1948 Act of the state Parliament. Like all local councils in Queensland it has a general competence to act and considerable power. Yet in practice the state government and its departments can always override it and their will and policy will prevail if there is conflict. A sign of the power of the state government was the sacking of the City Council over a development issue in 1978. An Administrator managed the city until the Council was reinstated after the city election of 1979. So, while local politicians and officials can have power, they can be curtailed by other power centres. These include the Minister of Local Government and his department, who have planning and other powers. Other departments will play the leading role depending upon the policy issue, whether it is roads, environment or police issues.

Queensland, like other governments, uses the statutory authority form of organisation to manage tourism. This is the Queensland Tourist and Travel Corporation (QTTC), which was established in 1979 and has been active at the local government level. Its main roles are promotion and development and these have affected the Gold Coast. At the city level there is also an independent organisation which manages tourism, the Gold Coast Visitors and Convention Bureau. This is a regional tourist association (RTA), which is supported by the industry, QTTC and local governments. It is responsible for the coordination and marketing of tourism for the coast and region. The Australian government can assist local government and Foreign Investment Review Board approval is required for foreign investment. Developers and investors at the Gold Coast have played a much more active role than local citizens.

In 1995, the city was managed by an elected mayor and fourteen councillors, and by appointed fixed-term officials: chief executive officer, seven directors and thirty-nine managers, with a staff of 2,300. The Gold Coast City Council was the second largest local government in Australia.

How managers manage

The city is managed through the seven directors with some functions important for tourism: 'One director was responsible for *Planning, Development and Transport*, which included: research, strategic planning, development, environment, directorate support, transport, statutory planning. One director was responsible for *City Projects*, which included: city projects, property, regional and economic development, directorate support.'

Management functions are also carried out by Council Committees made up of the elected councillors. Committees can be important in the formulation and control of policy. For tourism important committees include: Water, Wastewater, Beaches and Foreshores Committee, Planning and Development (North) Committee, and Planning and Development (South) Committee. Committees meet every three weeks and are open to the public.

The Council is also represented on the regional Joint Tourist Committee and on the Gold Coast Tourist Bureau. The city has corporate and operational plans and there is statutory planning, but there are no comprehensive tourism plans.

Managers manage through the provision of the normal services. Both the state and city governments have supported tourism and urban development and have provided the necessary infrastructure, such as water supply and roads. They have sponsored and subsidised tourist attractions, such as the Indy international car race. The state government manages its direct tourism support through the QTTC and with the City Council helps to support the Visitors' Bureau.

The city's budget in 1996/97 was A$424 million; therefore, unlike some local governments, the city has considerable resources and can hire, if it wishes, the expertise it needs. Queensland and the city, however, were slow to employ professional planners. There are no regional plans in Queensland and local government plans are limited. It is the market which has determined development and the City Council has responded to the desires of developers. Some political leaders, such as the former Mayor Bruce Small, have fought strongly for development against the wishes of some residents. He dismissed the outcry against high-rise development along the beach by saying that the shadows cast by the high-rise buildings on the beach in the afternoon would help to protect the tourists against skin cancer. The development ethos which has been so dominant in Queensland historically, and particularly under the National party state government until 1989 also prevailed at the Gold Coast, where the top priority was development, urban and tourist. The wishes of local residents were often neglected and the City Council was dominated by local business interests. Politically the prevailing philosophy was *laissez-faire*, market-led and free enterprise orientated, with government only intervening to assist development, not to stop or control it. The approach was disjointed, incremental and reactive, as can be seen in the development over the years. There was opposition to any suggestion of controlled or properly planned development. As Sir Frank Moore, Chairman of the QTTC expressed it:

> We are a private enterprise society. The last thing that I would want is that you get some kind of ghastly socialist planning which would decide who was allowed to go where. We are a free open society. We are a private enterprise society and it will respond to opportunities, as you find in private enterprise where people pay for their actions and mistakes, they are careful and cautious.
>
> (ABC Radio, 1989)

The city tended to agree with this kind of thinking. It did have planning powers in respect to land-use planning, but these were limited in their scope and there was no effective attempt to subject the area to a comprehensive, long-term plan. This in any case would have been difficult to enforce owing to the attitude of the state government and its power to override local governments. Furthermore, the city only controlled a long strip of land running alongside the ocean; the interior towards the mountains was controlled by other politically conservative councils. This changed in 1995 when Albert Shire was merged with the city, making a population of 320,000, allowing it the possibility to be more effective in its management of sustainable and balanced tourism development. Governments, like the Gold Coast and Cairns in north Queensland, have had problems funding the necessary infrastructure for the massive tourist development, and in 1990 the two councils unsuccessfully requested the Foreign Investment Review Board to limit foreign investment as they could not manage the infrastructure demands. In response to the costs of tourism and criticism from residents, the Gold Coast in 1992 introduced a tourism promotion fund (tax) of A$55 per year on those who benefit from tourism and A$45 per year on 'any premises which provides rental accommodation'. By 1995 this had been abolished and premises used for tourism were rated as commercial property.

What results? practice and performance

In theory, practice and performance should follow the principles. For example, politicians, public sector managers and the political and administrative system are expected to operate in the public interest. In many cases, however, in Queensland until 1989 they operated in the private interest of political leaders. The formal system and its mechanisms in state and local government such as town planning, rezoning, by-laws, road proposals, local government boundaries and responsibilities were overridden, if it was in the political or personal interests of the political power holders. Democratic systems and processes, and local governments and citizens were disregarded. Neither state nor local government encouraged public participation and any criticism was attacked.

Special legislation was pushed through the state Parliament, such as the 1987 Integrated Resort Development Act, to improve the effectiveness and efficiency of the policy process for tourism development. State and local government procedures can be slow, cumbersome and unclear, and developers want fast-track approval. The 1987 Act, however, insufficiently protected the public interest by curtailing local government power and the rights of local people. It was effective and efficient for the large, wealthy developers, who were also given privileges not available to ordinary citizens. No such priority or attention was given to the public service responsibilities of local government or to the poorer sections of local communities. Areas such as the Gold Coast therefore become the preserve of the rich and of overseas investors and tourists.

Another special Act which favoured private as against public interests at the Gold Coast was the 1985 Sanctuary Cove Resort Act, which gave special privileges to a developer close to the then Local Government Minister, Russell Hinze. Government loans were made available and public works were provided. When the development ran into financial trouble a further Act was pushed through Parliament to allow for higher-density building on the site (see Craik 1991).

The QTTC also used land public funds and land in its development activities, including the gift of Crown Land for shares in the Port Douglas Resort near Cairns. This resort later went bankrupt and the developer fled to Spain, refusing to return to appear in the courts. Large tourism development became a major segment in the power apparatus of the Joh Bjelke-Petersen government. The most senior public sector manager after his retirement joined the Daikyo company, the largest Japanese tourism investor, as their senior manager in Australia. There were accusations of widespread corruption, which led to the defeat of the National party government in 1989 and the imprisonment of the Commissioner of Police, Sir Terence Lewis.

In the public interest a city council should be concerned about the long-term as well as the short-term development of its area. Protection needs to be given to the city's resources, environment, amenities and the quality of life. Development needs to be balanced and should be ecologically sustainable. No one group should be able to dominate the area. There have been criticisms, however, of the management of the Gold Coast, of the lack of planning and a strategy for long-term comprehensive development. There has been *ad hoc*, piecemeal development, a failure to preserve open space or parks near the beach and a general deterioration and erosion of the beach areas. Criticism has also been directed at the increasing dominance of high-rise luxury development, foreign ownership and the number of Asians, and accusations of unfair Japanese trading practices. As a result of poor management, high-rise apartments and hotels have been built too near the beach, leading to serious beach erosion. This has forced the city into considerable annual expenditure to protect the beaches.

The public service principle requires local government to serve the community in a positive way, but especially those least able to take care of themselves. Maybe management has to provide a service because there has been a market failure or because there is no, or insufficient, financial return for the private sector to provide it. Tourism developers are out to make money, and providing public services or protecting public amenities is not high on their list of objectives. The city, however, has given most attention to big tourist and urban development, sometimes at the expense of poorer sections of the community, including the disappearance of facilities and a deterioration in the quality of life. Tourism, resort and casino development and international car rallies have done little for the homeless and jobless at the Gold Coast but they have helped to maintain the positive image of excitement, enjoyment and relaxation.

The evidence of wealth and conspicuous consumption, luxurious high-rise hotels and apartments, the development of the Spit, the only large nature area left in the city, for tourism, the development of the Waterways Authority and expensive canal estates, all contrasted strongly with youth unemployment, the poor facilities for those down and out and for pensioners and the disappearance of cheap accommodation, caravan parks and open space. The Gold Coast Visitors and Convention Bureau chief executive said in 1991 that resorts, hotels and holding apartments were competing to offer the best deal and they were sensitive to the needs of budget visitors and the hardships caused by the recession. Management are aware of the criticism but have been ineffective in dealing with it. This is partly because they wish to maintain the successful image of the area, which is essential for continual development and attracting greater numbers of tourists. Success is evaluated by tourism criteria, as against social or environmental criteria.

There has been effective management of the changes and the pressures brought about by the tourism success, but also of the population expansion of pensioners and others. The necessary stability, infrastructure and political and administrative environment has been provided. There has been a continual growth in tourist numbers, expenditure, accommodation and tourism attractions, but this has been more due to tourism demand and the activity of the independent Tourism Bureau rather than positive city management. There has been an increase in the range of overseas tourists as well as in investment, especially from Japan, since the 1980s, and more recently from elsewhere in Asia. Officials have developed the potential of the area and responded to the market. Particularly prominent are the Hilton Casino complex, and other five-star hotels, resorts, golf courses, marinas and attractions such as Seaworld and Movieworld. They coped well with the 1990s recession partly because of heavily discounted air fares. The recession in Japan leading to the selling of Japanese property, and one of the largest companies, Daikyo Australia, moving to Cairns, was partly offset by other, mainly Asian, foreign investment.

The Gold Coast has for a long period of time been regarded, rightly or wrongly, as Australia's premier tourist destination. However, the Gold Coast perhaps epitomises Queensland's future

velopment problem. The Gold Coast has tended to be attractive to the mass tourism market, and while mass tourism will undoubtedly be with us for a long time yet, there is a trend away from large-scale developments towards smaller, less contrived tourism destinations. The challenge for Queensland, as for the Gold Coast, is how to diversify the range of attractions open to the tourist while ensuring that development is more environmentally sound and community based than it has been in the past.

(Hall 1991: 57)

The City Council is responsible for the efficiency of its tourism expenditure, policy and management. Are the ratepayers receiving the best possible service at the lowest cost? Some citizens believed that they were subsidising the tourist industry, hence the pressure for the introduction of tourism tax. There is also the question of whether the city is getting the best return from overseas investment or whether most of the economic benefits are going overseas. In the longer term is it efficient to have such a high level of foreign investment? It is difficult to gauge the return from the supply of infrastructure facilities for tourism, subsidies for events such as the Indy Car Rally and the return in the long term as against the short term. Policies and expenditures which appear to be efficient in the short term may be inefficient over the long term. Over-building and approval of high-rise construction especially near the beach can be costly in the long term by lowering the quality of the tourist experience and discouraging return visitors or new tourists. In the long term maybe a better return could be obtained by supporting eco-tourism and cultural tourism, which would also be more in the public interest and would be providing a public service. Measures such as those by state government to help tourism, including subsidies to private airlines which then fail, and provision of government land, are not an efficient use of public resources. The Gold Coast could have managed its relations with both neighbouring local governments in Queensland and New South Wales and with the state governments more efficiently. Efficiency reflects the calibre of management but it can do little if the informal objectives of political leaders lead to inefficiency and corruption.

The accountability principle at the Gold Coast has been decidedly secondary to market demands for development. Both state and local governments, including public managers, have been used by political and economic power holders to further private interests. Audit mechanisms, elections, elected representatives, interest groups and the media have proved to be feeble in accountability. Little attention and superficial accounting has been applied to the return on public investment infrastructure, public expenditure on marketing and events such as the annual Indy international motor car race. In some local governments in Queensland electors have voted against candidates supporting high-rise development but this has not happened at the Gold Coast. While for some projects environmental impact statements have provided information, generally there has been insufficient information and public access to the policy process. The system has not operated in an open, democratic way with public participation. Those responsible for accountability and control have taken a narrow view of their responsibility in terms of public service, public interest and social and environmental issues, and have failed to protect the city and the quality of its tourism against the power of developers and the market. It may be possible to escape the consequences of increasing congestion, over-building and mass tourism in the short term but not in the long term. None of the management bodies responsible for tourism, political parties, state governments, various local governments, QTTC and tourism bureaux seem able to formulate and implement a long-term strategy for ecologically sustainable development and for the survival of the region as the premier tourist resort of Australia and of the southern hemisphere. It is surprising, if not alarming, that the City of the Gold Coast has no committee, department, director or senior manager responsible exclusively for tourism management.

Pattaya, Thailand

Why governments are involved

Since the 1960s Thailand has been one of the most successful tourism countries in the world with the number of visitors rising continually every year with one or two exceptions. It has been seen as a tourism model for development by other developing countries such as Vietnam. In Thailand, Pattaya was the brightest jewel of tourism, the fastest-growing and the largest tourist resort. Pattaya was seen as an ideal tourism product because of its exotic appeal, its sea, sand, sun and sex. It became world famous.

The Thai government supported tourism development because of its economic benefits, bringing into the country needed foreign exchange and investment, and public support was further stimulated when tourism became the top foreign currency earner in 1983, replacing rice exports. The Pattaya development and management reaction reflects the development of the long-haul tourism market and the strong demand for the Thai tourism product from overseas. Pattaya became the number one resort because of its ease of access from Bangkok and because it already had the necessary tourism infrastructure dating back to the Vietnam War period and to when Pattaya was used by the US military for rest and recreation (R and R).There was also pressure, from the tourism industry and particularly Pattaya and developers, for the government to support the industry.

Who is involved in tourism management?

The Thai national government is much more involved at the local level than are national governments in Britain, Australia or the United States. It has strong, hierarchically structured, independent ministries, which are active in the local tourism policy community. One of the largest and strongest ministries is the Ministry of the Interior, which controls the police and local government and appoints the provincial governors. Semi-autonomous government agencies are also important for tourism, such as the National Economic and Social Development Board (NESDB), the Tourism Authority of Thailand (TAT) and Thai International Airways. The TAT has a regional office based in Pattaya.

The mayor of Pattaya City, its council and officials are responsible for tourism management. Pattaya was recognised as uniquely important by the Parliament when it was given semi-independence from Chon Buri provincial governor and allowed to elect its own mayor, who headed the seventeen-seat Council, where eight councillors were non-elected members. A city manager is the key official hired by the mayor to administer the city at a salary which fluctuates with the city's revenue. Both mayor and city manager have to try and give satisfaction to a tourism industry which includes a wide range of investors and peak organisations such as the Pattaya Chapter of the Thai Hotel Association, all of which try to influence the mayor, the city manager and officials to act on their behalf legally and illegally.

How managers manage

In practice, managers leave the market to manage itself; they respond to demands and provide the necessary formalities. They are not active in controlling development and have rarely used their legal powers. Effective power has rested in the hands of the tourism developers and industry, supported overtly or covertly by local and national politicians. In theory, management was to be through the development plans formulated by the NESDB and the TAT, but these were never implemented. In 1983 a City Plan was formulated, and in 1986 adjusted to meet developers' needs or demands. According to the plan, the 22-kilometre-long beach of Pattaya and its green area was to be preserved for environmental and public entertainment purposes. Planning, however, remained an ineffective management process, set against powerful economic interests, and without the support of strong and honest political leaders. Long-term and strategic management is now part of the Eastern Seaboard Development Programme and Pattaya is planned to become the tourist and commercial area for the new industrial region.

Thailand has well-developed PSM processes at all levels of government and in its autonomous public agencies, led by many highly intelligent, well-educated, hard-working, honest managers and politicians. Expertise and other resources are available in the ministries and specialised agencies such as the Board of Investment, the NESDB and the TAT. The administrative system, however, is not always efficient or effective, it has its own values and corporate culture which are not necessarily attuned to swiftly developing areas, and sectors like tourism. There is little sense of public interest or public service. Organisations tend to be conservative, segmented, self-protective and resistant to change, and the management system is slow moving, bureaucratic and more concerned with preserving the *status quo*, or achieving consensus, than with taking and implementing difficult decisions. There is little sense of commitment and urgency in the system, but at times of crisis these qualities can come to the fore and stimulate efficiency. Reformers and dynamic, young, public sector managers have great difficulty in achieving formal public objectives against the strong, informal, private objectives which can predominate in the system. Dynamic managers and resources can be short at the point of impact and there can be conflicting objectives and priorities. The swamp-like nature of the bureaucratic system stops reform movements and smothers those who come within its power or terrain. It can also support corruption and self-seeking leaders. The Ministry of the Interior has suggested that the Pattaya City Act could be changed to help to solve problems. One city councillor said,

> We don't need changes in the law, only in the people who are responsible for carrying it out. We need a higher degree of skill

both among the civil servants working in the city and among councillors themselves who are unfamiliar with the bureaucratic system.

What results? practice and performance

Effectiveness

There has been a failure to implement plans and policies effectively. In 1978 Pacific Consultants International of Tokyo conducted a feasibility study and reported on Pattaya's tourism development. They reported on the problems of roads and traffic, fresh, sea and waste water, sewage and rubbish, especially plastics, polyethylene bags and papers. They reported on Pattaya's suitability for tourists, using 1977 data, and said, 'pollution was quite excessive compared to water quality criteria for ocean resort areas, Hawaii, Rio de Janeiro, Australia, USA and Japan. Pattaya Beach exceeds criteria at a number of locations for pollution, especially in front of Pattaya downtown.'

In 1989, when there was another Japan-financed study, by JICA, on Pattaya's tourism development, the situation had deteriorated further and spread. The resort has also suffered from electricity and water shortages; the latter problem has led to a proliferation of 'dangerously driven, noisy' water trucks. Hotels have installed water-treatment machinery but sometimes only operate it if an inspector calls. Due to the rapid development, even when there are drains they are too small to take the flow. Public infrastructure has not kept pace with public development, roads, street lighting, public transport, water treatment, rubbish collection, and street and beach cleaning. The lack of control and implementation of planning have led to excessive building, buildings too high and too close to the beach and the development of slums.

Efficiency

There has been an inefficient use of public resources, power, finance and personnel. Governments have been slow to provide facilities such as piers, training and educational facilities for hotel staff, and to upgrade the local U-tapao airport to international standards. Beer and girlie bars, prostitution, street walkers, drugs, AIDS, violence, and corruption among the police and public officials, have continued or increased. In January 1990, at least seventy policemen were to be transferred from Pattaya in an attempt to clean up its image of crime and police corruption, but only twenty-five were transferred because it was feared morale would fall too low. The tourism industry has also been suffering from a shortage of skilled staff and higher labour costs, and both the industry and the residents suffered from higher prices. Criticism has also been directed at the poor infrastructure for airport traffic and sub-standard airport facilities.

In 1989 the President of the Association of Thai Travel Agents (ATTA) accused PSM of lack of control. 'Look at Pattaya. It is so polluted because nobody seriously controls the environment and pollution there' (*Bangkok Post* 30 August 1989). He agreed with the TAT as to the deterioration of many tourist attractions in Thailand. Governments have been criticised by the media and industry for failure to implement the plan. The Board of Investment has also been criticised for being unable to judge the demand for hotels and for giving privileges to investors when there were more than sufficient hotel rooms, and for not giving privileges when there was a room shortage. The Public Works Department of the Ministry of the Interior has been slow to formulate and implement building regulations for resorts, and when they have tried to enforce them there has sometimes been criticism from Pattaya city councillors.

Control and accountability

Management appear to exercise little control over hotel and other development, but this would be difficult with powerful developers, such as the owners of the Ambassador City Hotel and Convention Centre erected at Jomtien Beach in the early 1990s. This claims to be the largest tourist project in Asia, in terms of land area, and provides 3,650 rooms and work for 5,000. Powerful interests are at work when tourism can bring at least Baht 8,000 million annually into the city.

Management and the Cabinet at the national level have failed to coordinate the many public bodies which are working, or should be working, in Pattaya. This is true also of the Ministry of the Interior, which theoretically and legally has responsibility for several departments, including provincial governors, police, planning and public works. The Public Works Department has not cleaned up the city, the Public Health Department has been very slow to act on AIDS, the Ministry of Commerce cannot or will not control hotel room rates, and the National Environment Board has had little or no impact. The population grew by 50,000 in three years (1986–89) up to 200,000, but public housing provided was insufficient and of poor quality. There has also been illegal building.

> One hotelier said that the Government and local city officials have neglected their responsibility for monitoring construction projects, and new hotels and condominiums have been allowed to operate without internal water treatment facilities.
>
> (*Bangkok Post* 1 September 1989)

The national government has been slow to increase its budget grant to the city which remained the same for ten years at Baht 30 million. In 1990 the city council requested Baht 100 million.

Public service

As a public service, the TAT has tried to stop sex tourism. It has, for example, opposed the open advertising of sex tours from Europe to Pattaya. The TAT has still continued to support Pattaya, including efforts to get charter flights into the area. The TAT has a regional director based in Pattaya so its management has been well aware of the situation. It has tried to placate the industry and claimed that Pattaya was still considered to be one of the most prominent destinations for the TAT. The TAT Governor, Dharmnoon Prachua-bmoh, said, 'Pattaya is the number one resort in the whole Asian region. I challenge anyone to find another place like it.' He said it was the second most popular destination in Thailand, with a character, flavour and variety that could not be matched anywhere else.

Some public service managers claim that many problems arise because of loopholes in the law. There is, however, a limit to how rigorously controls can be enforced in a democratic country with a tradition of free enterprise like Thailand.

Public interest

Managers have a responsibility to apply the law and regulations in the public interest. In Thailand and Pattaya there is a considerable amount of law and power in the hands of managers but often it has not been utilised. This is partly because of friction and the lack of cooperation between and within public agencies and the political leaders, including the mayor and manager of Pattaya and the Ministry of the Interior. The position of the City Manager, in particular, has been difficult and there have been resignations.

The mayor has been critical of councillors. For example, he accused one councillor of being 'currently involved in illegal contributions on Jomtien beach'.

Mayors have also said that the city has little power and they cannot strictly regulate the city growth, which is out of control mainly because of 'hidden powers and influence'. Part of this informal hidden power is money. It is said that anything is possible in Pattaya, even through PSM, if the price is right. There is no doubt that there is a tradition of venality and a lack of integrity in some public and private managers. This tradition is helped by the conflict and lack of unity within and between the two sectors. A very dynamic private sector responding to increasing demand has exploited unmercifully what was once a quiet fishing village with beautiful beaches. Governments, managers and even prime ministers have not been able to control these powerful forces. Many plans and policies have been produced by management but the prevailing political culture and the political and administrative system have been too weak to implement them. Disjointed incrementalism and almost unbridled development have been the norm.

Press coverage of Pattaya has perhaps sensationalised its problems; it is still a very popular and attractive tourist resort. Thailand and Pattaya have been fortunate in gaining from the turning away of tourists from problem-ridden tourism areas, such as Sri Lanka and the Philippines.

Performance

The ultimate test of performance is the impact of tourism, and the ultimate test of management is how adequately it responds to the problems brought about by that impact and how it protects the long-term future of the city.

A test of the commitment of governments to policy implementation can be partly measured by public expenditure. Therefore it is a good sign that since 1994 more public finance has been available to Pattaya and some improvements have been made: 'The Pattaya waterfront was improved . . . so as to revive tours of Pattaya so that it could recover its reputation as a famous tourist attraction' (TAT *Annual Report 1994*: 21). Only time, however, will tell whether management at the local level, following the principles of public interest, public service, effectiveness, efficiency and accountability, can bring the standards at the resort up to the level of competitors.

SUMMARY

Local governments are important, for they represent the people at the level where tourism and policies have a direct impact. Policies have to be implemented at this level and local citizens can have the power to influence results. Local governments have responsibilities to the citizens as well as to assist the tourist industry and can act as a bridge between citizens and industry. Politics, ideology and objectives can be important but, as at the national level, public managers should act within the five principles.

Participants will vary with the local area and the policy, but political and business leaders and local council committees can be important in the formulation and implementation of policy. Management and the industry will play a crucial role in implementation but citizens should not be neglected. Managers have to enforce the law and regulations. Local offices of national agencies and conservation groups may also be active.

How effectively management operates will depend upon its skill in balancing various political, economic, social and legal pressures and conflicting interests. Market forces and power groups in the local community, tourism developers and state and national governments can be pushing for tourism development. Yet, as the Newcastle case study shows, unless the tourism product is there, or can be produced by managers, development will be stagnant. Local people may support these demands for economic reasons but significant interest groups and citizens can be against tourism, and the burden of resolving the conflict and opposing forces often becomes the responsibility of management. There can also be conflict among local government representatives and managers about principles and the value and form of tourism. At the local level management has many responsibilities in providing basic services, and tourism has to be balanced with these. Local managers have the opportunity to be closer to the people and to have a better understanding of their needs and problems.

At the local and national level there are tourism policy communities which overlap and relate with one another, and decisions are taken and policy implemented through the operation of these communities. These communities include public and private managers who must cooperate to ensure effectiveness and efficiency and the future of tourism. Managers can have power through their official positions and resources of knowledge, skill, finance and law.

The results in terms of the practice of management are dependent upon the power available to local managers to be able to balance political demands and principles and those of the industry. Effective management practice also requires sensitivity, commitment, skill and, in tourism, initiative. In two of the case studies results in terms of performance at times have been excellent; management has been effective in boosting the number of tourists. In Pattaya, however, using public interest criteria performance at times has been abysmal, as local communities and environments have been damaged or destroyed by uncontrolled growth in tourism. The private sector is normally the driving force behind this growth, and the next chapter discusses how public managers manage their relationships with this sector.

SUGGESTED READING

Adams, I. (1990) *Leisure and Government*, Sunderland, England: Business Education Publishers. Chapters on local government, central government and tourism.

Ashworth, G.J. and Tunbridge, J.E. (1990) *The Tourist – Historic City*, London: Belhaven.

Buckley, P.J. and Witt, S.F. (1985) 'Tourism in difficult areas: case studies in Bradford, Bristol, Glasgow and Hamm', *Tourism Management* 6(3).

Carroll, P., Donohue, K., McGovern, M. and McMillen, J. (eds) (1991) *Tourism in Australia*, Marrickville, NSW: Harcourt Brace Jovanovich.

Craik, J. (1991) *Resorting to Tourism: Cultural Policies for Tourism Development in Australia*, North Sydney: Allen & Unwin.

Hall, C.M. (1992) *Hallmark Tourist Events: Impacts, Management and Planning*, London: Belhaven Press.

—— (1994) *Tourism and Politics: Policy, Power and Place*, Chichester, England: John Wiley. Contains a chapter on tourism and the local state.

Heeley, J. (1979) *Regional and Local Planning for Tourism: A Historical Perspective*, Glasgow: University of Strathclyde.

Hewison, R. (1987) *The Heritage Industry: Britain in a Climate of Decline*, London: Methuen.

Hitchcock, M., King, V.T. and Parnwell, M.J.G. (eds) (1993) *Tourism in South-east Asia*, London: Routledge.

Law, C. (1993) *Urban Tourism: Attracting Visitors to Large Cities*, London: Mansell.

7 Public management and the private sector

This chapter explains:

- why the relationship between public and private sector is so important
- who are the people and the organisations involved, and their diversity
- how the relationships between the public and private sectors are managed
- what is the practice and performance.

WHY: RESPONSIBILITY, MUTUAL IMPORTANCE

Responsibility of governments

Governments have a responsibility to manage their relations with the tourism industry for the public good, which should also include the good of the industry. How far that responsibility will extend will depend upon the ideology of the government of the day and the prevailing political culture of the country. While one government may tend to be non-interventionist and leave the industry to compete in the international and domestic market place, another government may be active in supporting the industry in various ways.

The US federal government, for example, has not been active in support for the tourism industry, while Cuba under Castro has owned and supported the industry totally. Under the 1981 National Tourism Policy Act the US government formally accepted considerable responsibility for tourism, but informally the situation is different. Tourism industry critics have complained about the lack of political interest, low budgets and priorities given to tourism. The Under Secretary of Commerce for Travel and Tourism, Greg Farmer, in 1994 'agreed with the tour operators that the country [the United States] doesn't put enough resources into the market place because it doesn't recognise the economic significance of tourism' (*Japan Times* 1994).

In Britain the Young Report reflected the ideology of the Conservative government.

> It may be asked why the Government should involve itself directly in this topic, which is primarily a matter for private enterprise. Indeed, the Government believes the best way it can help any sector of business to flourish is not by intervening but by providing a general economic framework which encourages growth and at the same time removing unnecessary restrictions or burdens.
>
> (UK, Cabinet Office 1985)

Other governments believe intervention is necessary, because if tourism is left to the private sector and to market forces the public interest will be sacrificed to private interests.

It is expected that governments will support economic development and will attempt to maintain a healthy balance of payments. This leads governments to support tourism as a growth industry and as one of the chief currency earners. In 1988 the President of the United States, George Bush, was therefore prepared to make a television commercial for the tourism industry: 'Today there are more reasons than ever to visit America, and there's never been a better time than now. So what are you waiting for, an invitation from the President!' Mrs Thatcher, as the British Prime Minister, give a similar invitation to visit Britain, in her address to a joint session of the US Congress. Support can be financial by way of grants, subsidies, lower taxes and investment capital, while government-owned land may be made available. Physical infrastructure and an administrative system and process can be provided to help industrial development. Governments are responsible for reducing the administrative and other burdens on industry by reducing regulations and providing a 'level playing field'.

Tourism is more than an industry or a series of industries in the private sector. It is an activity and experience which affects many individuals, communities and organisations which are not involved in tourism for economic gain but for other reasons. The tourist alone is participating in tourism for pleasure, relaxation, escape and for other reasons. Governments therefore in their management of the private sector must not lose sight of the non-economic side of their responsibilities. The Tourism Society, based in London, has been one of the most critical observers of government and tourism in Britain, and in the following Memorandum to the Department of Employment (December 1989) it stated what they believed were the Government's responsibilities (see Box 7.1).

Other organisations and governments reflecting different views and political cultures, such as that of the United States, would consider that several of these tasks were not essential national tasks and could be better performed by the private sector.

Importance of industry to the public sector

It is the industry, particularly the private sector, which plays the leading role in the development of tourism and which provides most of the investment, capital stock of accommodation, hotels and resorts, theme parks, travel agents and tour guides and most of the transportation. For the industry to develop, private managers should have initiative, ability and experience. The industry has the knowledge of markets, of the customers and the product; it has the skills and the dynamism necessary to operate in the highly competitive market place. These same skills are necessary to deal with natural or political disasters which can hit the industry, ranging from cyclones to military *coups*. It is to gain these skills as much as investment that countries such as China establish joint venture hotels. The industry can market the tourism product in a foreign country or region without provoking an adverse reaction which could happen it if was marketed directly by government. Because they are not tied to a public bureaucratic system with its hierarchy and management principles the industry has the freedom and flexibility to take risks, and it is prepared to take risks for profit, which would be unacceptable for PSM. Industry is also important in other ways, according to Grant (1987: 37): 'There is an exchange relationship from which government secures three types of benefit: information for policy design; consent for policy clearance; and cooperation for policy implementation.'

As the former USSR found, it is extremely difficult for public management to achieve objectives efficiently in today's swiftly changing, highly complex, intensely competitive international market system. Management needs information, consent, cooperation and other forms of assistance from industry. The tourism industry also needs, as acknowledged by the British Tourism Minister Norman Lamont in 1984, to be given the same kind of treatment as other industries. PSM should give equal treatment to tourism; there should be a level playing field. If the industry is totally or mainly owned by government, as in China and Vietnam, it must have considerable

Box 7.1 The need for national policies, and essential national tasks, Britain

We identify ten tasks in this section which are, in our judgement, essential for securing the future growth and prosperity of tourism and for regulating its negative effects. These tasks can be fulfilled most effectively only at national (GB/UK) level. Of course, recognising the current political climate, they can be fulfilled less adequately, as now, at the level of England, Scotland and Wales (and Northern Ireland).

None of the tasks below can be split up and devolved to regions, although in some cases their implementation can and should be:

Policy: The national importance and the effects of the tourist industry require that there must be a national tourism policy. It should be evolved by a National Board in accordance with broad policy guidelines stated by government.

Strategy formulation, implementation and control: The formulation and promotion of strategies to implement policy, through a regional system of tourist board and other agencies as appropriate. To ensure efficiency and accountability in the spending of public money, this task must include the monitoring and control of implementation.

Development and marketing initiatives: The selection, formulation, and implementation of development and marketing schemes where these have an obvious national dimension for initiation and control of implementation.

Co-ordination: Essential national co-ordination between the many and disparate agencies and organisations involved with aspects of tourism, For example, Government Departments (Dept of Env. and DTI); national agencies (Countryside Commissions, Development Agencies, Forestry Commissions, Sports and Arts Council); national trade associations (BHRCA, ABTA, BITOA), and the major national and multi-national commercial sector organisation.

Quality standards: The definition and promulgation of quality standards, codes of conduct and other regulatory means, where only a national body can act as an unbiased arbiter in the interest of the consumer throughout the country.

Tourism information services: The establishment and maintenance of a comprehensive, standardised, impartial consumer information network.

Research: The specification, analysis, interpretation and dissemination of data required for policy formulation and development and marketing purposes. This to include the conduct of surveys or use of agencies as necessary with commercial participation where possible.

Development expertise: The exercise of the national tasks will generate information and expertise at the highest level. They are necessary to provide national services to investors,

> financiers, developers, businesses in the industry, and in support
> of other bodies as required, so as to improve the tourism product
> and the efficiency of both development planning and marketing
> throughout the industry.
>
> *Education and training*: The size of the industry, its need for an
> educated and trained workforce at all levels of maturity and
> skills, and the existence of national agencies involved in
> provision require a continuing national contribution.
>
> *Leadership*: Given the disparate nature of the industry and in
> relation to highly competitive and rapidly changing world
> markets for tourism, the exercise of leadership is vital for its
> future prosperity and growth.
>
> (The Tourism Society, viii, 1990)

autonomy if it is to provide the tourism knowledge, skill and
dynamism which is needed, but which is lacking in the traditional
government department with its bureaucratic methods, hierarchy and
slow-moving regulated procedures.

In its relations with government, industry should respect the public
interest and the political culture. There should be fair and just treatment of the community, of guests, hosts and employees. Industry
should respect and preserve the natural and cultural environment and
strive to make tourism and its activities beneficial to all concerned.
The peak bodies of the tourism industry are in a much better position
than public managers to monitor, control and secure compliance
to principles from recalcitrant members of the industry. Industry
cooperation is necessary for policy implementation.

According to the 1987 Report of the Australian Inquiry into
Tourism (volume 1), the role of the private sector is 'to provide tourism
facilities and services to the travelling public while maximising financial returns'. This role engenders ideas and leads to the initiation of
new projects in which the private sector is able to recognise the market
need or niche – as, for example, in the development in the 1930s
of youth hostels, and in the 1980s backpackers' hostels. The private
sector formulates and implements the project, and takes the financial
risk. Private management provides the tourism experience and skills
but also the specialised technical skills through consultants, planners,
architects, engineers, designers, lawyers, project managers and builders.
Governments cannot provide all of these functions nor the whole
range of other service functions involved, such as accommodation,
food and beverages, transportation and retail shopping. The movement towards privatisation of public organisations is a recognition of
the value of private sector management.

Importance of the public sector to the industry

The industry cannot survive without the system and the infrastructure of support and security provided by the public sector. If governments can stop violence or terrorism and provide security they can boost tourism, as Egypt did between 1994 and 1995, raising the number of arrivals by 21.9 per cent. Within the system in particular the industry needs certainty, consistency and continuity from public management, whether it is to do with laws, taxes, immigration, transportation or attitudes. The private sector managers need to know the public parameters in which they can take decisions. Industry needs a stable legal and financial system within which it can operate, which will give tourism activities legitimacy. The tourism industry needs government permission and support for most of its development, such as the building of hotels or development of resorts. According to BTA Chairman Duncan Bluck:

> whilst of course, the tourism industry is primarily a private sector industry, it is essential that there is a Government involvement at all levels, designed to ensure that the infra-structure in every respect is best suited to help the growth of this important industry.
> (British Tourist Authority *Annual Report 1985*: 6)

The marketing of tourism, especially overseas, is a good example of where government intervention is necessary. Because of the diversity and differences in the industry it is difficult to get agreement and raise funds for marketing promotion, and therefore government organisation and funds are necessary. This was recommended in the 1965 Report which brought the Australian government and its management fully into tourism.

> (ii) Adoption of an intensive promotion programme in overseas travel markets correlated with development of travel attractions and facilities in Australia. Assurance of adequate funds is essential to plan and execute a successful overseas promotion.
> 2 Provide the financial requirements of the proposed Australian Travel Authority to the extent needed over and above the contributions by the states and territories and from private industry.
> (Harris, Kerr, Forster and Co. 1965: 4)

The United States under the 1981 Act gave assistance to the industry in various ways, including international marketing, provision of information, and assistance to states for regional promotion.

Grants and taxes

The industry has always been eager to gain funds from public sources, and the British government's deeper involvement with the industry in 1929 and 1969 reflected this. In many countries this public funding of the industry has taken the form of pump priming – that is, getting projects started.

The Chairman of the Australian Travel Industry Association, Sir Frank Moore in 1992 was quite clear about what the industry needed from governments, including the tax provisions.

'The industry had to "work smarter" in the 1990s but would need assistance from Commonwealth and State governments.'

'We don't want government hand-outs,' Sir Frank said. 'What we do want is for governments to tax us as little as possible and then get out of the road and let private enterprise get on with the job.'

He said the increase in depreciation and investment allowances in the Government's One Nation statement earlier this year had not gone far enough.

'What's the good of giving us anything if it doesn't work, and it doesn't work at 4 per cent,' he said. 'It might work at 7.5 per cent.'

Australia's Asian neighbours were more flexible and supportive of their tourism industries, providing a much higher level of incentive to tourism investors.

Sir Frank said it was critical for State governments to examine the basis of assessment for land tax and rate bills, at present based on the highest essential use for a block of land rather than its actual use.

This meant hotels were often liable for the same sort of charges payable by a 50-storey commercial office building, he said. Some hotels in Sydney were having to pay $18 a room per night in government fees, based on a 100 per cent occupancy rate: if a hotel was only 50 per cent full it would be forced to pay charges amounting to as much as $36 a room.

The Government should also look at the question of payroll tax and pay awards within the industry, Sir Frank said. 'For every 100 days of work, because of the work practices we presently have, we pay for an extra 63 days for them to do nothing at all,' he said. 'That's why it costs so much to put up five-star hotels.'

Since the 1980s particularly, and because of high unemployment, governments have increasingly seen the industry as being important in job creation. Often the new jobs have been created with the help of government grants. The British Minister for Tourism, Viscount Ullswater, wrote in 1990 that the industry supported 1.5 million jobs and contributed over £22 billion to the economy. In 1989, 191,000 people were officially regarded as self-employed in tourism-related industries, 18 per cent more than in 1981. He claimed that the industry was facing a demographic time bomb, hence the stress on recruitment and training. The Minister continued:

> What then is the Government's role in this? Part of the answer is to be found in the work of the Training Agency and the new Training and Enterprise Councils. Of equal significance is the emphasis now given to the Regional Tourist Boards, and the overseas offices of the British Tourist Authority following the recent review.
>
> (The Tourism Society 1991: v)

Stability and freedom

The industry needs government financial support but it also requires stability, certainty, freedom, reliability and quick decision making. Instability at the political and bureaucratic level can lead to a loss in market share, as in Queensland, according to the industry Regional Tourism Association. 'The state had three tourism ministers in the past three years, with five board chairmen and three chief executives leading the Queensland Tourist and Travel Corporation in the past six years' (*Courier Mail*, 4 June 1996). Stability is related to an environment of security and safety where laws are enforced and natural and cultural resources are protected. The public service principle leads governments to provide laws to protect the consumer, such as licensing and insurance of travel agents and the official grading of tourist accommodation.

While the industry needs support, history has shown that, because of the dynamic nature of the industry and intense competition, what is needed as much as anything is freedom for the tourism industry to respond to market demands. Public managers at times find it difficult to give this freedom; they want to retain their power over industry, sometimes for covert, informal reasons such as wanting to protect departmental interests rather than the public interest. This danger has been recognised in the management reforms of deregulation, corporatisation and privatisation. The United States has deregulated the airlines and relaxed tourism immigration formalities, which have stimulated tourism growth, yet there are growing controls and constraints in other areas such as environmental protection and labour relations. State and local governments continue to tax the industry.

There are times when the industry itself needs PSM to enforce regulations and principles against members of the industry.

Five main roles may be defined for government in relation to business: as a policy maker; as sponsor; as a regulator; as a customer; and as an owner. As a maker of economic policy, government substantially influences the context in which enterprises make decisions.

(Grant 1987: 36)

Industry needs PSM as a policy maker, but also as a sponsor, in the sense that it is only governments which can sponsor tourism and negotiate airline routes with another government. Public tourism managers can sponsor tourism within the broader public system. UK Conservative government tourism ministers have used the term 'sponsor' to indicate a much reduced government role in tourism. It can help to educate public organisations about the value of tourism. The industry needs PSM to act as a bridge to foreign countries, to the public sector and to the broader community. The public sector communication and coordination systems and skills are needed for successful tourism. In the customer role, governments can buy specialist tourism services such as marketing or consultancy. Because of the increasing economic importance of tourism, most governments in recent years have had to play a more active mandatory role as regulators. The industry in Australia claims that it is over-regulated by state governments, national parks and local governments on environmental issues. 'On average tourism operators pay about 5 per cent of their total earnings towards environmental regulations. Other industries pay far less – mining pays about 1 per cent, agriculture about 2 per cent, and manufacturing less than 1 per cent' (Managing Director, Tourism Council Australia, *The Australian*, 13 July 1996). Government can still be a substantial owner in the tourism industry mainly through public transport systems.

In practice, government and industry are dependent upon each other, and public sector and private sector managers must work together to achieve tourism objectives.

WHO: THE INDUSTRY, GOVERNMENT BUSINESS ENTERPRISES

The line between the private sector and the public sector is not clear. Tourist organisations can be owned jointly by both sectors; a publicly owned hotel can be managed by private management; a publicly owned airline can be listed as a private company and managed as such. Government business enterprises can be managed and operate like a private organisation, with private objectives, values, attitudes and behaviour and little or no concern for the public interest or public service.

Characteristics

The tourism industry is distinguished by its tremendous diversity, complexity and propensity for change. To deal with an industry with these characteristics calls for reciprocal qualities in public management and its processes. The tourism industry is made up of significant sectors of several other industries, such as transportation and leisure, and these industries have customers who are not tourists. Managers must be concerned not just with the industry, but also with the policy community, the tourism community and the general public. Included in the 'who?' must be citizens, tourism workers, trade unions and interest groups.

Diversity is the main characteristic of the tourism industry – diversity in almost every way: in activity, from accommodation to car hire to beach sale of food, transportation from international airline to river canoe operator, travel agent, tour operator, restaurant owner. Size will vary from international hotel chain and airline to a one-person, part-time business selling handicrafts to tourists. There is the big investor, the multi-million international corporation, and the woman renting out a room on a part-time bed and breakfast basis. The tourism operation can be owned by an individual, or by a public or private organisation. The owners can be local, national or international investors. A tour company owned and operating locally may differ from one owned nationally and operating nationally but the same public principles will apply to either. There is also tremendous diversity in the way these organisations relate to the different levels of government.

Coupled with the diversity of the industry is its complexity, which adds to the difficulties government has in its responsibility to assist tourism. There is the complexity, for example, within the huge network of travel agents, with their relations with their customers, one another, their peak organisations and with the public sector. This complexity is intensified because of the different levels of governments and their organisations and also relationships with communities, interest groups and the media. Public managers cannot be aware of all the complexities of the industry but should be aware of the most significant

the perspective of public sector objectives. Part of the complexity
~~ intermingling and overlapping of the private and public sectors.
In tourism, the mixture of the two sectors and their interdependence
is strongly pronounced. Participants can wear one or more hats;
the chairperson of the national tourism organisation can also be the
head of a large private organisation. Participants can operate at all
levels performing different functions and having different objectives. A
national elected representative supporting the national public interest
at the national level may also be vigorously pursuing his personal
interests through his local tourism business. Public officials such as
policemen with the formal legal objective to uphold the law may
also be corruptly protecting illegal gambling and sex establishments.
Managers move freely between the public and private sectors, and this
can make their values, objectives and behaviour more complex than
the managers who spend their whole careers in one sector. Managers,
generalists or specialists, can be formulators and implementors of
policy, all adding to the complexity of tourism.

The nature of the industry, its environment of competition and
market, public and government demand, mean that it is always in a
state of change. It is always under pressure to respond to the market,
as countries, regions or types of tourism rise and fall in popularity.
There can be considerable volatility and flux in the industry. Tourist
organisations are vulnerable to internal and external pressure and
must be strong to survive, and flexible enough to respond to the
pressures and challenges. If not, they can collapse, as did one of the
most famous pioneering airlines, Pan American. Normally tourist
organisations have no control over the external factors but they
should be effective enough to respond positively to them. Management should be flexible and supportive, and act as a facilitator for
the industry as it struggles or plans to meet challenges. The history
of the industry is one of change and striving to respond to demands
such as those of the 1990s – eco- and adventure tourism, tourism
for the disabled and retirees, theme parks and 'user pays' and new
destinations such as Indochina and Eastern Europe.

The world-wide movement towards privatisation has brought
changes for tourism and management. British Airways, the British
Airports Authority and Sealink Ferries, for example, have been sold
by the British government and become private companies. A regional
tourist board can become a private company and can be so poorly
managed as to make bad property deals and go bankrupt. In England
this happened with the Thames and Chilterns Regional Tourist Board
covering Bedfordshire, Berkshire, Buckinghamshire, Hertfordshire

and Oxfordshire. This region was merged with the Southern region. All these changes test the response and quality of public and private sector managers.

In all the diversity, complexity and change the public managers must decide who are the most significant actors and who are the most important power holders, but they must also be sure to whom their responsibility lies. Airlines, local, national and international, are some of the most significant and powerful actors in the industry not least because of their close relationships with public managers. There is a wide range of interest groups putting pressure on governments and the industry. Not least are the various national and international environmental groups which are growing in significance and influence. Those actors least able to protect themselves, such as the low paid, child workers and indigenous peoples in need, should be given particular assistance.

Local people can also possess power and their opposition has been known to stop tourism development. Similarly, individual tourism operators have been able to curtail the activities of powerful peak organisations or national tourism offices. The activities of poorly paid, poorly educated Thai hotel workers during the democracy period in the 1970s severely affected the powerful Thai tourist industry, and the Australian airline pilots during their 1989 national industrial dispute withdrew their labour and crippled the tourist industry. Small investors operating deck chairs on the beach adjoining a luxury tourism complex, because of their behaviour and attitudes, can create major problems for large investors and their managers, if the beach is an integral part of the resort. Trade unions can also be significant power holders. Power can come, and be expressed in many different forms, and managers have to decide what is legitimate power, and whether its use is legitimate.

Peak organisations

A peak organisation seeks to represent all the companies within that industry. There are several peak organisations in the tourism industry. Membership is normally voluntary but needs to include a high proportion of the industry for the organisation to be effective and have influence with government. Examples of such organisations include the American Society of Travel Agents, the Australian Hotels Association, the Australian Federation of Travel Agents, the Association of British Travel Agents (ABTA) and the Thai Hotels

Association. There are also industry-wide organisations which include all sectors, such as the Australian Tourism Industry Association, the Travel Industry Association of America and the Inbound Tourism Organisation of Australia (ITOA) which concentrates on inbound tourism. It is possible for government tourism corporations, and even governments, to be members of such associations.

The peak organisations perform the important functions of bringing together the majority of the members of the sector, acting as collectors of information and communicators with members and governments, helping to formulate the collective view of the members and policy of the organisation. These organisations are normally supported and favoured by PSM, for they ensure that public objectives are met more effectively and efficiently, they provide necessary information to PSM and communicate and support government views and policies to the industry. Public management tries to keep in touch and consult with peak organisation managers, and this places peak organisations in a position of power. It is easier for management to maintain contact with one large organisation rather than many small organisations; also the bureaucracy of a large public organisation shares similar objectives with the bureaucracy of a large private organisation, they are for quiet, efficient processes which do not rock the boat and keep most people happy.

The ABTA, founded in 1950, is an example of a one-sector peak organisation. It represents both tour operators and travel agents in the United Kingdom. Ninety per cent of the industry belongs to ABTA, including approximately 5,000 retail members.

Box 7.2   Travel agents' main purposes, Britain

The ABTA's main purposes are

- To promote the interests of all members in their relationship with each other and with other branches of the international travel industry, such as airlines, shipping companies, railways, coach companies and hotels.
- To maintain Codes of Conduct governing the activities of tour operators and travel agents for the benefit of members and the travelling public.
- To maintain liaison with governments and organisations concerned with the development of travel and tourism both in the United Kingdom and abroad.

(Association of British Travel Agents 1990)

The Association does more than liaise with government. It actively tries to persuade governments to support its industry. It is therefore essentially an interest and lobby group with all the advantages and disadvantages of such a group.

Developing countries and new industries see the need for associations to bring pressure on governments. In 1993, the Thai Amusement and Leisure Park Association was founded to exchange information and technology among members, to develop the country's amusement industry and to bring their interests before governments. Although the industry is small now when compared to the size of the population, it is expected that people will move from natural tourist destinations in the future to amusement parks. The new Association has sixteen members, as follows: Magicland, Siam Park, Safari World, Samut Prakarn Crocodile Farm and Zoo, King Kong Island, Oasis Seaworld, Pata Zoo, the Mall Water Park, Samphran Elephant Ground & Zoo, Mahachai Park, Porn Prom Paradise in Chiang Mai, Imperial World (Samrong), Bang Pakong Crocodile Farm and Zoo, Million Years Stone Park, Pattaya Crocodile Farm, Pattaya Water Park.

An all-industry group is the Australian Tourism Industries Association Ltd (ATIA). The board membership of 1992 gives some idea of the 'who' of the Australian tourism industry, and where power lies in the industry (see Box 7.3). It is important that the heads of other peak organisations are on the board as well as representatives of the powerful airline industry. The board included some of the most talented and experienced people in the industry but no woman, environmentalist or public servant. Some sub-committees, however, did contain such representatives. The primary objective of the ATIA is the development of a profitable industry, and this is reflected in a board membership of business people. It is not a public board like the ATC, which contains a cross-section of the tourism community.

Small organisations and individual entrepreneurs can often feel alienated and neglected by the peak organisation and public organisations such as national or regional tourism boards. It is not easy to get the industry to join together in a one-industry or an all-industry peak organisation even though the industry leaders and tourism minister may agree on the need for such an umbrella group. Private organisations value their freedom highly and fear that such organisations could lessen their independence. Thailand was still struggling in 1993 to establish an all-industry organisation which would include the fifty-six one-industry nation-wide travel associations and the Thai

---

Box 7.3 Australian Tourism Industries Association Board, 1992

Sir Frank Moore, AO, Chairman Director, Jupiters Ltd
Capt. Trevor Haworth, Deputy Chairman, Managing Director, Captain Cook Cruises
Mr Fred Basheer, National President, Australian Hotels Association
Mr Graham Couch, Chief Executive, Flag International Ltd
Mr John Dart, OBE, RFD, ED, Executive Director, Australian Federation of Travel Agents
Mr Julian Hercus, Deputy CEO – Commercial, QANTAS Airways Ltd
Mr Jon Liddicoat, Chief Executive, Best Western Hotels
Mr Geoff McGeary, Director, Australian Pacific Tours
Mr Bob Roberts, Director – Corporate Services, Ansett Transport Industries
Mr John Rowe, AM, Managing Director, Sydney Convention & Visitors Bureau
Mr Nick Tait, General Manager – AUST/NZ, British Airways
Mr Tony Thirlwell, Director of Marketing Services, Qantas Airways Limited
Mr Len Taylor, Managing Director, Inbound Tourism Organisation of Australia
Mr Brian Wild, General Manager – Australia, Continental Airlines

---

Travel Agents Association, which had grown from 220 members in 1984 to 386 in 1993. It was suggested that the eight to ten main industries could join first.

Unlike Thailand, since 1982 the United States has had a specific organisation to present a unified point of view of the industry to the federal government in Washington, DC. The Travel and Tourism Government Affairs Council represents all sectors, including transportation, food and beverages, accommodation, attractions and travel agents.

Individual organisations

The structure of the tourist industry covers a vast spectrum of private and public sector enterprises, and what distinguishes them from other industries is that they are mostly small, disparate, and spread throughout the land in every community from inner city to country. Britain is a good example of the widespread nature of the industry.

In each of the main sectors, however there are a dozen or more major companies such as THF, Rank, British Airways, Intasun, and Madame Tussauds; they are all highly influential. But even the top 100 or so companies probably account for less than a third of tourist spending; they cannot and do not speak for their own sectors and certainly not for the tourist industry as a whole.

Government acknowledges that the tourist industry is comprised mainly of businesses in the private sector. Some of these businesses are wholly or for the most part involved in tourism (dealing with staying and day visitors), while others are only partially involved although they are still essential elements of a successful tourist industry.

(The Tourism Society 1989: 3)

Box 7.4 Tourist and partial tourist organisations, Britain

The wholly involved sector comprises upwards of 50,000 mainly commercial businesses (the exact number is not known), including:

- hotel, guest houses, and other forms of serviced and self-catering accommodation
- holiday caravan parks and holiday centres
- commercial attractions ranging from theme parks to industrial heritage and amusement parks
- tour operators, travel agents and other travel organisers.

Other essential facilities and services only partially used by tourist and day visitors comprise a further 150,000 or so different organisations and establishments, many of them provided in the public sector including:

- restaurants – cafés – pubs and clubs
- transport operators (air, sea, road and rail)
- leisure and sports centres – country parks
- outdoor sports facilities such as golf courses and sailing marinas
- museums and galleries and the arts and entertainment.

(The Tourism Society 1989: 3)

PSM must manage not only the individual organisations and the individuals involved in tourism, locally, nationally and internationally, but they must also manage relations with the numerous interest and other groups, including trade unions and environmental and community groups. The 'who' will include international hotel and resort chains whether operating on a franchise or licence or directly by a parent company in the United States, Japan or Europe, such as the Hilton, Sheraton, Hyatt, Novotel, ANA or Meridien.

Government business enterprises

Among the 'who' in the tourism industry are the government-owned business enterprises. These can take the form of a statutory authority under a special Act of Parliament or Congress, or an ordinary company under the normal commercial law of the land. They can be joint ventures, wholly or partially owned by government, or owned by government but managed by the private sector. Joint venture hotels, for example, are common in China. As business enterprises they are expected to operate like a private enterprise, to be revenue producing and making profits, but also to follow the five principles.

If, however, the main objective is to establish an infant industry, governments will accept financial losses until the enterprise gets established. Some government business enterprises can be established to support essential but loss-making services, or to achieve more efficient management of public money entrusted to the enterprise. Under new managerialism (see Chapter 3) business enterprises are becoming more popular with governments, and these trends are bringing pressure on national tourism office managers to perform more like private managers. Their organisations are expected to produce revenues, and ideally to pay for themselves without receiving public funds. In response to this pressure the British Tourist Authority Chief Executive states:

> More generally, we will be adopting an even more commercial approach and seeking higher levels of private sector support for our initiatives. The fact that we can generate £23 for every £1 of public money we invest demonstrates how effective a partner the BTA can be for private sector companies and, in general, the British economy.
>
> (BTA *Annual Report 1995*)

There is a wide range of government business enterprises, including hotels, airlines, airports, development finance, local government piers, tourist attractions such as parks or caves, golf courses and marketing boards. Amtrak in the United States is such an organisation, operating through the National Railway Passenger Corporation since 1970. The Australian Senate classified the Australian Tourist Commission (ATC) as a business authority.

> The essential feature of these authorities is that they perform business-type activities which could be performed, or are being performed, by the private sector. Characteristics which they will usually, if not always have in common are that they are incorporated,

at least partly self-financing, staffed outside the Public Service Act
and autonomously managed with ministerial power of direction.
(Australia, Parliament, Senate Standing Committee on Finance
and Government Operations 1979: 9)

This reflects the theory that lies behind this form of organisation.
They should be similar to private enterprises in their freedom to
compete in the market place without the constraints of the traditional
government department. As a public enterprise, however, there
are certain community service obligations, and the enabling Act,
and general policy guidelines of the Minister, must be followed.
Depending upon the nature of the enterprise they are expected to
raise some, if not all, of their finances from business activities. Tourist
boards have always been dependent upon government for some of
their finances. The key test of the vitality of any business enterprise is
its ability to compete in a dynamic market place in the situation of a
level playing field where it has no special advantages or disadvantages
as compared to those of its competitors. Tourist organisations have
to operate in a highly competitive environment against one another
as well as against overseas countries and resorts. The industry and
the boards must always be market driven and like any other market,
customers-tourists must be encouraged to buy the product, to visit and
enjoy the tourist attractions available in the host country, rather than
elsewhere.

Some government business enterprises are part of the tourist
industry and are managed and compete like any private enterprise –
as, for example, publicly owned airlines or railways. They will be
managed to achieve a profit, and perhaps there will be no community
service obligations, but if there are, this should be stated clearly in the
annual profit and loss account. Public airlines can be so imbued with
the private sector ethos that they can be unwilling to curtail profits
and increase seat capacity in order to carry tourists at lower fares.
Ideally, government business enterprises should be managed and
monitored as if they were private enterprises.

HOW: POLITICS, FREEDOM, DEPENDENCY, REGIONAL BOARDS

How public managers are involved in tourism will depend upon the
political culture of the country and the ideology of the government
in power. The political culture of the United States means that
management there is much less interventionist than in France, while

the ideology of Britain's Mrs Thatcher placed greater emphasis on the private sector. The public sector is also affected by the pervading management trends such as privatisation, deregulation and marketisation. Relationships with industry are also conditioned by public sector principles. The pursuit of the public interest or accountability by management can complicate and prolong the policy process for the industry. For example, for a tourist company to get permission to develop in a specifically designated historical or nature area can be time consuming. Yet this procedure is necessary if those areas are to be protected.

There are formal institutions, processes and laws within which PSM and the industry operate but there are also the informal relationships of shared objectives, needs and values. Institutions and regulations may be formal and static but relationships and processes are often informal, flexible and dynamic. This partly reflects the nature of the tourism industry which, if it is to survive, must always be dynamic and open to change. The diversity of the industry with its different objectives requires a fluid, open and cooperative relationship between public and private managers. PSM, at least, must always create the framework to enable the industry to respond to the market. This entails giving considerable freedom to the industry; even if they are not private organisations as can be found in China and Vietnam, they must still have freedom to compete. Peak organisations will strive to have good relations at the national level where laws and major policy are formulated. Many of the participants at this level must also work with other organisations at other levels to achieve implementation. In Britain and elsewhere, one problem for the industry is the relatively short time, of two to three years, for which senior civil servants stay in tourism positions. The two sides do not have enough time to get to know each other. Which public or private organisations will participate and how, will depend upon the policy area. There are the tourism policy communities which will change according to the issue, and there are tourism policy networks which keep PSM and the industry in touch with each other.

Ministers have undertaken a wide range of engagements to promote the work the industry is doing. The importance of tourism to the national economy is now more widely recognised by the press, the public and by people looking for careers. During the past year, the Secretary of the State for Employment has held meetings with colleagues in other Government Departments to ensure that cooperation between government and industry is working effectively. The Ministers for tourism in England, Scotland, Wales and Northern Ireland have met to ensure that policies are consistent and to discuss their common interest in tourism issues.

(UK, Department of Employment 1988, *Tourism '88*)

While politicians tend to be involved in occasional meetings and talking with industry, some managers can be involved in an almost daily round of consultation, negotiation and cooperation.

All participants, public and private, are dependent upon one another. They all have something to contribute to tourism but some are more influential and active than others. Influence comes from resources such as legal power, finance and expertise, and these are held by both PSM and the industry. For example, while a national tourism board may have legal powers and direct access to the political leadership it does not have the expertise and the knowledge of the industry. Because the sectors are dependent upon each other their power and independence is constrained. These constraints, coupled with the nature of the tourism industry, means that the success of the industry depends upon a good working cooperation from all sides. There must be good communication and trust and a willingness to negotiate, bargain and have informal as well as formal exchange agreements. The public sector needs the cooperation of industry if policies are going to be implemented effectively. This was shown in the attempt to introduce an arrival tax in Australia. The Federal Department of Finance introduced an arrival tax on tourists landing at international airports. The tax was the idea of the Australian Treasury to raise more money; there was little consultation with the industry, which was strongly opposed to the tax; the airlines refused to collect the tax and it was difficult for PSM to administer it. The tax was eventually withdrawn.

For tourism organisations to be accepted into the policy community they must be seen as responsible, reliable and prepared to recognise the legitimate claims of public interest and service. Credit card companies, for example, are accepted as being responsible and their cards are used extensively in tourism. As the Visa company expressed it, 'Visa wants to show and back it up that we are a responsible corporate citizen of Thailand.'

Joint ventures

This is a common management device for private companies to engage with public organisations in tourism projects. The private company will invest in the projects, but in particular they will provide the management skills needed in the development, marketing and operation of the joint venture. A joint venture in Vietnam planned in 1994 by the American company BBI Investment Group is based on a 67 per-cent share, with Quang Nam-Da Nang Tourist Company and the People's Committee of Quang Nam-Da Nang Province to hold 33 per cent. It was considered to be equal to the largest single investment in Vietnam by a foreign company and would consist of four hotels, a conference centre and a golfcourse to be located on a beach near Da Nang.

Regional tourist boards

These boards are a good example of how the public and private sectors together manage tourism. In England, for example, there are eleven regional tourist boards. These have gained more power with the reorganisation of the national boards. The autonomous boards are comprised of public and industry representatives. Seven of twelve English boards were chaired by managers from the industry. Policy is decided by the part-time boards and the day-to-day management is carried out by full-time professional managers. These organisations are expected to work on behalf of the whole region and to be expert, independent and responsive to market demands. Their two key objectives in 1988 were 'to spread the economic and employment benefits of tourism more widely across the UK, and to encourage tourism outside the main holiday season' (UK, Department of Employment 1988).

The importance of support from the national government can be seen from the table of sources of income (see Box 7.5), but the income from the commercial activities of the regional tourist boards themselves exceeds the income from the national boards. Income from their own resources increases the independence of the boards. National governments can exert excessive control and direction over boards. In the English case, however, the national government, for ideological reasons, and to cut national expenditure, tried to curtail its own responsibilities and to pass those on to regional boards. To achieve national uniformity and support tourism services, national governments have to provide some funds to the regional boards. Some regional boards are weak in resources, leadership, management and local government and industry support. There can be political interference and an over-dominance by local government members which can lead to a high management turnover. There needs to be a high level of cooperation and trust between government and industry members on the regional boards. Boards can be an excellent way to achieve public and industry cooperation.

The following statement in the 1990/91 *Annual Report* of the English Tourist Board (ETB) is a good example of how the different public organisations and the industry are actually involved in tourism. The issues management considers to be important, including finance, are discussed.

Box 7.5 England's regional tourist boards

During the year, the Board devolved further responsibilities to the 12 regional tourist boards, providing funding of £6.4 million. However, the total cost of supporting the new arrangements was £7.4 million. Nearly half the payments were in the form of performance related contracts for services carried out by the regions on the Board's behalf. The agreements were designed to ensure a uniform approach to priority activities such as Tourist Information Centre networking, business advice and information collection. They proved successful and further contracts were negotiated for the year starting in April, 1991. They cover employment and training, corporate communications, travel trade development, tourism signposting and the development of direct marketing databases. Other funds were allocated through a bidding process for specific projects. This allowed the Board to give greater support to local area initiatives, strategic TICs and market research.

Great emphasis was placed on monitoring the effective use of Board funds. The contracts set out specific tasks while support for regional marketing programmes was linked to achievement targets. In addition, an evaluation programme was devised for selected activities to begin in April, 1991.

During the year, three more regions elected industry representatives as chairmen, taking the total to seven out of 12.

The increase in ETB funding to the regions made a considerable impact, increasing their level of activity and their ability to generate additional support from partners, particularly the private sector. While commercial membership subscriptions increased by 7 per cent to £1.74 million, local authority subscriptions remained static. This was due, primarily, to a reduction of over 200 per cent in the contribution to the London Tourist Board from the London Borough Grants Scheme, the withdrawal of Derbyshire County Council from membership of East Midlands Tourist Board, and reduction in funding from Cumbria County Council to Cumbria Tourist Board.

Regional boards' commercial activities continued to grow steadily, with commercial income reaching £9.3 million. Taking into account the transfer of Victoria TIC from ETB to the London Tourist Board from 1 April 1990, this represented a 7 per cent increase over the commercial income achieved in 1989/90.

The chart below indicates the levels of income for the regional boards from local authorities, commercial members and their own commercial activities.

Regional tourist boards' sources of income	Commercial members' subscriptions (£)	Local authority subscriptions (£)	ETB funds[1] (£)	Other income (£)	Total (£)
Cumbria	100,200	74,900	511,000	540,100	1,226,200
East Anglia	65,600	92,600	452,100	458,900	1,069,200
East Midlands	49,000	69,900	414,700	315,200	848,800
Heart of England	126,800	153,800	611,700	756,800	1,649,100
London	609,000	294,000	727,300	1,650,000	3,280,300
Northumbria	62,000	265,600	362,300	246,300	936,200
North West	105,000	244,400	461,800	1,027,800	1,839,000
South-East England	125,900	185,400	508,900	659,700	1,479,900
Southern	105,800	86,000	542,800	1,435,700	2,170,300
Thames & Chilterns	129,600	48,000	334,300	872,900	1,384,800
West Country	135,300	142,600	810,700	765,700	1,854,300
Yorkshire & Humberside	126,000	189,200	681,200	544,000	1,540,400
Total	1,740,200	1,846,400	6,418,800	9,273,100	19,278,500

[1] Includes funds for Local Area Initiatives and Strategic TICs totalling £0.75 million.
Includes the operational income attributable to Victoria TIC which transferred from ETB to LTB on 1 April 1990.

(ETB *Annual Report 1990/91*: 21)

There are now eleven regional tourist boards, as Thames and Chilterns has been merged with Southern, which becomes Number 7 on the revised list, and South-east England becomes Number 11 (see Box 7.6).

WHAT RESULTS? AIR TRAVEL, INCENTIVE TRAVEL

Airlines and airports

Why governments are involved

The airline industry is crucially important, especially to the international tourism market, but also to the domestic industry where countries are large, such as Australia, Canada and the United States. Even though the biggest section of the market is normally domestic

Box 7.6   Regional tourist boards

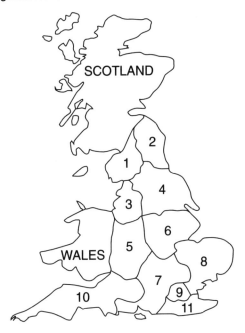

1 **Cumbria**
2 **Northumbria**
  (Cleveland, Durham, Northumberland, Tyne & Wear)
3 **North West**
  (Cheshire, Greater Manchester, Lancashire, Merseyside, High Peak, District
  of Derbyshire)
4 **Yorkshire and Humberside**
  (North, South and West Yorkshire and Humberside)
5 **Heart of England**
  (Gloucestershire, Hereford and Worcester, Shropshire, Staffordshire,
  Warwickshire and West Midlands)
6 **East Midlands**
  (Derbyshire, Leicestershire, Lincolnshire, Northamptonshire,
  Nottinghamshire)
7 **Thames and Chilterns**
  (Bedfordshire, Berkshire, Buckinghamshire, Hertfordshire, Oxfordshire)
8 **East Anglia**
  (Cambridgeshire, Essex, Norfolk, Suffolk)
9 **London**
10 **West Country**
  (Avon, Cornwall, Devon, Somerset, Western Dorset, Wiltshire, Isles of Scilly)
11 **Southern   7 (revised)**
  (Eastern Dorset, Northern Dorset, Hampshire and the Isle of Wight)
12 **South-east England   11 (revised)**
  (East Sussex, Kent, Surrey, West Sussex)

tourism, governments give priority to attracting overseas tourists. International airlines themselves can be major earners of foreign currency for the home country, or at least they help to reduce the foreign currency deficit on the overseas account. While airlines and the tourism industry are important for economic reasons, airlines are also important national flag carriers. They can boost national prestige and pride by showing the national symbol around the world, such as Qantas with its famous kangaroo and British Airways with the British flag. There is normally a strong political commitment to the national carrier and that is why it is sometimes subsidised by governments or allowed to run at a loss, and allowed to behave in a very independent fashion that is sometimes contrary to the wider national interest. Governments control the landing rights of airlines coming into their own country and they have often protected the national carrier first, and restricted other airlines flying in, at a loss to the tourist industry. Public and private managers have had to fight hard to obtain a greater access for foreign airlines in order to boost the number of incoming tourists.

Airlines are also very big business. Their marketing budget is much higher than that of the tourism industry. Their investment in aircraft and the national investment into airports is immense; they provide considerable employment, often at a highly skilled level such as pilots, engineers and experienced cabin staff. National airlines, whether they are public or privately owned, require considerable government attention because of their economic and political importance. It is only national governments which can negotiate with other national governments over issues such as landing rights in their respective countries. The airline industry is important politically, for if it is inefficiently managed it can create problems for the minister and the government.

Airports are crucial for the transportation and communication needs of the national economy and also for the tourist industry. Heathrow Airport, London, was the busiest international airport in the world with 44,968,000 passengers in 1992. O'Hare Airport in Chicago is busier but passengers include many domestic travellers. The economic importance of airports can be seen in the case of Heathrow, which employs 54,000 people and whose business amounts to 16 per cent of British international trade turnover. In 1987 it was calculated that if Heathrow could add five extra runway slots it would help the British economy by £180 million per year.

Who is involved

The airline industry is a mixture of public and private, international, national and local interests. Airlines can be joint enterprises, as was Qantas, the Australian airline, which in 1993 was 25 per-cent owned by British Airways (BA) and 75 per cent by the Australian national government until the privatisation of its share. Qantas is managed under the private company form but other airlines are under the public corporation form. In the United States airlines are owned by the private sector. Airlines can also be part of a larger transport or tourism organisation.

Privatisation is the current political and management fashion, and many countries are selling off their national airlines to the private sector as in Britain, Singapore, Japan and Thailand. In the United States however, the airlines have always been owned privately. Airline companies can offer charter flights if approved by governments, and these have been important for the growth of tourism. The rapid growth of tourism in countries like Spain in the 1960s and 1970s was possible, not because of regular scheduled airline flights, from northern and western Europe but because of the dynamism of private charter flight companies. Governments have to try and maintain the balance between the regular airlines and the chartered airlines companies. Relations between the two sectors of the industry can become bitter, as was seen in the conflict between BA and Virgin Airlines, owned by Richard Branson, and it can continue when they are competing through scheduled flights.

Within the airline and tourism policy community are various public and private organisations, managers and politicians. One of the most important organisations is the Ministry of Transport. This is normally a very large, long-established, powerful ministry, strongly supported by its industrial groups such as aviation. The ministry is dedicated to protecting its position and its clientele groups, and it has been highly defensive of the airline industry. Like other ministries it has a high opinion of its position, importance and expertise. Its vision, however, can be too narrow and damaging to other interests such as tourism. The corporate culture can be conservative and based on serving vested interests. This culture has led to a policy of total support of national airlines in opposition to the national policy of tourism growth.

Among those interested will also be related but maybe semi-autonomous public agencies which manage the airline industry and airports, such as the Civil Aviation Administration of China

(CAAC). CAAC has overall management responsibility for almost thirty airlines in China. There are many vested interests in the industry, including powerful trade unions, and military officers who wish to move into lucrative management positions in the airline after their retirement from the air force. For many years the president of Thai Airways International was the commander-in-chief of the Thai air force. Management of the airline industry internationally, including agreements for special tourism fares, is conducted by the International Civil Aviation Organisation (ICAO) from its head-quarters, which helps to bring together the policy community.

Others involved must include airport authorities such as the British Airports Authority (until it was privatised in 1987) and the Australian Federal Airports Corporation which owns and manages twenty-two of the twenty-three leading airports in Australia, which also underwent privatisation. Most airports were managed by national governments using statutory corporations, but in the United States local and state governments have owned and managed airports often through statutory corporations. The fastest-growing airport in Australia for tourist arrivals is the tropical, far north Queensland airport of Cairns managed by Cairns Port Authority. Sydney, the number one arrival airport for international visitors, with 2–3 million arriving in 1992, is managed by the federal government.

How managers manage

Through various organisations, processes and networks, management provides the direction, communication, coordination and control functions needed in the industry. It has the responsibility to provide the necessary infrastructure, protect the local community and environment and support national and local economic development. The test of the good manager is the ability to balance and reconcile the various opposing forces. This is done partly through the typical management device of autonomous statutory organisations which manage, and the appointment of representatives of various sectors to serve on the governing boards. Board members should improve the effectiveness and efficiency of the airline but they can also do the opposite. For example, on the board of Thai Airways International there was conflict between the Ministry of Transportation and Communications, and the Ministry of Finance, each represented by their Permanent Secretaries. Each had a different view of the airline and of who should be the senior managers. In 1993 Thai reported its worst financial results ever, which were blamed on poor management, but vested interests and management internal conflicts were also responsible. Normally the board would be a part-time policy board with the chief executive officer (CEO) of the airline or airport as a member or an observer. The CEO should have considerable freedom to manage the day-to-day business of the airline.

For success, the airline industry must be very much market driven because of the competitive nature of international air travel. Airlines therefore have as their first priority the financial return on the air route, and the profits of the company as a whole. They much prefer to have fewer flights filled with higher-fare business travellers, or fully paid economy flights, rather than many flights filled with tourists paying special group air fares.

Tourism managers have to struggle to gain acceptance by the airlines policy community, which have their own objectives and do not always take kindly to what they see as tourism interference. In order to be effective and efficient it is necessary for the tourist industry and its public managers to be accepted as a member of the airline policy community and to be automatically seen as part of the policy network. Airlines are normally very strong politically, they are conservative and dominated by self-interest, and are not particularly open to outside pressures. They are also strong within the public sector, with interlocking relationships with the transport or aviation ministry. This rigid, strong situation is, however, under criticism. For example, a 1994 Report on government-owned European airlines was highly critical of their costly and uncompetitive operations and heavy debts. It was suggested that government airline subsidies be cut and moves made towards privatisation.

As part of the airlines policy community, management can influence and help the airlines to become more profitable and competitive by boosting the number of tourists travelling by air. Qantas and Japan Air Lines (JAL) resisted the efforts of the tourist industry, the tourism minister and tourism PSM to increase the number of flights from Japan to Australia, to boost the number of Japanese tourists. The catalyst who broke the resistance and pushed through an increase in the number of flights between the two countries was a very determined new tourism minister in Australia. Airlines also resist opening their territory to new operators, and tourism PSM has to fight these national organisations and their sponsoring ministry to gain access for new airlines.

Public management can spend considerable time negotiating deals with foreign countries and airlines and national airlines, agencies and tourism groups. They then have to monitor, control and ensure that agreements are implemented. Strong interest groups such as the air-line trade unions must also be managed and kept happy. Airlines are a people-orientated industry, so good staff management is essential to maintain morale and cheerful, efficient service to passengers. The poor image of the former USSR Aeroflot was partly caused by surly, unfriendly, inefficient staff.

What results? practice and performance

The practice of PSM towards airlines has tended to be conservative and protective but unresponsive to the needs of tourism and market demands. One of the biggest problems facing tourism management in recent years has been the failure to provide sufficient modern airports to cope with the huge growth in tourism and air traffic. This is true of London, Sydney, New York or Tokyo. Everywhere there is conges-tion, in the air and on the ground, and delays can be longer than the actual flying time. Since the early 1950s British governments have been trying to solve the problem of congestion and there have been numerous public inquiries into proposals for new airports and runways. One solution has been to open other airports near London and the regions, but most airlines still want to use Heathrow.

Part of the problem is the huge cost of airport development, the long time-scale needed actually to become operational and strong opposition to airport development by local residents and some public managers. These managers question the value of airport development when there are serious social problems in the country such as poverty. Pressure for airport development is accentuated by the intense competition between airports internally and internationally, as between London, Paris and Amsterdam. Bangkok competes with Singapore and Kuala Lumpur.

There are also the high costs of air traffic control systems and the costs which can be inflicted on the industry by strong, militant trade unions. In Australia, the 1989–90 pilots strike was disastrous for the tourism industry. There can also be conflicts within the public sector, such as which organisation should manage duty-free goods facilities. In Thailand, for example, Thai International and the Thai Airports Authority fought for the power to control the lucrative duty-free business. Management can also be made more difficult by internal conflict and bureaucratic politics, as with Thai International between military and civilian managers in 1993 and accusations of 'nepotism and favouritism' in the airline. Politicians can be corruptly involved as in the case of the former Prime Minister of Japan, Kakuei Tanaka, who was accused of taking millions of dollars of bribes from the US Lockheed Corporation, so that he would persuade a Japanese airline to buy Lockheed aircraft. This was the so-called 'peanuts' case, as he signed receipts for so many peanuts, which signified so many millions of dollars.

An international recession can hit airlines hard, forcing some to go into bankruptcy and others to merge. Military conflicts can also cause problems, as with the 1991 Gulf War. One of the most important public policy changes affecting airlines has been deregulation. In the United States this has led to cheaper fares but also to huge losses and the failure of some of the biggest and oldest airlines, including Pan Am. In 1978 the US Airline Deregulation Act allowed PSM and the US Civil Aeronautics Board to start dismantling the legal and administrative structure in order to allow airlines to compete freely in the market. Deregulation spread to New Zealand in 1983, Canada in 1987 and Australia in 1990. In May 1986, the European Court of Justice ruled that in principle price-fixing airline cartels were in breach of Treaty of Rome rules on free competition. This has been supported by the European Commission, but some European governments have been reluctant to deregulate because of resistance from large and powerful government-owned airlines and their trade unions. France was one example, with the government trying to protect Air France against BA and going against a European Union decision. WTO, the World Bank and the International Monetary Fund have pressed for the ending of bilateral restrictive air agreements and for an open skies policy and lower fares which would boost world tourism.

The industry has been subject to scrutiny by regulatory bodies such as Prices Surveillance to protect the public interest. However, it has been the pressure of the market and the world recession which has brought about mergers between domestic and international carriers of the same country and airlines buying into foreign airlines, such as the £665 million which BA paid for a 25 per-cent share of Qantas in 1992, beating off a bid from Singapore Airlines. Other challenges to the public management of airlines include dangers to air safety and terrorism threats.

Governments have been more concerned about protecting their national airlines and their positions in airports than in the broader public interest or service, or effectiveness and efficiency.

Incentive travel market

This branch of the tourist industry is a good example of what can happen in practice as PSM and the industry act together. Incentive travel is a relatively new, but a very profitable and a growing sector of the market. It does, however, require close cooperation between public and private managers for it to be successful.

Incentive travel is a system where companies such as insurance and car dealers reward, or give incentives to employees, where they have achieved targets, such as the sale of a number of cars, or raising the sales figures beyond or up to a set target. It is based on the belief that employees will work harder if there is a possibility of overseas or domestic travel reward. It is based on the avarice of the employee, but it also aims to build up loyalty to, and morale in, the organisation. In the very competitive US business market of the 1960s it was found that incentive travel rewards schemes stimulated production and improved results.

Why governments are involved

This market is important because it gives such a lucrative return on the number of tourists. For example, it is said to be well above the return of convention visitors, who themselves spend three times as much as an average tourist.

In 1992, for example, an incentive visit of 4,500 Japanese saleswomen from the lingerie company Charle were estimated to have spent A$10 million in Sydney. Of the 2.3 million visitors to Australia in 1992, 230,000 were incentive visitors. It was estimated that 20 per cent of all tourism receipts came from incentive and convention visitors, and this amounted to A$500–600 million. In a period of recession, and when traditional visitors to Australia, such as honeymoon couples, appear to show no growth, incentive travel appears to be growing. In 1992, for instance, the number of honeymooners visiting Australia increased by 19 per cent and tourists from Japan by 11 per cent, but in 1993 the market was flat. Yet about 80,000, or 20 per cent, of the total Japanese tourists arrived on company-sponsored tours.

One of the principles of the tourism industry is the ability to meet competition, and the industry move into incentive travel shows that Australia is meeting the challenge. Industry must always be prepared to think up something new to give it the competitive edge. In the airline business, which also helps the tourism trade, the challenge has recently been frequent flyer schemes. In the United States in 1991 incentive and convention expenditure declined by 4 per cent, but actual trips were up 9.7 per cent to 83,400. Australia has benefited from expansion in the Asian market, especially Japan.

Who is involved?

PSM should be involved in assisting the industry to meet the competitive challenge. Japan, for example, needed to send more tourists overseas to reduce its foreign exchange balance. In April 1993 the Japanese Tax Office extended its tax concessions by allowing companies to claim up to four nights for incentive programmes, and this further stimulated the Japanese market. National tourism organisations receiving incentives brought pressure on the Japanese Ministry of Finance to remove all restrictions. Government tax policies and offices can help tourism development. Tax offices in Australia, however, can be very suspicious of incentive or convention expenses unless they are within the guidelines of necessary business expenses. Officials of receiving countries need to be flexible enough to modify their normal procedure and so be able to receive large numbers of tourists at any one time, and they must be prepared to drop or adjust customs and immigration regulations. Thailand, for example, when introducing convention travel had to be prepared to allow certain goods and persons into the country for long periods, which was not allowed under the existing regulations.

The NTOs are the key bodies for researching and identifying demand possibilities in different markets. They also need to undertake the long-term, more detailed research requirements and identification of market trends. New Zealand, recognising that tourists today are more conscious of environmental problems, has been marketing itself as a 'green and clean' destination. NTOs should always be aggressively seeking out new customers. As the US incentive market declines and as the growth in Japanese tourism decreases, NTOs must be prepared to tap the new, growing middle-class markets in Thailand, Malaysia, Taiwan and South Korea. NTOs often establish specialised departments to manage this lucrative business and the Australian Tourist Commission has established Incentives and Convention Offices in the United States, Japan, Singapore and Hong Kong. The industry has also established specialist organisations such as the Australian Incentive Association (AIA) and the Professional Conference Management Association of Australia.

How managers manage

These days management must use the most up-to-date technology to keep it in touch with potential tourists. The ATC, for example, has an in-house data base, 'Meetings and Incentives Direct Access System', mainly concentrating on North America. Whether the incentive company uses a travel agent, an airline or an NTO to organise its incentive programme, it requires the cooperation of the public and private sectors. Managers have to work very closely together at all stages of the programme. Public and private managers should be able to manage their staff at all levels so that they provide efficient and friendly service to the tourist. This was underlined in the AIA 1993 Conference, 'People Power – People, Productivity and Prosperity'. Tourism is very much a people industry; it is labour-intensive and this means that the people, the employees, have power to affect the industry for good or ill, its prosperity or failure. Power lies with the ordinary people in the industry, for it is they who have the face-to-face contact with the tourists at the front desk, restaurant and bar, not the senior executives. If an incentive or other programme is successful it can have favourable repercussions, as when the President of the Charle Corporation, Mr Masaharu Hayashi, endorsed Australia as a first-class destination to his corporate peers. In tourism, personal and word-of-mouth recommendations are important marketing channels.

Tourism management must take the comprehensive and long-term view of tourism but also of what is in the public interest. Managers must play the major coordinating role for the public sector including local government, but they are also the link and coordinator with the industry. The industry has many associations but the incentive and convention sector is also highly segmented. Because of the nature of incentive and convention tourism the whole tourism community must be involved, receiving and giving benefits. In New Zealand the government provided NZ$1 for every $2 provided by the industry. The tourism community should be prepared to bring in the buyers free of charge, or for a nominal charge, to show and explain the product. This sector requires much more specific research and marketing and public infrastructure than general tourism. Singapore is one of the leaders in incentive travel because its management had the foresight and the government was prepared to back them with these resources. Australia, Britain and Thailand have been much slower in providing the resources needed for incentive tourism. Even with resources incentive tourism poses a major challenge for management because of the great numbers of people involved very intensively for a short period. The perception the tourist has of a country is important, as is their actual experience of services such as immigration, customs and transportation. Public managers need to be aware of how tourists perceive the performance of their organisation. Australia, for example, improved its image and performance, ranking in the low twenties in 1989 and becoming the third most favoured nation by US incentive and convention tourists in the early 1990s.

What results? practice and performance

Incentive tourism illustrates the importance of the partnership of industry and PSM. Neither can achieve their objectives without the support of the other. This partnership can take the form of joint ventures, if not always in organisational form certainly in expenditure. The complexity of the industry and public sector and the challenges and problems they face are made more difficult because of the long time-frame of incentive tourism, its size and international nature. Domestic incentive tourism is easier. It is essential that objectives are made clear and management networks are efficient.

Success in incentive tourism is determined by close relationships and strong support within the tourism policy community with the crucial leadership role taken by the NTOs and the peak organisations. Industry leadership, initiative, flair and specialised knowledge are required but also diligent, long-term research and sensitive marketing with the skill of specialised offices and officers. Because of legal and the other obstacles, very long-term planning, marketing and difficulties of coordination and communication with various levels of government and industry, incentive and convention tourism requires particularly dedicated management. More pressure can be placed upon management, because often prominent political and community leaders are involved in greeting large incentive and convention groups.

If this type of tourism is not managed efficiently it can damage the prospects for future business. This is particularly serious if governments have invested heavily in convention premises and other infrastructure, as happened in Manila under the Marcos regime. Management in Australia was slow to move into incentive tourism because of the limits imposed by its political culture, the federal system, lack of commitment by governments and limited vision of public and industry management.

SUMMARY

Tourism requires a good relationship between the public and private sectors if it is to survive and prosper. Governments acknowledge that they need the economic returns from tourism and the industry, which alone has the necessary expertise, capital and entrepreneurship. While governments can support the industry, they should also serve the consumer and the public interest. The industry is dependent upon government to provide a stable and secure environment and infrastructure.

A tremendous diversity of people and organisations are involved in tourism in both the public and private sectors. Participants include large government ministries and powerful international corporations but most of the private operators are small. This can make the industry peak organisations important and influential if they are united. Government ministers and ministries have power, but it is often the national tourism organisation which has the expertise, and direct relationships with the industry. Airlines are important and can be powerful. A growing number of interest groups are active in conservation and other areas which can stimulate community activity and affect tourism.

Relations between the two sectors need to be close, continuous and harmonious through organisations and processes both formal and informal. Management should be based on trust with consistent but flexible policies responding to the market and the actual needs of the industry. The ideal relationship is based on partnership and exchange, on a community of interests which operates effectively through networks. It is a dynamic power relationship; it is not static. Public management has to balance the essential freedom of the industry with public principles, including the need to protect those adversely affected by the industry. Lack of decisions by management leaves tourism to the market and private sector.

In practice, public management has not applied principles strongly to the industry. The main emphasis has been on effectiveness as measured by the number of tourists and hotel rooms. Efficiency, including the return on public investment, has only been given serious consideration in recent years. In practice, market forces have dominated and there has been little control of tourism development and its consequences. Considerable freedom has been enjoyed by the industry as laws and policies have either been non-existent or lightly or ineffectively implemented.

Public interest and public service principles have not always been given sufficient emphasis or have been seen mainly in economic terms. Insufficient attention also has been given to formulating clear national objectives and guidelines, and management has tended to play a minimal, reactive role, or no role in many situations. Despite its economic importance, the industry has not been strong politically so government has been slow to act on its behalf.

The results and performance of the industry have been good, with growth in tourist numbers, expenditure, investment, and employment. Part of the success is due to the industry continually moving into new products, more openness by airlines and gradual recognition by the public sector of the importance of the industry. Yet in countries like Britain and the United States national governments have cut their support to the industry and pushed management and responsibility more on to the industry and state and local governments. The devastating impact of tourism in some countries has led to greater controls over tourism development, and this is discussed in the following chapter.

SUGGESTED READING

Baldwin, R. (1985) *Regulating the Airlines: Administrative Justice and Agency Discretion*, Oxford: Oxford University Press.

Doganis, R. (1992) *The Airport Business*, London: Routledge.

Findley, C.G. (1985) *The Flying Kangaroo: An Endangered Species? An Economic Perspective of Australian International Civil Aviation Policy*, Sydney: Allen & Unwin.

Grant, W. (1987) *Business and Politics in Britain*, London: Macmillan.

—— (1989) *Government and Industry: A Comparative Analysis of the US, Canada and the UK*, Aldershot: Edward Elgar.

Holloway, J.C. (1994) 4th edn, *The Business of Tourism*. Chapter on the industry, including the aviation business.

McIntosh, R.W., Goeldner, C.R. and Ritchie, J.R.B. (1995) 7th edn, *Tourism Principles, Practices, Philosophies* New York: John Wiley. Chapter on how the tourism industry is organised, including the airlines.

Page, S. (1994) *Transport for Tourism*, New York: Routledge.

Sampson, A. (1984) *Empires of the Sky: The Politics, Contests and Cartels of World Airlines*, London: Hodder & Stoughton.

Stewart, R.G. (ed.) (1994) *Government and Business Relations in Australia*, St Leonards, NSW: Allen & Unwin.

Wilks, S. and Wright, M. (eds) (1987) *Comparative Government –*

Industry Relations: Western Europe, the United States and Japan, Oxford: Clarendon Press.

Wilson, G.K. (1990) 2nd edn, *Business and Politics: A Comparative Introduction*, London: Macmillan. Chapters on the United States, Britain and Japan.

8 Management of tourism control

This chapter explains:

- why public sector management (PSM) control of tourism is so important
- who are the actors involved
- how PSM manages its tourism control responsibilities
- what are the results in:
  Vietnam
  environmental sustainable development.

Control and accountability are important functions of PSM. To control an organisation or official is to have the power to coerce, persuade, force or direct to act, or not to act, in a particular way. It is the responsibility of managers to control tourism in the public interest, but it is the responsibility of other organisations in the public sector, especially elected representatives, to control managers. Management has to manage control devices such as the Tourist Police of Thailand, who are there to control the illegal activities of those who would prey on tourists. Ultimate control is when a manager directly allows or stops an activity, such as the development of a resort complex. Regulation is a common management device used to control activities such as tourism, to ensure that the public interest is protected or that a public service is maintained. In recent years there have been movements towards deregulation.

Accountability is defined and discussed in Chapter 3. It is not direct control but it can have a control effect over public organisations. It is one of the five principles guiding management, for it is necessary that they account for their actions. Accountability requires reporting, which indicates the performance of an organisation or official. It can be achieved through parliamentary inquiries, annual reports, financial statements and management appraisals.

There can be permanent, regular controls of management through ministers or the auditor-general and through the operation of the hierarchy in the organisation. Temporary controls can operate by means of an *ad hoc* committee of inquiry, or be imposed after a protest rally or march against a tourist development.

Box 8.1 Control and accountability

1 Tourism PSM control
   • of the tourism industry
   • of other public managers.
2 Government and PSM control of tourism public management.
3 Accountability of
   • the tourism industry
   • PSM
   • tourism public management.
4 Formal or informal
   Permanent or non-permanent, *ad hoc*.

There can be situations of non-control, where management leaves the area completely to the industry, and in some circumstances management has no or little control owing to external factors such as international market movements, or a climatic or an airline disaster: these can be ruinous for tourism. Control can be exerted by non-governmental bodies and by external factors, such as public opinion, mass media and interest groups. Managerial accountability to test efficiency and effectiveness can use performance or financial audits. Formal control of the executive, including managers, is the responsibility of the judiciary and the legislative body. Ministers and local government leaders are responsible for controlling managers at their respective levels while upper-tier governments have some control over lower-tier governments. Managers can have control over tourism directly, indirectly and via local government. Control can be formal, such as through institutions, and informal, such as through a corporate culture.

In recent years there have been fierce controversy and substantial criticism of the lack of public control of tourist development. Development of tourist resorts, marinas and golf courses has been very destructive of the natural environment and the life style of the people. Rich foreign tourists are seen as benefiting at the expense of the poor local people. There has also been insufficient control of sex tourism and the spread of AIDS. In developed countries there has been criticism of the damaging effect of mass tourism on historic cities and areas of natural beauty.

WHY CONTROL? PRINCIPLES

Public interest

There are various reasons why governments and management intervene and exert control in the tourism sector. There are public interest responsibilities imposed on PSM by law and regulations and by their political leaders which require them to control tourism activities. The political culture, system and public expectations may require action, or no action. Management has the responsibility to control factors which damage the public interest, people, communities and culture, national resources and the environment. Control systems try to ensure that development is sustainable on long-term ecological as well as on economic and social grounds. They try to ensure that there is the appropriate balance between short-term and long-term objectives and that development is sustainable. Managers can be responsible to intervene, for often it is only they who have the power, knowledge and resources to investigate, report on and control tourism issues. This is particularly so when the industry is weak or is being used by foreign companies for their own purposes. Management may have to protect the infant industry to allow tourism to compete in the international market. Whether it is the development of golf courses in Thailand or the mass of tourists and their coaches and cars destroying the character and peace of a historic English city like Cambridge, there is the same call for control in the public interest.

In tourism, environmental and community issues have more than obtained a place on the policy agenda – they have become pressing political issues. Governments and management have responded to pressure and passed legislation, have established new regulatory bodies and have at times given high priority to these concerns. Tourist pressure on areas of natural beauty, wilderness regions and historic cities, and excessive development and foreign investment, have stimulated opposition, and sometimes anger and nationalism. It is the threat of change, and the lack of consultation by private developers and management, as much as the actual impact of tourism on local communities, with the consequent social and economic problems, which engender unhappiness and animosity. To avoid these situations control systems which will help to ensure that managers follow legal and democratic principles in practice are essential. If it is said that tourism enjoys no respect in society, managers should accept some responsibility and examine how control systems can improve the situation.

Public service

Control is also required as part of the public service responsibilities of PSM. Managers should protect and try to raise the living standards of the poor and to protect those least able to protect themselves. There are cases where local people have lost their land or their rights to traditional land to tourism developers. Large investors can have too much power and can abuse it. Small investors also can abuse their position, and their activities can be destructive of the natural environment, such as when fishermen collect coral from a tropical reef for tourists.

There can be a public service obligation to help the unemployed and the poorer regions of the country and management can use tourism development to help to meet this obligation. There are also questions of equity and how to protect those in need. These lead governments to control wages and the conditions of tourism workers. Educational campaigns, health facilities and enforcement of laws can be undertaken for sex workers. Public service is also provided by consumer protection, through the public licensing of travel agents and grading of hotels.

Effectiveness

One of the first principles of PSM is effectiveness – that is, to implement objectives and policies effectively – and this requires an efficient control system. This system operates within the context of protecting and serving the public interest. The effective application of public interest objectives will vary according to the politics and power operating within the society. Management's power to control tourism is also limited by these factors. Among the influences on the effectiveness of management is the incidence of poverty or economic need in the tourism area, social movements, Western values, materialism and the mass media. All social ills are not due to the ineffectiveness of management. Social values and value systems are powerful control mechanisms and managers will try and utilise them. The failure of laws, policies and plans to have the expected effect can be due to the operation of these other forces, it is not due solely to the ineffectiveness of implementation and control. Yet it is the responsibility of managers to achieve and main...

...

It is not sufficient for management to formulate policy or to rely upon legislation but it should monitor and, if necessary, control implementation and enforcement. Public standards, for example, must be maintained and public safety protected. Ineffective management control allowed the Royal Plaza Hotel in Nakhon Ratchasima, Thailand, on 13 August 1993 to collapse, killing more than 130 people. In the 1970s ineffective enforcement by management of the fire precaution system allowed a large hotel in Tokyo to catch fire, killing several people. It is against the public interest for the tourist industry to be allowed to erect unsafe hotels or operate unsafe tourist ships.

Efficiency

Efficiency is another principle which management should follow; that is, there should be a reasonable return on the costs incurred. Objectives should be achieved at the lowest cost, and certainly the costs should not be excessive. Public money and resources are being used and management is responsible for their efficient use. There has been criticism of the efficiency of tourism marketing as to whether the results justify the expense and whether there are cheaper ways of achieving the same objectives. The national tourism boards of Britain were considered to be inefficient by the Thatcher government, which established inquiries to investigate their operations and management.

It is not easy to find the appropriate control mechanism to evaluate clearly the benefits or results obtained from public expenditure and the use of public resources in tourism. What is spent is can be known but not the benefits of expenditure on markets, facilities or environmental protection. Under critical and cost-conscious governments management are placing more emphasis on efficiency and struggling to find better ways to measure efficiency and the return on public expenditure.

Public, unlike private management, takes into account the social costs incurred where they attempt to control a tourism project. It is difficult to measure the costs of mass tourism on small rural communities or the costs on the spiritual life of a medieval cathedral or Buddhist temple. It might be easy to calculate the cost of mass tourism to Hadrian's Wall in Britain, in terms of car parks and toilets and costs of the upkeep of the wall, but you cannot calculate the cost of the loss of atmosphere caused by mass tourism.

Accountability

Accountability is another principle which guides PSM (see Chapter 3). It is fundamental for preventing the abuse of power and for ensuring instead that power is directed towards the achievement of the public interest and the provision of a public service with effectiveness and efficiency. It can include evaluation. Accountability therefore is a form of control. It restrains management generally and managers of tourism in their behaviour. Accountability can help tourism to be managed in the public interest. Managers can be held accountable for their management based on agreed principles.

Sometimes, however, the biggest problem is how to control public bodies or governments which are abusing their powers, not following the law, refusing to consult those affected, going against public opinion and which are ineffective, inefficient and corrupt. A control system must be strong and independent enough to subject public bodies and governments to scrutiny and control. This system can include the legislative body, the electoral system, the legal system, public opinion and the mass media. There are also the various public regulatory bodies, which are autonomous and have a responsibility to scrutinise and control, such as national environmental agencies. In recent years various interest groups have been much more active and influential and have been an important control factor often influencing and supporting management and the formal control bodies as they try to monitor and control tourism power holders.

WHO IS INVOLVED?

Five main groups are involved in the public control of tourism: the public sector, industry, local people and tourists, interest groups, public opinion and mass media. These can be at the international, national or local level. The public sector includes government at all levels, and their public agencies, and national and regional tourist offices and officers. Some agencies may be in favour of tourism development while others could be opposed. Industry includes large and small investors, individuals and the peak organisations, but what they all have in common is the objective of making money, a desire for economic gain. Industry is normally under the controlling direction of management but industry also exerts control over managers, in so far as alert managers will be responsive to the needs of the industry and the market situation within the overall context of the public interest. Management should encourage industry to be self-regulatory, and self-regulation is one of the main functions of peak organisations which exert control over their members. Environment and community considerations may rate a low priority. Local people are affected directly, either gaining beneficially or losing in economic and social terms. Local communities vary from those which are wealthy in Northern Europe and wish for no change, to poor communities of fishermen and farmers who are eager for economic development. Some are opposed to tourism for they wish to retain their life style which tourism would disrupt, others are strongly in favour because of the promise of economic gain. Local government should represent all the people but can be more representative of the wealthier people in the community, which can include people in the tourist business. Management should try to mitigate the adverse effects of local government policy on the poor in the community. The power of local management and their control over tourism will differ according to the national system and political culture.

Tourists themselves may need protection from those engaged in the industry. Management can control the industry to ensure that tourists get value for money, receive good service and enjoy safety and security. The tourists themselves ultimately control the industry, for if they are unhappy with the product they will not revisit and can tell others about the industry's defects.

Interest groups are active in the tourism area, particularly in the environmental and conservation field, and they bring pressure on governments to act in favour of the groups' interests. Trade unions can also bring pressure on governments to act on their behalf, which could introduce controls over the industry. Groups can be permanent or *ad hoc*; they can act formally or informally.

Public opinion and the mass media can aiso have a powerful influence on public management and tourism. Opinion is expressed through the national and local media, by direct contact with those engaged in the process, by means of letters, processions, protest rallies and direct action. Public opinion and the media are important control mechanisms, because of their effect on politicians, officials and the industry, who are anxious about the effect of criticism on their image and on their election or promotion opportunities. Managers can make extensive use of media officers, news releases, and public relations, sometimes in a genuine attempt to inform and educate, but at other times as placation or propaganda, trying to keep the truth and the real issues from the people and in order to hide corruption.

The five groups are all dependent upon one another and act to control or restrain one another's activities. Management has the overall responsibility for control and holding them to account. Control agencies such as a prime minister's office and the ministry of finance have responsibility for the oversight of other public agencies and the control system. There are also other agencies which have been specifically established to act as control bodies, such as audit commissions and the Management and Coordination Agency of Japan.

An active and strong tourism minister can be important in controlling or influencing the industry, the public sector and tourism management. In Thailand, for example, Meechai Wiravaidya in the 13 months until March 1992 was active as Tourism Minister in socio-health issues and in the control of sexual diseases by means of education, publicity and the law. Tourism management was unhappy about his emphasis and what they perceived as the damage to the tourism image, but as minister he established the priorities for control.

Numerous governmental environmental bodies have also been established around the world specifically to protect and regulate areas of natural beauty or of natural importance, to protect beaches and to stop the pollution of air and water. They have to administer and enforce the law, advise on policy, issue licences and educate the public and the policy community.

Public control can be exerted over special sites and areas by designating them as national parks, wilderness areas or heritage sites. This can help to protect them against damage by excessive tourism but still retain them as a tourist attraction. These are national assets which should be protected against damaging development for tourism or other use. Botswana has been successful in protecting its wilderness areas and controlling tourism by only allowing low-volume, high-cost tourism. There can be problems, as in Kenya, with political interference in national park protection. Political interventions in Thailand by the tourism minister in 1993 brought pressure on the national parks to be opened up for tourism. In this case public managers took opposite sides; the national tourist office supported by tourism developers were opposed by the national parks department and environmental interest groups such as the Wildlife Fund Thailand and the Committee for Natural Resources and Environmental Conservation. All public agencies have some control responsibilities because of the public interest/public service requirement. Yet their interpretation of those principles can be narrow and in terms solely of departmental interests.

Specific public agencies such as development agencies can be used for the development of tourism but also as control bodies, as in

Mexico. Foreign investment is important for tourism but can be controversial and economically and politically damaging if not controlled. Australia has the Foreign Investment Review Board (FIRB), which includes one public servant, with its secretariat provided by the Foreign Investment Branch of the Australian Treasury. The FIRB gives independent advice to the government on tourist investment but the government must decide what criteria should be used in the decision. In 1986, in order to encourage more investment, control was eased by the criterion 'not contrary to the national interest' which replaced the 'economic benefits' test.

The five main groups are related with one another in a tourism community based on tourism control.

HOW TO CONTROL: FORMAL AND INFORMAL

Control can be influential because of the position or character of the controller, such as a strong senior minister. The method of control can be formal or informal. Ultimate control in some ways is by market forces and tourism managers will utilise market forces to control the industry.

Formal controls

A national constitution can allocate control to various levels of government and can guarantee various rights to the people. Power, coming from the constitution, can be used to control tourism development, such as land held for aboriginal people. The legislative assembly has power to control through legislation and allocation of finance. It can check and scrutinise the public sector through motions, debates and questions. Most of the scrutiny and control power is used through committees of the parliament or congress which have power over persons and papers; that is the right to call for and to investigate all relevant persons or papers. In Australia, Britain and the United States these committees have been useful in examining the management of tourism. They have allowed the elected representatives to scrutinise policy and performance and to receive evidence from management, the industry and other interested parties.

Democracy

Citizens can control governments and policies in a democratic system when, by means of an election, they replace one government with another. In Queensland citizens have voted out local councils because of their dissatisfaction with high-rise and tourism development. In Australia the membership of federal and state tourist boards have been changed by newly elected governments with different political ideas. Democratic controls can operate effectively when an administrative system is open and understandable and when relevant information is available to the citizen. Management which is serving the public will be open and transparent. An administrative process which is hidden and closed and occurs in secret leads to distrust and can protect self-serving interests and corruption. A democratic system helps to control the policy community, the process, management and power holders. It also helps management in its control responsibilities. Supportive and vigilant public opinion, media and interest groups can also assist.

If local people are kept informed they can be the most effective and efficient defenders of the public interest at the local level. They can be educated about the benefits and disadvantages of tourism development and should be allowed to participate as fully as possible in the policy process. Local and national officials should also be educated and trained to control tourism. Most local government management is more active in tourism development than in control, but the normal controls do apply, such as planning and environment and zoning controls. Local government is under great pressure to take action against the tides of tourists who are threatening or damaging many areas of the world.

The judiciary

Judicial control over tourism management takes place by means of courts and legal tribunals. It is, however, not always easy to enforce the law even with the use of special tourist police such as in Thailand and Greece. Judicial action can also be expensive, time consuming and not always effective. If a hotel is illegally built too high and too near the beach, it is not easy for the court to order that such a building be demolished. The correct processes, or due process in the United States, freedom of information, legislation and an ombudsman can assist the citizen and help to control the industry and public organisations.

Ideology

Control and accountability are affected by political culture and ideology. The use of the autonomous statutory board as a tool of management reflects the belief that this type of organisation is better able to control industry and public expenditure. In recent years the new managerialism has reflected the ideology that government is too big and is interfering too much with business, and that the best government is the least government.

This was reflected in the new managerialism of President Reagan and Prime Minister Thatcher, with cuts in public expenditure, de-regulation and the stress on the 'user pay' principle. They believed that government control should be severely curtailed, with organisations forced to justify themselves through competition in the market place. The ideology was that they would become 'lean and hungry', and therefore more efficient and effective. This ideology, however, can weaken the principles of public interest, public service and responsibility. Between 1979 and 1990 Mrs Thatcher who had strong ideological views, privatised much of the public sector, curtailed the activities of the British Tourist Authority and the English Tourist Board and tried to move more responsibility on to the industry, local government and the regional tourist boards. These control effects were sometimes counter-productive.

Management

Management has a whole range of powers it can use in tourism control. For example, it can refuse to issue necessary licences or approvals. In 1993 Malta, because of a surplus of accommodation and a desire to lessen mass tourism and increase luxury tourism, banned the building of any tourism accommodation except for five-star hotels. Managers can make regulations and take regulatory action. Land zoning and other standards can be applied, environmental impact statements can be required. Special *ad hoc* task forces can be established for specific functions or major problems. Information, coordination, coordination monitoring and feedback are all essential parts of the control system. They must be continuous to be successful. Successful control also requires that policies and plans are realistic and that management has the capability to implement and control.

Informal controls

Control of tourism and of management can be formal and direct through ministerial direction, regulation and the administrative hierarchy. Yet often the most effective and efficient form of control of both the tourism industry and management is informal. Because tourism, its activities and the public sector are so diverse there can be a limit to the effectiveness of formal control mechanisms. Therefore, for reasons of efficiency and effectiveness much discretion is left in the hands of management.

Informal controls are often internal and can be self-enforcing. They can include individual and organisational values, norms and objectives involving integrity, honesty and public service. Normally these values and objectives reflect the prevailing national beliefs. Privatisation was expected to change and control public organisations through the introduction of a new corporate culture. Managers and others can be socialised into a system and organisation based on principles which can instil dedication and a sense of responsibility to the public. Formal training may be used, but this is most effective when it reflects the informal socialisation process. Informal controls can be based on fear, mutual respect or shared values and objectives. As part of the policy community with the public sector the tourism industry is conscious of its dependency upon government and the need for mutual trust. If informal controls are operating there will be automatic respect for rules and regulations, and management will not need to enforce them formally. Each side is eager to maintain its reputation of honesty and regard for shared values. If they do not 'play the game', they could lose the benefits arising from being a member of the policy community. Informal factors can be positive and support principles but they can also support self-seeking managers, private organisations and corruption.

In practice, how effectively a control system operates and whether controls are actually implemented will depend upon where power lies in the system. Public interest can be neglected because of the power of political or economic interests. Often managers can only advise political leaders as to what is the public interest and the correct action to take; the actual decision must be taken by the politician. Political will is important in enforcement, but so also are the circumstances. An accumulation of factors, inducing time delay, delaying tactics by interested parties, conflicting objectives and interests and unforeseen factors can lead to non-enforcement. The rapid natural growth of tourism has found several control systems ineffective and inefficient in both monitoring and controlling tourism development.

WHAT RESULTS? VIETNAM, ENVIRONMENT

Vietnam

Why control?

The government of Vietnam, like that of other countries, is involved in the control and development of tourism mainly for economic reasons. Vietnam is one of the world's poorest countries due to military conflict stretching over forty years until 1979. A highly rigid centralised planning and economic system and ideologically based economic policies contributed to a disastrous economic performance which in the 1980s resulted in famine conditions. The American economic embargo until 1994 was another factor. GDP was about US$200 per capita. Unemployment and underemployment was very high and the situation was made worse by a high birth-rate and deteriorating social services.

The Vietnamese situation was similar to that of many other developing countries, including Cambodia and Laos. The country had huge debts to the former USSR, Western countries and international financial institutions dating back to before the fall of Saigon in 1975. These, coupled with the shortage of foreign exchange, a balance of payments problem, the need to replace infrastructure and the standard of living have forced the government to develop tourism.

In 1990 Vietnam lost the substantial aid it had been receiving from the USSR and had to try and obtain aid from the West and international institutions. UN agencies, the IMF and the World Bank are now giving aid but they expect the government and public management to control inflation and support controlled market reforms and industries such as tourism. It is only public management that can deal with these international institutions, establish a favourable climate to attract foreign investment and institute an effective and efficient management control system.

As with many other countries, developing and developed, Vietnam is concerned to provide jobs for the vast numbers who are unemployed and to help the poorer regions of the country. A major problem for developing countries is people leaving the poverty of the rural areas in the poorer regions to move to the large cities, but where there is also high unemployment. Tourism development in the poorer regions can provide employment and an economic stimulus and prevent people moving to the larger cities, such as Ho Chi Minh City and Hanoi.

Control is needed to prevent damage to the economy and society by the wrong kind of, and excessive, investment, which can cause inflation, strain the existing infrastructure and cause social unrest. Vietnam is in the transition stage from a tightly controlled state economy to a more market-controlled economy and requires sensitive and at times strong management control. Tourism also needs sensitive and positive control if its full potential is to be realised and damaging effects kept to a minimum.

Control in developing countries must be active for the private sector, and society does not normally provide monitoring or control functions. Tourism, for example, cannot just be left to the market, or to international or local developers. Market forces will not pursue the public interest or provide the public services needed for the poor and those in need. It is only PSM which has the authority and knowledge to protect the local people and to conserve the natural and historic heritage of Vietnam. This heritage is fragile and easily destroyed if overexploited. The coral reefs of Ha Long Bay, listed by World Heritage, have been damaged as tourism has developed. There is a fear, for example, that the old city of Hanoi, with its charm, old Chinese and French buildings and spaciousness, will be destroyed. Because of the economic need and the desire for rapid development it is easy to give up natural assets to developers. It is easy to forget the social needs of the people and be unaware of the destruction of communities and culture. This is why management should have efficient control systems and the commitment to protect the public interest. Public protection should also be available to poor farming and fishing communities and workers in the sex industry, all of whom are easily exploited.

Vietnam has the ingredients for an excellent tourism product but it should not be damaged by over rapid or insensitive development. Management should aim for quality in tourism. Control is also needed to protect the tourism image of Vietnam; a good image is essential for successful tourism. There is great pressure on management to push tourism development through quickly because of intense economic and social need and tourism competition. Care, however, must be taken that this does not lead to the downgrading of public objectives or to the inefficient and ineffective utilisation of scarce public resources and capital.

Management in Vietnam has suggested that the Thai model of tourism should be followed. Thailand has been very successful in attracting tourists and developing the industry but it has involved heavy social and economic costs. These costs have been incurred partly because of the lack of an effective control system and this is one of the lessons Vietnamese management could learn from Thailand.

One of the most important reasons why effective PSM control systems are so important is the need to control management itself. Good, efficient, honest management is vital to any country, but especially to developing countries where the private sector and democratic institutions are so weak. Government leaders in Vietnam have attacked corruption and unsocial behaviour in the civil service, state enterprises and local government and among Communist party cadres many times since the mid-1980s. Control must start from the top, and national management must be honest and effective in controlling lower-tier governments and the powerful state enterprises.

The opening up of Indochina to foreign aid and investment and the lifting of the American embargo in 1994 raises major control problems, if the investment is not to have disastrous economic and social effects. Officials may have authority to make decisions but lack the knowledge and skills to evaluate and deal with the often complicated and technical proposals of large foreign investors. Managers at both the national and local level are eager to get investment but do not always understand the possible repercussions and side effects of such investment. These situations require good control and monitoring systems especially from the centre, where political and technical authority can be available to assist tourism projects and to stop mistakes and abuses.

Who is involved?

Those who are involved in the tourism control community include the parliamentary and Communist party institutions, the political leadership and lower-tier governments. Control responsibilities also lie with the managers of government ministries, financial institutions, state enterprises and provincial and local governments. There are agencies responsible for controlling development through planning, the environment and investment. The government tourism industry sector should also be regulated, including the airlines and regional tourism enterprises.

Saigon Tourism is the biggest enterprise, owning over 100 hotels and managing many other tourism activities. But there are also several other tourism businesses operating in Ho Chi Minh City. Control should also be directed at the growing private tourism sector including joint-venture enterprises with foreign companies.

For example, the most luxurious hotel in Hanoi, the Pullman Metropole, is a joint venture with a French company. Joint-venture enterprises are common in the tourism industry in Vietnam. Growing fast are local private enterprises such as small guest houses and coffee shops, and a multitude of individual traders offering various services to tourists. These are difficult to control, as are the illegal drug, gambling and sex enterprises.

Figure 8.1 indicates some of the organisations and forces which help to control and monitor tourism activity. This activity operates like a community, or a system of accountability, where all are connected to one another directly or indirectly through organisations, principles, politics and practice.

How they are involved

Communist party

How the tourism control system works in Vietnam is not clear because there are so many informal factors. In theory, one important control organisation is the Communist party of Vietnam which, through its various levels, runs parallel to the formal political and administrative system. The party partly controls by deciding what is in the public interest and for the public service and what should be the policy objectives. The Sixth Party Congress in 1986 decided that tourism was in the public interest and that Vietnam should be open to all tourists. To create favourable conditions for foreign tourists to visit Vietnam it was decided to improve entry visa application formalities for all foreigners regardless of nationality, and to allow all overseas Vietnamese irrespective of expatriation date to enter Vietnam for tourism. It was expected that tourism would be of service to the public through investment and employment.

According to the General Secretary of the party, Do Muoi, the party does not replace other organisations in the political system, it leads the political system and at the same time belongs to that system. It maintains close ties with the people and is subject to their supervision and it also must operate within the framework of the constitution and the law.

Control is exercised by the party through its leadership role. The main directing organisations for management in the political and administrative system are the Party's Central Committee of 161 members and the Politburo of 17 with its Standing Central Committee of 5 established in 1996. These bodies parallel and have considerable

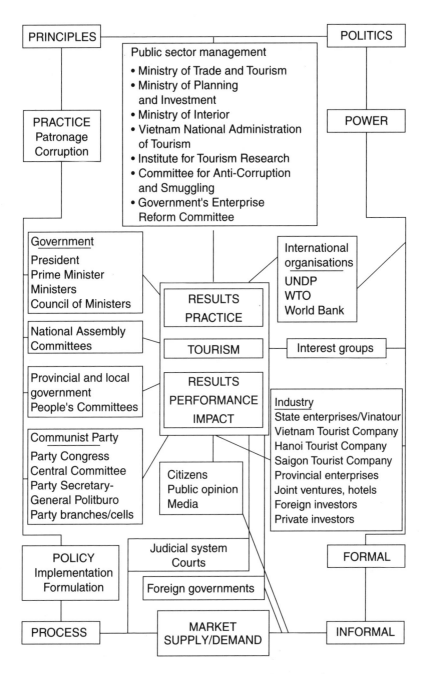

PRINCIPLES ———— POLITICS

Public sector management
• Ministry of Trade and Tourism
• Ministry of Planning
  and Investment
• Ministry of Interior
• Vietnam National Administration
  of Tourism
• Institute for Tourism Research
• Committee for Anti-Corruption
  and Smuggling
• Government's Enterprise
  Reform Committee

PRACTICE
Patronage
Corruption

POWER

Government
President
Prime Minister
Ministers
Council of Ministers

International
organisations
UNDP
WTO
World Bank

RESULTS
PRACTICE

National Assembly
Committees

TOURISM

Interest groups

Provincial and local
government
People's Committees

RESULTS
PERFORMANCE
IMPACT

Industry
State enterprises/Vinatour
Vietnam Tourist Company
Hanoi Tourist Company
Saigon Tourist Company
Provincial enterprises
Joint ventures, hotels
Foreign investors
Private investors

Communist Party
Party Congress
Central Committee
Party Secretary-
General Politburo
Party branches/cells

Citizens
Public opinion
Media

POLICY
Implementation
Formulation

Judicial system
Courts

FORMAL

Foreign governments

PROCESS

MARKET
SUPPLY/DEMAND

INFORMAL

Figure 8.1 Vietnam tourism: public sector control community

overlapping membership with the Cabinet of the government. The senior leadership responsible for the control of management and policy are the President, the Prime Minister and the ministers. The General Secretary of the Party is obviously very powerful, but under the new policy of party–state separation he is only responsible for policy and control in an indirect way.

National Assembly

The elected parliamentary body, the National Assembly, legislates to give effect to party decisions and policies. Under the more open system which has existed since 1986, the National Assembly can be used to express criticism and dissatisfaction, which has a control effect and can stimulate management to take action or stop behaving illegally. It also performs this function through its standing committees.

Tourism management

The tourism minister, and the management of the tourism ministry, are responsible for the implementation, monitoring and control of tourism policy and development in Vietnam. Tourism is part of the Ministry of Trade and Tourism, which emphasises its importance in the economy and the earning of foreign currency. Before, tourism was part of the Ministry of Culture, Information, Tourism and Sports. Tourism is now part of a more powerful ministry but the minister and management have wider trade responsibilities, thereby lessening their ability to control tourism. Because of the desperate need for investment and development they tend to respond favourably to most tourism proposals.

An important control body is the State Committee for Cooperation and Investment (SCCI), established in 1989. It has a particular responsibility for tourism, which was designated as one of the five priority sectors for foreign investment. Vietnam is heavily dependent upon foreign investment for any significant tourism development and the SCCI must examine, evaluate and monitor the proposals such as the various hotel developments in Hanoi and Ho Chi Minh City since 1989. There are also State Committees which have control functions, as on cooperation and investment. The State Planning Committee still has the potential to play an important role. Direct responsibility for tourism in every aspect lies with the General Department of Tourism (Vietnam Tourism), which is headed by a Director-General and two Deputy Director-Generals, one of whom manages tourism in

South Vietnam. They are responsible for the overall management of tourism in Vietnam – for its marketing, development and regulation. They have powers of control and approval over items such as contracts and agreements.

Local government and state enterprises

Hands-on control and implementation, however, lie with the lower tiers of government and the state enterprises: several of the provinces, including the cities of Hanoi, Haiphong and Ho Chi Minh City, and lower-tier government are active in promoting and developing tourism. They also have control responsibilities which can often be neglected in the dash to obtain development. Local government management is responsible to an elected People's Council and appointed People's Committees. Under these committees are executive subcommittees and various companies, some engaged in tourism. Some state enterprises also are active in tourism ventures. Examples of tourism state enterprises are the Vietnam Tourist Company (Vinatour), Hanoi Tourism Company and Saigon Tourism. There are many joint ventures, such as the Song Be Golf Resort between the Protrade state enterprise and a Singapore company. It is not easy for management to control such developments because of their size and powerful political connections. Environmental control is the responsibility of the Department of Nature Resources and Environment within the Ministry of Sciences, Technology and Environment.

Planning

Public management can also use planning as a form of control: national, regional, land use and sectoral. Planning has been used with success in Japan and France and is used extensively in developing countries. Vietnam has now moved away from the highly centralised planning system which dominated its development in the past. It still, however, has a long-term plan and has a tourism plan drawn up in 1991 partly by the United Nations Development Programme (UNDP), the World Tourism Organisation (WTO) and Vietnamese government organisations. This was replaced by a new plan in 1996.

Four tourist regions have been designated and they will be given priority for receiving investment:

- zone 1: Hanoi, Haiphong, Hongai
- zone 2: Danang, Hue

- zone 3:   Camranh, Dalat
- zone 4:   Ho Chi Minh City, eastern and western provinces of South Vietnam.

The plan or strategy is up to the year 2000. There are also development plans for such tourist attractions as Ha Long Bay, Hue and Nho Trang. The problem for management, however, as in Thailand, is how to implement these plans. Implementable plans need sound information and technical advice based on good research. The Institute for Tourism Development Research in Hanoi has tried to provide the service but is short of resources and expert staff. They also have to work with and are dependent upon the assistance and proposals of local management and people.

Legal system

The law may be used by PSM to control tourism – for example, the 1988 Investment Law. This law is generous in tax concessions, repatriation of profits and investor freedoms, and especially so if investment is to sectors of priority public interest or remote regions designated as needing more intensive public service. Yet if the law is to be effective and not abused it must be effectively monitored and controlled. There must be an effective accountability system. Law however is sometimes difficult to enforce or it may be that there is no actual law to cover the situation. The duty-free shop at Hanoi Airport was given a five-year contract, but after only three years the Commerce Ministry issued a licence to another company to operate the shop. The legal system was unable to protect the first contract.

In the swift movement towards development since 1986 the legal system has failed to keep pace with the changes. Improvements continue to be made to the laws and legal system but much depends upon the vigilance, initiative and commitment of managers.

Local government and state enterprise managers are responsible for enforcing law and implementing public policy, yet their priorities are economic development and the economic pressures operating on them are immensely strong. There is a long and strong tradition in Vietnam of regional and local autonomy and resistance to national government control. All these factors make the enforcement of laws and implementation of plans extremely difficult.

Problems

Regional and local organisations are politically strong at their level locally but nationally also they have influence through their representatives in both the National Assembly and Party Congress. This autonomy can be strengthened by being independent of national government finance for tourism projects. Local and enterprise managers enter into agreements and start tourism projects but these can be contrary to national policy and investment and environmental law. At times agreements made by the national government may not always be honoured in practice by the local management. Tourism control limitations in Vietnam include the following:

> In order to allow tourism to expand rapidly, many actual limitations have to be overcome: the government should as soon as possible study, build up and promulgate a Law on Tourism with concrete policies covering the administration of tourism and of this business; it should make clear, concise and once for all the planning of tourism development all over the country as well as in each region; emphasis should be placed upon tourism development coupled with preservation and development of national culture, with protection of the environment and nature; it should build up and implement soon priority policies covering tourism involving branches concerned with immigration procedures, visa issuance, international flights regulations, customs policies. . . . Accordingly, local tourist organisations should invest to improve the quality of their services, starting with their personnel, their material and technical facilities, their products.
> (*Panorama Magazine*, 'Vietnam Fair and Exhibition Centre'
> 1992: 121)

Since 1986 the former highly centralised planning and control system and intervention by the Communist party have been severely curtailed. The current control system allows much more freedom to the industry to respond to market demands and competition. Indirect control has been strengthened through elected bodies, the media and training schemes.

In allowing 'tourism to expand rapidly' the control system should hold to the five principles as much as ever, but their application requires managers who are sensitive and responsive to the needs of both the people and the industry.

What results? practice and performance

What has happened in practice with tourism control in Vietnam is considered within the five principles.

Public interest

It is much easier to present results in terms of numbers of tourists,
foreign investment, currency earnings and the number of hotels rather
than to calculate how effectively management has been able to protect
the public interest. Management has to be effective in achieving
tourism policy objectives but it also has the important basic objectives
of protecting the society and improving the living standards of the
people not just in the short term but also in the longer term. This will
involve ensuring that tourism policy objectives are consistent with
national objectives. Yet it is easy for objectives to conflict, such as the
objective to double gross domestic product by 2000 but also to protect
the environment. Short-term objectives can be in conflict with long-
term objectives. Public interest as defined at the national level can be
difficult to implement and control at the local level.

It is in the public interest to support sustainable development,
but the push for rapid tourism development works against this. The
Environment Law of December 1993 reflects the concern about the
deteriorating environment and the need to support the 1991 National
Plan for Environment and Sustainable Development. Yet in practice
there is a lack of commitment to conservation and a shortage of
expertise and effective enforceable controls. There is not always
an understanding of the fragility of eco-systems and the importance
of natural and historic resources. There needs to be a much stronger
control system, clearer priorities and stronger political support for
management as it tries to protect the public interest.

At least in Vietnam all land is still owned by the state in the public
interest. This means that unsuspecting farmers cannot sell the land
to tourism developers and lose their livelihood, as has happened in
Thailand. In Vietnam, farmers hold the land on long or life-term
leases. Some Communist party members believe that state controls
are ineffective, and the Thai model of unrestricted growth has brought
excessive social problems. They would prefer that the Bhutan model
of control and restricted entry, as in Laos, should be followed.

Public service

In theory, following the ideology of the Vietnamese Communist party
it could be expected that the public service principle would be closely
followed by the party and management. This is particularly so in a
one-party state where the party claims it holds the monopoly of
power so that it can serve the people and maintain stability. The wars
with the colonial French government and the former regime of South

Vietnam were fought to stop the exploitation of the people and corruption and to provide service to the people instead. Management controls have not sufficiently taken into account the social and environmental effects of tourism development. The so-called 'trickle-down effect' of public and private investment appears to have been negligible.

When Vietnam first opened up the country to Western tourists it only gave access to expensive tour groups. A change of policy allowed entry to individual backpackers, whose expenditure goes more to poorer local people. As most tourism investment has been in Hanoi and Ho Chi Minh City it has done little to help rural areas. What is now needed is a programme to build up tourism in the poorer regions and countryside, which employ two-thirds of the labour force.

There is also a concern as to whether the conditions of workers are protected and whether they are being exploited by local and foreign companies, including some in the tourism industry. In December 1993 the Prime Minister acknowledged that government must 'protect rights of workers as well as those of employers'. Managers had not modernised laws or procedures to deal with the new economic system. Party slogans are no substitute for management action.

Because of poverty, the slackening of the strict social control and the growth of wealth and tourism in the cities, 'social ills', crime, drug trafficking and prostitution are now flourishing. This is a sign of the failure of management to be able to control these movements. It also shows the need for a more vigorous public service to those in need, including beggars, children, the unemployed, disabled former soldiers and AIDS victims. Credit card fraud is also growing.

Political stability is sometimes given a higher priority than public service. In 1988 a Vietnam government management report said, on the socio-economic impact of tourism: 'In the future, even if she handles several hundred thousand or a few million foreign visitors a year, Vietnam can hardly become a hotbed for social ills as she is a socialist state always capable of drastic control measures.' This confidence has been misplaced and suggests inexperienced, over-confident management unaware of the realities of the tourism situation. Control measures in Vietnam, as in many other developing countries, have proved to be ineffective. Management and 'many cadres' are engaging in corruption and using their position and power for their own personal benefit. In these organisations public service principles and goals have been displaced. As the Minister of the Interior told the National Assembly in December 1993, corruption cases had doubled in 1993 and 'counter measures have not brought about any significant changes and the situation remains very serious'. This was reiterated at the Communist party Congress of 1996.

Effectiveness

Management in Vietnam has been effective in achieving the objectives of increasing the numbers of tourists, foreign currency earnings, foreign investment, hotels and hotel rooms. Tourist arrivals in 1986 were 54,353 and in 1994 approximately 1 million. Business turnover increased by nine times between 1990 and 1994. Between 1991 and 1995 there was a 39 per-cent annual rate of increase in foreign tourists, well above that projected by experts in 1989. There is now a good range of accommodation from luxurious hotels to private guest houses and an increasing range of services including high-quality restaurants. Some regional development has taken place, especially in Hue, Halong Bay and Vung Tau. Management in marketing, in the airlines and immigration has showed marked improvements. More important has been the freedom which management has been prepared to give to the industry both public and private, which means they have been better able to respond to market demands and competition and so improve the quality of the tourism product. Control by PSM has continued in various forms but they have been curtailed and modified under pressure from the market. Security is still a concern for the Interior Ministry, the police and conservative management, and efforts have to be made by tourism management to ensure that this control does not damage the effectiveness of their management.

Efficiency

A major responsibility of management is to control for efficiency. Do the benefits justify the costs? Is the public getting value for money? The control of joint ventures in tourism is easier because the foreign investor only invests on the basis of an efficient enterprise and a good return on the investment. Foreign investors are welcome not only because of their investment but also because of their expertise, which brings the efficiency that often local management control cannot provide. There is a control problem, however, when the foreign investor is dishonest or greedy, the return on the public investment is low, social costs are high and labour is unfairly treated. To help in efficiency control the National Assembly has established Economic Tribunals which will mediate in disputes. Big infrastructure projects are difficult to control, for it is almost impossible to pinpoint responsibility because of the numerous enterprises and centres of authority involved. There is also the problem of how to enforce efficiency not only on the most senior management but also on those at the local and enterprise levels. In these cases an old Vietnamese proverb is appropriate: 'The emperor's rule stops at the village gate.' Local managers do not welcome control, neither do energetic managers fighting to compete in the tourism market. It is possible, especially in developing countries, that some managers are more impressed with new buildings, tourism vehicles and aircraft than with actual efficiency.

Where resources are scarce management has to be particularly careful in managing control, taking social and other costs into account. Projects need to be justified on social as well as on economic grounds. Plans to develop five golf courses and resorts which involve huge investment mainly from overseas raise questions about the immense public costs of the infrastructure. Would this investment have been available for, and should it have gone into, rural or other development? Management cannot take these decisions: they have to be taken at the highest possible political level, but management can advise and take responsibility for efficiency control. Environmental costs can be taken into account. Obstacles to efficiency in Vietnam are not just of poor or non-existent hard infrastructure such as roads and electric power but also because of the lack of soft infrastructure such as administrative and legal systems and ability. Excessively costly management can also be inefficient and bureaucratic. Profits can be potential rather than actual. Control agencies at the centre and in tourism do not always have the necessary authority, expertise or resources or sufficient coordination. A lack of effective planning and legal sanctions, clear guidelines and objectives and efficiency awareness make management control difficult. The wrong kind of control, however, and too much interference can hamper efficiency. As one World Bank Report stated there is 'too much government in some areas resulting in too much unnecessary and inefficient regulation and interference with market activities'.

Accountability

Accountability has received more emphasis since 1986, with a strengthened parliamentary, legal and administrative system. February 1994 saw the first conviction of a senior member of the government and Central Committee of the party. A former Minister of Energy was found guilty of corruption and sentenced to four years in prison in an open trial. More criticisms are now raised in the National Assembly, the Party Congress and the press. An interesting attempt to control took place in 1986, when Nguyen Van Linh, the General Secretary of the party, under a *nom de plume*, wrote a very critical, regular newspaper column attacking corruption and abuses in government. Nguyen recognised that the old formal system of accountability was inadequate to deal with the new dynamic economic regime. Tourism, for example, was a new phenomenon, involving foreigners, massive investment and possible threat to the security and stability of the state. Before then a highly centralised rigid planning system had helped to enforce accountability.

Although the system of accountability has grown stronger it has not kept pace with the abuses thrown up by the tremendous increase and changes in the economy, nor with widespread corruption and the collapse or inadequacy of the old systems of control and accountability. Management and systems of accountability need the support of the political leadership to be effective.

Performance

The five principles have been applied in Vietnam, but it is only effectiveness which has been given emphasis. In practice, the other principles have only been given half-hearted commitment as against the priority given to economic growth. Tourism development is similar to what has happened generally in Vietnam, particularly since 1986, when economic reform really took off. Traditional management controls through the party, centralised planning system and social discipline were not able to cope with the changes brought by the economic reforms, the growth of the economy and corruption. It is difficult for the management of developing countries like Vietnam, with their poverty and need, to control rapid economic development and its effects. Normally management is not strong enough to control because of the prevailing economic, social and political forces, and sometimes management does not want to control but to enjoy the economic benefits.

It is important for management to get the right balance between control and freedom, for the tourist industry is very competitive and must be free to respond to market demands. The main justification for the development of luxurious resorts and golf courses is to enable Vietnam to compete internationally. Yet it can be asked whether there is enough public participation in this kind of decision.

Does the control system allow for adequate attention to be given to the public interest and public need? Has Vietnam learnt from the Thai experience and the adverse effects of tourism development?

The tourist industry should be able to operate on a level playing field similar to that of other industries and its competitors. Management controls should be restricted to matters of public interest and public service, taxes, protection of labour, the environment and the enforcement of laws. The same controls will be applicable to all in the industry; there should be no political favouritism.

Control can be more effective if there is one ministry responsible for tourism alone, with a senior minister who is strongly supported by the Prime Minister. Clear guidelines and objectives can be established and monitored. The public interest and public service in the widest sense will be the key objective for management, not just economic objectives. Corruption and self-seeking should be vigorously fought. The Communist party can follow its beliefs and support the people in practice and provide strong leaders of integrity and commitment to the people. Without this backing, control and accountability cannot be successfully achieved.

Environmental control and sustainable development

An operating definition of sustainable development

The development of tourism is a good example of the control challenge facing public sector managers, who must support both tourism development and an attractive, sustainable environment on which tourism is crucially dependent for its success. Some kind of definition is required; management must know what it is working on. As a starting point, the definition of 'sustainable development' put forward in the Brundtland Report is useful.

Economic, social and cultural development should be pursued but it must include ecologically sustainable development (ESD) (Australian

---

Box 8.2 Definition of 'sustainable development'

Humanity has the ability to make development sustainable – *to ensure that it meets the needs of the present without compromising the ability of future generations to meet their own needs.*
(World Commission 1990)

Government, Ecologically Sustainable Development Working Groups, 1991). It should include the total natural environment but also social equity and local communities. The World Tourism Organisation (WTO) in the Manila Declaration of 1980 accepted that all resources are a common heritage for all humanity.

It is, however, the government and the top policy makers in the country who should establish the operating definition. The definition should have authority and legitimacy, and it is only the government working through democratic channels which can formulate an operating definition. For sustainable tourism development it can be useful if as many groups in the country as possible are allowed to participate and to make a contribution. To achieve a national consensus the formulation process should be bottom-up as well as top-down. The process is not just to formulate a definition and policy but it is also to inform and make the country aware of the importance of sustainable development. This type of process may help to create the climate which will make the actual implementation of the policy more efficient and effective.

The definition can emerge out of the national planning process and form part of national objectives and strategies. Planning can help to formulate and establish operational definitions and strategies (Inskeep 1991). Even Australia, which at the federal level has never had a national plan, now has a National Strategy for Tourism.

In tourism the term 'environment' is used in the widest sense to cover not only the natural environment and its resources, and historical and cultural resources, but also the local people, who are a living part of the environment.

An inventory may be made of the various significant natural, historical and cultural resources of the country, particularly those which are unique to the country and are of outstanding quality. These resources will range from natural resources such as islands, forests and beaches to historic cities, cultural sites, living communities, such as the city of Venice, and indigenous people, such as the hill tribe people of northern Thailand. Environmental managers will be involved in drawing up the inventory and in formulating the definition, and they will also be responsible for supporting and protecting these resources, sometimes from potentially destructive tourism development.

Various objectives and priorities will be established based on an inventory of the resources, the development needs of the country and ESD. The response to the demand for hotels, resorts and other developments will recognise that some national resources are irreplaceable and there should be limits to their development.

The operating system will also cover the objectives of the government in terms of the number of tourists, their expenditure, hotel rooms, the regional and seasonal spread, employment and especially foreign currency obtained as against public expenditure. An operating definition is dynamic, and it can be applied by management in the actual operating situation where tourism development is highly competitive and always changing.

Elements of sustainable development essential to any definition

First, there must be the element of effective responsiveness in an operating definition to the following:

- the demands of the market for the tourism product;
- the market is very competitive, so management responses need to be effective, swift and efficient;
- the needs of the people for economic development;
- pressure from the tourism industry for development.

Second, management should be sensitive in the development of the environmental resources available and in their response to the volatile tourism market, including demand, need, quality, quantity and price. Sensitivity is required to achieve the correct balance between tourism development and environmental sustainability. Sensitivity to the needs and wishes of local people is also necessary.

Third, commitment to the goal and the maintenance of a high-quality tourism product and a high-quality environment and ESD. A political and management commitment is required which will provide the necessary resources to implement tourism and environmental policy, and support the balance between the two. A commitment to equity, to the welfare of the local people and to future generations is essential.

Fourth, long-term planning or a strategy is necessary for ESD. Management must not just strive for successful development but also for successful sustainable development, which requires a long-term vision. Too often tourism developers and governments have only been concerned with short-term gains at the expense of long-term sustainable development. Long-term planning is necessary for infrastructure such as airports. Planning proposals, such as on convention centres and theme parks, can help to make such activities acceptable to politicians and officials.

Fifth, the management resource element is also essential for sustainable development as much in quality as in quantity. PSM must have experience, ability, and the innovative talent necessary for the competitive situation. Management should be able to administer complex, sometimes conflicting situations, and have the skill to manage the relationships of the public and private sectors and be able and prepared to give freedom and support to the industry in the competitive market situation.

The most important trade-offs that must be made in managing sustainable development

Governments can trade off certain resources to the private sector to receive benefits in return. From the private sector, governments receive that vital entrepreneurial drive and skill which takes the initiative in development. Received also are management resources: know-how, ability, experience, knowledge, contacts – international as well as national – development and marketing skills, entrepreneurial initiative and flair. Private development produces foreign currency and capital, employment, regional development, and capital structures such as resort hotels which cannot be taken out of the country. The adverse trade-off for development can be exploitation, abuses, corruption, with local people losing their land, culture and supportive communities.

Trade-offs given by the public sector include: permission to develop tourism facilities, public land sold or leased at low prices, community rights curtailed on behalf of the private developer, fast tracking of development so avoiding bureaucratic delays. Resources provided include infrastructure, roads, airports, water, sewage disposal, grants, tax concessions, services of managers and specialists including customs, immigration, planning, education and training. Freedom is given to the private sector, including allowing foreigners and autonomous agencies to pursue their own objectives, initiatives and developments. This freedom, however, can make the provision of unified, uniform and equitable management more difficult.

Government has responsibilities to stimulate development, but also to protect the national heritage and the welfare of the people. It must balance competing needs and assess the value of the various trade-offs. Too often in tourism, economic development has been pursued with adverse environmental and cultural effects. For example, sex tourism might help tourism development but it can be devastating to local communities, particularly since the emergence of the AIDS disease.

The most effective mechanisms for providing financial and other support for sustainable development

The most effective mechanisms are those in which policy makers at the centre establish clear priorities and guidelines which show clearly the needs of ESD. An effective policy formulation mechanism will be open and will encourage active participation from all sections of the policy community, so engaging their support and the implementation of policy objectives. It will be dynamic, managing the continual tension between tourism development and ESD. This involves much effort being given to communication, cooperation and the exchange of information and research, all with the objective of avoiding or solving conflicts and gaining support for ESD.

The most effective mechanism to obtain financial and other support will involve the president or prime minister in backing ESD. Their strong and clear direction and control will achieve the necessary support. In 1992 Thailand reconstituted the National Environment Board to make it more effective and made the Prime Minister the Chairperson. Alternatively, one senior Cabinet minister can become responsible for sustainable tourism development only. Australia appointed a senior minister responsible solely for tourism to the Cabinet for the first time in December 1991. Previously, tourism had been the responsibility of a junior minister, not in the Cabinet, and responsible also for several other policy areas. Use can be made of government ministries, such as the Department of the Environment in Britain covering several policy areas, but these can become too unwieldy, bureaucratic and slow to respond to the needs of the situation.

The most effective mechanisms may involve the use of autonomous specialised public agencies, whether in tourism development, environmental protection or national parks management (Elliott 1987). These agencies have specific objectives, adequate resources, specialised staff and dedicated chief executives committed to achieving organisational objectives. Their effectiveness comes not only from their political support, technical knowledge and research capacity, but also from their excellent understanding of, and links with, both the public and private sectors, local communities and non-governmental organisations (NGOs). Agencies are aware and can respond more quickly to the operational situation, take the initiative and help to coordinate the policy developments needed. They can monitor, control, evaluate and ensure that guidelines are followed by both private and public organisations. Effective agencies will have the resources to control vested interests and destructive development, overcome bureaucratic resistance and inefficiency, so allowing competitive but sustainable development.

Environmental agencies such as national park agencies have been successful in administering, sustaining and developing parks in many countries. As with the parks, the designation of special environmental areas can help in providing effective protection in places of great natural beauty, at historical and cultural sites and monuments. International pressure or World Heritage listing can also assist conservation administration.

Effective mechanisms will include various types of planning, including regional planning, which should be integrated with other uses and utilise Environment Impact Assessments (EIAs). There can be incentives to control and protect environmentally sensitive areas. Areas can be designated as being representative of an ecological system. Developers need considerable freedom if development is to be sustained and fast-track development can be encouraged, but they, and polluters generally, can be penalised if they damage the natural or cultural environment.

Resources, especially financial grants and taxes, are very effective in getting organisations to follow policy and guidelines. NGOs, local government and communities where the actual impact takes place need to be effective participants in the process to ensure that resources and power do not remain completely at the national level or in the hands of big ministries and developers.

The most important issues to be resolved in public sector/private sector relationships in sustainable development

The most important issue which must always be resolved is the conflict between development, which is normally from the private sector, and the possible negative effect on the environment for which the public sector is responsible. The pressure for development can be intense, coming from the developers and local people and often supported by politicians and administrators. The possible danger to the environment is not given high priority. In fact, in poorer communities environment protection can be seen by the locals as stopping the escape from the poverty trap which tourism development offers (de Kadt 1979).

Large tourist resorts can be environmentally friendly in themselves but can be unfriendly to the wider region by destroying the fragile eco-system. Smaller investors offering services on a beach can also degrade the environment but to a lesser extent. There is also the conflict between intense tourism demand at peak periods and the sustainability of popular historic cities and cultural sites. The issue is how to resolve the dispute and how to achieve a balance between two opposing demands. Furthermore, the line between the private and public sector is not clear, for many public organisations, including government tourism offices, local governments, government-owned airlines and hotels, are in the business of pushing tourism development. Sometimes the conflict can only be resolved through the use of power, including public opinion and protests.

Another important issue which must be resolved is the nature of the relationship between the public and private sectors. Essentially the relationship is one of partnership in development and environment protection. The role of the public sector will depend upon the particular country, but it is accepted that a government will provide the basic infrastructure and administrative services. Tourism development should not be penalised or unduly favoured; it should be treated and assisted as any other industry. The cost of complying with environment regulations such as EIAs should not be excessive.

A crucial issue between the two sectors is in their response to the market. It is important that management should support and complement rather than distort or contradict market mechanisms. The relationship should allow the private sector considerable freedom to respond to competition and to develop within environmental guidelines.

There is pressure on governments to cut the size and involvement of the public sector in the economic area, and this is reflected in policies such as privatisation, corporatisation and 'user pay'. Governments in the past have been slow to apply cost benefit analysis to infrastructure and certain services because costing benefits can be difficult, but this is an issue which must be faced by administrators. The price of many resources has been, and for some is still too low, leading to overdevelopment. To know the benefits of tourism development or of non-development requires an assessment of the costs or benefits foregone by the community. The basic question is always who pays and who benefits, and management has the role and responsibility to try and answer the question. ESD involves questions of equity and the well-being of people today and of future generations.

Another important issue is that of the implementation of public objectives, policies, plans and strategies. So often the public sector will expend considerable resources, including time, to draw up plans and to lay down guidelines, only to find that the private sector, and sections of the public sector, do not implement or follow public policy. There are various reasons why environmental policies, in particular, are not always implemented. One is that governments give overriding priority to development and pay only lip-service to environmental protection. Development in tourism is normally private sector led but the private and public sectors can be working together to the detriment of the environment. Because tourism is such a new and rapidly growing industry PSM and the courts do not always have the power or the appropriate instruments to enforce implementation. Legal and administrative processes can be inefficient and long-drawn-out, so making them ineffective. Officials and politicians can become too closely aligned with the private sector, leading to corruption and a disregard of public responsibilities. There can be a lack of effective control over localities and public agencies. The public regulatory agencies can lack resources and power, captured by the industry, become too bureaucratic and over time lose their initial enthusiasm. Normally it is the relationships at the local level which are crucial for implementation, and if those relationships are dominated by economic development issues environmental protection will often be disregarded. On the other hand, strong local opposition with a commitment to the environment can stop tourism development.

There is a lack of coherence in the organisation of both the public and private sectors, with a great diversity of organisations and objectives. In the private sector, small investors are not part of the decision-making system, and among the larger investors even within peak representative organisations, such as the hotel associations, there is still no unity of purpose. The same problems afflict the public sector: there is a multiplicity of public organisations with different objectives whose activities impinge upon tourism.

All public agencies pursue their own objectives, and some behave like private organisations concerned only with development so neglecting other public objectives such as environmental conservation. They can be unduly secretive and closed so there is not the openness or transparency of administration that would inspire trust and confidence from the private sector. In this situation it is difficult to communicate and get coordination and agreement within and between the sectors. If objectives are in dispute or unclear this can lead to costly conflicts, complexity, fragmentation, delay in the formulation and implementation of decisions, the overlapping of functions and the lack of integration of tourism development and environmental conservation.

The public and private sectors need to resolve questions about management techniques used in development. There are inadequacies, such as in planning, which can have too narrow a focus and fail to take an integrated approach covering the wider society and its changes. A similar problem arises with EIAs, which can fail to take into account region-wide issues. There are also difficult issues such as the pricing of environmental and ecological resources and the carrying capacity of tourism areas. These and other controversial issues place strains on the relationships between the public and private sector, and pose challenges to administrators and specialist advisers.

Factors in successful sustainable development

Several interrelated factors are necessary for success on which management needs to concentrate (Williams & Shaw 1991). First, it has to be decided what is success in tourism development. One evaluation of success can be the amount of foreign currency earned, the number of tourism visitors, money spent per head, length of stay, capital invested, number of new hotel rooms, and growing tourism regional development. These are the criteria normally used by governments and national tourism organisations. In this sense tourism has been the leading success story in the past decade, as can be seen from the statistics (WTO).

A second evaluation can be based on the long-term sustainability of tourism. Has it continued to develop or even survived, have tourists revisited and new tourists arrived? Sustainability does not receive the attention it deserves from governments which are more interested in the current tourism numbers and foreign currency received.

A third evaluation of success is whether tourism development has followed the principles of ESD: has the environment been conserved or improved? It is not easy to draw conclusions, because often the sustainable nature of the environment undergoing tourism development will only become known over a longer period of time and there are insufficient data on ecological systems to evaluate their sustainability. These difficulties can be used as an excuse to avoid evaluation, or because the answers are politically embarrassing.

Then there should be an acceptance and a basic commitment to the industry and to ESD. This acceptance, which can move on to active commitment to ESD, is brought about by a change and pressure from public opinion, fostered by public environmental and tourism ncies, NGOs, education and the media. A transparent, open, ticipative and consistent management system helps the educational process and the winning of acceptance and commitment. An important factor in gaining acceptance of tourism and ESD is to show how important they can be economically. Over the past decade an increasing number of countries have become committed to conservation but more need to err on the side of caution in approving development (*Annals of Tourism Research* 1987). The tourist industry is also becoming committed to conservation, as reflected in the growth of eco-, green, nature and heritage tourism.

Further public management should know the national environmental resources and the dangers of development; they have the responsibility and the capacity to conduct the necessary research. This knowledge can be expressed as an operational definition, with strategies, plans and a listing of priorities for development and protection. It can establish a climate of opinion conducive to ESD.

Another important area for success is the relationship between the public and private sectors and particularly the freedom allowed to the industry, both private and public, to pursue development within broad guidelines. Most of the tourism success of the past decade has been due to the dynamic nature of the private sector, which has been able to respond to the market and has not been held back by the unduly heavy demands of public bureaucracies. In Australia, the most successful and largest resort area, the Gold Coast, Queensland, prefers to respond to entrepreneurial proposals rather than plan for tourism and the environment. At the federal and state level in Australia there are no clearly defined or comprehensive goals for tourism or the environment and therefore no operational plans. This is similar to the position in Britain and United States.

There can be successful tourism development and ESD when there is competent management and coordination of the many diverse bodies, public and private, related to tourism. Over the past decade NGOs have become increasingly important and played a part in development. Tourism is accepting more readily the ESD message, as seen in the Code of Environmental Practice drawn up by the industry in Australia in 1990 (Australian Tourism Industry Association 1990).

Successful sustainable development can be achieved with an effective control system. It is the central authorities which have the power, responsibility and legitimacy to take and implement the difficult ESD decisions, such as phasing out development and declaring development free zones. The declaration of protected areas has been a successful control device, whether as historic city centres like Stockholm or national parks as in the United States since 1872. Yet no success story is total and it requires a constant battle to continue to achieve objectives (Soden 1991).

Autonomous agencies with specific responsibilities, and authority over policy areas including ESD, can be successful, such as the Great Barrier Reef Marine Park Authority in Australia. Some of the most successful control operates through financial penalties or rewards, where grants or subsidies are given. Users and polluters have to pay for their activities. The number of tourists can be reduced by an increase in charges, so conserving the environment, and fees raised are used for conservation. Other control or implementation devices include the carrying capacity determinations for tourism areas, EIAs and regulations controlling rubbish, sewage and other types of pollution.

In successful ESD there is acceptance and implementation at the local level, by local governments and communities. Local people are involved in the formulation of national policies and priorities and in their enforcement through both small and large investors. There is an understanding that ESD is necessary for the future of their communities even if they have to surrender possible current benefits. Conflicts over environment in the past have contributed towards success, for they have helped to educate and sensitise communities, developers, local and central politicians and administrators to the importance of ESD.

Failures in sustainable development and why they were unsuccessful

Locations

In coastal areas, including islands, the three Ss of sun, sea and sand have attracted millions of tourists over the decade, such as Benidorn in Spain and Pattaya in Thailand. Unspoilt beach areas have been intensely and often insensitively developed with too many buildings, too close to beaches and built too high. There is water, beach, air and noise pollution. At times the infrastructure has lagged behind development or has not been maintained, including sewerage, water and power facilities, roads and rubbish clearance.

Local communities, their economies and culture, have been disrupted or destroyed. Fishing and rural communities and the ecological systems on which they depended for their livelihood have not been able to withstand the onslaught of tourism. Tourism has helped to erode traditional culture and values but at the same time has stimulated activities such as handicrafts and dancing. Prostitution and crime have increased in some tourism areas. Local people have found that the change in the environment has taken away their traditional occupations and pushed up the cost of food, materials and land.

There has been a failure to conserve many of the world's historic cities and monuments against the increasing numbers of tourists. Fragile areas cannot cope with the density of visitors at particular times of the year, with their transport and service requirements. The character of the areas and the quality of the experience have been lost.

Similar failures have also occurred in the lack of application of ESD to areas of wilderness, forests, deserts and mountains. This has happened in rich and poor nations. Examples are the over-use of the European Alpine regions at weekends and the Nepal mountains during the trekking season.

Why ESD has been unsuccessful in the past (see Farrell and Runyan 1991)

First, economic growth and development were given overriding priority by governments; there was no continuous, strong commitment to ESD. Political, public and economic opinion brought little pressure, for they also were mainly committed to tourism development. Environmental agencies did have a commitment but the majority of public agencies were concerned about achieving their own objectives. Governments have paid lip-service to conservation but it is only more recently that NGOs, public opinion and protests have been able to get governments to consider ESD. In south Florida, for example, it has been difficult to protect the fragile barrier reefs against the annual 1 million tourists and a tourism industry which is worth US$2 billion a year in the Keys region.

Second, there was either a failure to provide plans and clear environmental objectives, or the plans were not implemented. Much tourism development was left entirely to the industry, with conservation getting little attention from governments. Conversely, some government plans were too comprehensive and detailed and unrealistic in practice. Land-use plans were common at the local level but they gave little attention to the environment and even less to ESD. Plans were not integrated with other development or regional-wide issues.

Third, the formal control system has been ineffective at all levels of government and ill prepared not only for mass tourism but also for small developments or backpacker tourism, which can be just as devastating to a fragile ecological system. Central agencies have either not had the commitment to conservation or have lacked resources. Laws have often been non-existent, unclear, inappropriate or applied too slowly. Parliament and the media have not pushed consistently for control and the industry has been opposed to government intervention. Financial inducements and environmental costings have also been weak. Control agencies have lacked power, resources and sufficient expertise for such a dynamic and complex industry as tourism and ESD. At times they have been too bureaucratic and slow and too close to the industry and therefore unable to act as an effective monitor or control body. These agencies have not had the required status or influence in the political administrative system and have failed to achieve the necessary cooperation and coordination among rival public bodies and the industry. For example, on one tourism island in South-east Asia nine public agencies were using nine different maps.

Fourth, ESD has been unsuccessful, for it has failed at the local level where the impact is most felt. Local governments have often not had the resources, skills or contacts necessary either to understand or implement ESD or resist developers, and central authorities have failed to support them. Where local people were actually operating ESD because of traditional knowledge their views were not sought and their opinions overridden by governments and developers working together. Governments have failed to protect and educate local people about ESD, AIDS, or the lease or self-development of their land rather than sale of it. Local people and modernisation can be just as destructive of the environment as tourism. Local development decisions in themselves may appear to be minor but they can have cumulative effects, as in Australia when it was found that 60 per cent of wetlands on the south and east coasts had been destroyed.

Fifth, ESD has been unsuccessful because of the operation of informal factors. Hidden agendas have been followed by politicians and managers, which rated economic development high and conservation low. There has been politicisation of the system and development has been encouraged or allowed, to the personal benefit of politicians and administrators. Self-seeking and greed have led to corruption and bribery, the non-enforcement of law and the rejection of public interest and responsibility. The management culture with its own informal interests, closed nature and secrecy and the self-seeking and rivalry of public agencies have not controlled but

often even supported unsustainable development. This has stimulated
the growth of NGOs and alienation among citizens.

There is a growing acceptance of the crucial economic importance
of environmental control and sustainable development. Coupled with
this is a growing understanding that if the quality of life of the
modern world is to be improved development must be ecologically
sustainable. Governments are only beginning to accept that tourism
development can be part of that quality of life, but it can only be
sustained if it is based on ecologically sustainable development.

Box 8.3 Check-list for the public sector management of environmental
and sustainable development: tourism development and the environment

1 Establishing the definition
   (a) Different definitions
       (i)   ecologically sustainable development (ESD)
       (ii) local communities
   (b) Inventory of assets
   (c) Objectives: development needs and ESD
   (d) Dynamic
   (e) How?
       (i)   government – authority, legitimacy
       (ii) participative process
       (iii) educational
       (iv) planning, national strategy.

2 Elements of ESD
   (a) Responsiveness to markets, industry and local people
   (b) Sensitivity
   (c) Commitment
   (d) Long-term planning
   (e) Administrative resources.

3 Trade-offs
   (a) From private sector:
       (i)   entrepreneurial drive
       (ii) experience
       (iii) foreign currency
       (iv) capital
       (v)   dangers
   (a) From public sector:
       (i)   legal framework
       (ii) infrastructure
       (iii) freedom
   (b) Government responsibilities.

4 Effective mechanisms
   (a) Will establish

    (i)   clear guidelines
    (ii) open, participative system
    (iii) dynamic process
(b) Will contain
    (i)   strong political support
    (ii) senior minister with one-sector responsibility
    (iii) one-sector ministry
(c) Autonomous specialised public agency
    (i)   national tourism board
    (ii) environmental agency
    (iii) environmental area
(d) Planning and financial mechanisms.

5 Important issues – public/private sector
  (a) Conflict development and environment
  (b) Pressure
  (c) Adverse effects
  (d) Abuse by public organisations
  (e) Partnership
  (f) Markets
  (g) Costs and benefits
  (h) Implementation
  (i) Coherence
  (j) Inadequacies.

6 Success
  (a) Criteria
    (i)   economic
    (ii) sustainable tourism
    (iii) ESD
  (b) Acceptance and commitment
  (c) Knowledge
  (d) Relationships
  (e) Effective control system
    (i)   protected area
    (ii) autonomous agency
  (f) Local level implementation.

7 Failures
  (a) Where?
    (i)   coastal areas
    (ii) local communities
    (iii) cities
    (iv) lack of ESD application
  (b) Why?
    (i)   economic priority
    (ii) implementation failure
    (iii) ineffective control system
    (iv) local level failure
    (v) informal factors.

SUMMARY

Control is necessary to encourage or enforce the application of the five principles. Some policy items are too important or sensitive to be left to the market or the industry, including tourism development in areas of outstanding natural beauty. Accountability is a fundamental principle in the control of PSM.

Political leadership at all levels of government is crucial if control is to be effective. Management organisations at the centre are important for accountability and efficiency but regulatory bodies and tourism management can be used for direct or local control. Local governments and organisations such as national parks are important control agents. Both the industry and public organisations are controlled to a certain extent by interest groups, public opinion and the mass media.

Control management is formally through instruments including laws, regulations, permissions, plans, strategies, policies and finance, such as grants or charges. There is also informal control such as the need to maintain trust, and this will constrain behaviour. The Weberian model using the hierarchy can also act as a form of control in public organisations. Successful control is the right balance between freedom for the industry and the implementation of principles. Control operates at all stages of the administrative and policy process, starting with formulation. Public sector managers responsible for control are accountable to, and controlled by, ministers and elected representatives; politicians can be controlled through public opinion and elections.

The practice of public control systems, especially in developing countries such as Vietnam, has been unsatisfactory. Management has found it difficult to enforce principles and policies against strong economic forces, vested interests and corrupt politics. Control of beach development, for example, has often only paid lip-service to environmental sustainability. Another problem has been the difficulty of calculating the non-economic costs and benefits of tourism and of making a clear evaluation of impacts. Care needs to be taken that control does not make tourism too costly or unable to respond to market forces.

In terms of performance and the impact of tourism, economically the performance has normally been good but environmentally it has often been poor. Especially in the Third World, environmental control and sustainable development need to be more effective to protect natural and cultural assets on which the future of tourism depends. In many countries tourism benefits have not come to the poorer members of the community yet they have had to pay high social costs.

> The resident peoples fail to share fully in the benefits of progress realised under colonial rule – partly because they were unable to match the economic experience and financial and political resources of alien competitors and partly because population increases which accompanied improved order and sanitation prevented any significant rise in per capita income.
>
> (Cady 1964: 587)

SUGGESTED READING

Annals of Tourism Research (1987) Tourism and the Environment, Special Issue, vol. 14, no. 1.

Cater, E. and Lowman, G. (eds) (1994) *Ecotourism: A Sustainable Option*, Chichester: John Wiley.

de Kadt, E. (ed.) (1979) *Tourism: Passport to Development?* World Bank and UNESCO, Oxford: Oxford University Press.

Economist Intelligence Unit (1992) *The Tourism Industry and the Environment*, London: Economist Intelligence Unit.

Edington, J. and Edington, J.C. (1986) *Ecology, Recreation and Tourism*, Cambridge: Cambridge University Press.

Hall, C.M. (1992) *Wasteland to World Heritage: Preserving Australia's Wilderness*, Carlton: Melbourne University Press.

Harrison, D. (ed.) (1992) *Tourism and the Less Developed Countries*, London: Belhaven Press.

Hitchcock, M., King, V.T. and Parnell, J.G. (1993) *Tourism in South-East Asia*, London: Routledge.

Hunter, C. and Green, H. (1995) *Tourism and the Environment: A Sustainable Relationship?* London: Routledge.

Lea, J. (1988) *Tourism and Development in the Third World*, London: Routledge.

Mathieson, A. and Wall, G. (1982) *Tourism: Economic, Physical and Social Impacts*, Harlow: Longman.

World Commission on Environment and Development (1990) *Our Common Future*, Melbourne: Oxford University Press.

9 Conclusions ... and the future?

This study has shown that tourism could not survive without public sector management (PSM). What form that management will take will depend upon the political and administrative system, the political culture and ideology and where power lies. Politics is found as much in administrative systems as in political systems. Therefore management, as it works to put principles into practice, must operate within a political environment and in situations of power and conflict. This book suggests that there are certain principles, which PSM in particular, should aim to follow. Whether these principles, or others, are acceptable, or how they are followed in practice will vary according to how they are evaluated by governments, as seen in the United Kingdom, the United States and Thailand.

PRINCIPLES AND PRACTICE

All political systems are based on certain principles. In an address to the World Tourism Organisation (WTO) the Secretary General of the United Nations stressed the importance of ethical principles in the management of tourism (Boutros-Ghali 1994). Several international declarations have also laid down principles, such as those from the Osaka World Tourism Forum in 1994 and from Manila in 1980. The centrality of principles is one of the main differences between the public sector and private sector manager.

In practice, the role of management is made more difficult because of the politics, complexity and fragmented nature of the public and private sectors. There is also the pressure to perform well in a highly competitive, dynamic market situation in partnership with the local industry. This study through its frameworks, guidelines, analysis and sectoral approach tries to bring some coherence to the management and politics of this vast and complicated tourism industry.

Why governments try to manage tourism is very much based on the power of the growth of tourism and the economic benefits which flow from it. This is as true of Vietnam and Thailand as it is of Australia and the United Kingdom. Tourism has almost been seen as a panacea for economic problems of failing economies, foreign exchange deficits, high unemployment and economically poor regions. Management has also become involved to control the expenditure of public money on tourism. While basic services and infrastructure are provided for the industry, tourism is more than an economic activity and there are public responsibilities and principles which are also applicable. Often it is only governments which have the power to manage the policy area. Increasing controversy over tourist development, congestion and environmental damage have also forced management to become more involved.

It is important in tourism management that the most significant organisations and actors are identified. These will vary according to the national political system and policy issue. Some countries have a ministry or department which has several responsibilities, of which tourism is only one. Tourism management, however, is strengthened if the minister and ministry are responsible exclusively for tourism. A strong, committed minister can make a key contribution. In many countries the national tourist organisation (NTO) is the active manager especially in marketing, but it does not normally have much power within the political or administrative system. Powerful ministries in the system such as finance and transport can either hinder or help tourism management.

Local governments are essential organisations in the implementation of tourism policy and the control of tourism development. They, like national governments, are subject to pressure from different types of interest groups active at the local and national level. Local people should be able to participate in the policy system either as individuals or through groups. Tourism would not exist without the multitude of organisations and individuals providing the many services which go together to make the tourism product and the industry. Although the government input is necessary, it is the industry which provides the initiative, enterprise and normally the direct tourism investment required.

HOW MANAGERS MANAGE

The success of tourism has depended upon management's achieving the correct balance between support and control, and freedom for the industry. How this balance is managed will depend upon how far governments are interventionist or non-interventionist and what their commitments and needs are. The commitment of Australian governments to tourism is much stronger than that of the US government. Management operates through formal and informal systems and mechanisms. The formal system, following Weber, uses organisations, such as NTOs, to formulate objectives and implement policy. Representatives from the tourism industry and other industries can be drawn into the formal system by means of part-time appointments to national tourism boards, as in the United Kingdom, Thailand and Australia.

In practice, managers can find the informal system just as important as the formal. The fragmentation and complexity of the tourism community require good communications and continual informal contacts and relations between members of the policy community. Effective communities are based on mutual respect, understanding and trust. Managers in both the public and private sectors need to be very aware of their dependence upon each other and the importance of partnership and exchange. Government provides the support and infrastructure, while the industry provides investment and entrepreneurial skills. Managers manage in a highly competitive and dynamic environment, so they need skill, discretion and flexibility.

In many ways managers act as a bridge, and try to achieve a balance between the public sector, the industry, political leaders, interest groups and the community and between hosts and guests. Managers are responsible for policy formulation, implementation and control, on the basis of principles. They have to explain the position of the industry in the public policy-making process, and the public policy to the industry.

Management can try to enforce principles and policies through the formal power of laws, regulations, finance and the giving or withholding of approval of schemes. Yet these efforts can be limited because of the power of economic and political interests, and because tourism is a 'new' industry without its own united powerful industrial and political sponsors. In practice, managers are under considerable pressure to respond to market forces and to increase the number of tourists. They may wish to follow rational policies and plans but are often forced to respond in a disjointed, incremental way to power pressures. It is much easier to respond to immediate pressure rather than to fight for longer-term objectives.

Limitations are placed upon tourism management by political constraints, shortage of resources, lack of government commitment or policy guidelines. The policy of a national government can be to have no policy, and basically to leave tourism to the private sector and to other levels of government.

THE RESULTS

It is not easy to evaluate the results of the public management of tourism with any accuracy because of the imponderables, conflicts and contradictions within the policy system. Whereas some costs can be easy to calculate financially, other costs and benefits are difficult to calculate or evaluate. Yet in the public sector particularly, there is a responsibility to evaluate or to account for the management of the sector.

First there can be an evaluation of the practice of management – has the practice followed the principles and the guidelines of Box 1.3? This can be seen as an internal perspective. Second, there can be an evaluation of the performance – have objectives been achieved, what have been the actual results and impact of the management practice and the policy?

PRACTICE

Public management practice is expected to follow the principles of public interest and public service but these are open to interpretation and citizens' expectations. Often a policy can only be judged to be in the public interest in hindsight, after its impact has been revealed. Managers can also be judged as to whether they followed an open, fair and democratic process in their policy formulation and implementation. Have they adequately represented citizens and the public interest as against economic interests, or have they acted mainly as gatekeepers to the administrative system on behalf of developers? How far have managers tried to follow standards of integrity and impartiality and to achieve a beneficial balance between the industry and citizens?

The establishment of systems, national objectives and priorities, plans and strategies for tourism development have either been neglected or proved to be inadequate or irrelevant, as in Thailand. Systems of control and accountability have proved to be weak and ineffective in some areas of development, tourism growth and quality standards, as in Vietnam.

Principles can overlap and support one another but can also be contradictory. The practice of democratic process can lessen the efficiency of a project. Evaluation and control becomes more crucial as tourism increases in importance and scale and when the environment resources are in limited supply and vulnerable.

Government and management have given emphasis to the economic development of tourism and have been relatively effective in achieving their growth goals. They have been less effective in controlling the efficiency of management and in the use of, and in the return from, public funds. Public interest has been seen mainly in terms of tourism growth and there has been a tendency to neglect the wider public interests, including social and environmental issues, traditional culture and the poorer, least organised sections of the society.

Tourism practice in terms of effectiveness and efficiency can be rated highly because of tourism growth but not so highly in terms of public interest and social need. Management effectiveness can be curtailed by the lack of political support, as in the control of tourist development. There has been an almost inbuilt tendency to over-develop both in developed and developing countries. A lack of clear objectives, plans and policies have not helped management, and sometimes management has not understood the needs or respected the rights of the public and industry.

PERFORMANCE

The performance of the tourist industry since the end of the Second World War has been very impressive, as can be seen in the increase in the number of tourists, spending, foreign currency earned, hotels built, capital investment and employment. There has also been a gradual improvement in the level of services provided by the industry and the public sector and in the growth in the range of attractions, and types of tourism available. Public and private managers have become more sensitive about dangers to communities and the environment. On the positive side tourism has helped to stimulate local economies and handicrafts, has raised living standards, opened up more employment and educational opportunities and led to more cultural diversity and freedom.

Although the growth of international tourism has been very substantial in recent years, many traditional domestic tourism areas have seen a decline in the number of visitors. These resorts have failed to compete with overseas resorts, with their beaches and sunshine. Cities which have tourism potential, such as Newcastle upon Tyne, have failed to realise it. Even when there is growth it can have mixed effects, especially when management has failed to implement principles and plans, as in the case of Thailand.

The negative side of tourism has been gaining increasing publicity involving controversy, conflict and politics. Unbridled tourism development had caused destruction and substantial damage to the natural environment, not least in developing countries. It is doubtful whether countries newly moving into tourism like Vietnam have learnt the lessons of past mistakes. Well-established areas like the Mediterranean, with 120 million visitors per year, are heavily polluted. The coasts and islands and heritage areas of the Caribbean, Greece, Spain, the United States, Australia, Thailand and the United Kingdom have deteriorated under the impact of mass tourism. Management is now supporting environmental sustainable development, but in too many areas there has been overbuilding beyond the carrying capacity of the area, deforestation and decline of wildlife. The development of expensive resorts, golf courses, casinos and theme parks for foreigners can be an affront to the economic poverty of local people and may be politically and morally undesirable.

The negative effects of tourism on local communities and the life of the people can reflect the lack of power in the hands of managers or at the local level. Congestion of people, vehicles or aircraft has been destructive of quiet and traditional life styles and a quality tourist experience, whether on the ski slopes of the European Alps or in the world's historic sites and cities. The local atmosphere and character have been lost, to be replaced by a dull, uniform conformity. Poorer communities often have no choice, they have little power to stand against economic forces. They also suffer because tourism pushes up the cost of food, materials, land and labour and adversely affects their social and cultural life. There has been a movement away from traditions and religious and other values and vigorous local communities have disappeared; others have become more materialistic, hedonistic and less independent with weaker family networks and community support systems. Social problems have arisen because of more permissive attitudes towards alcohol, sex, prostitution and gambling. There has been a rise in crime, drug use and sexual disease, including AIDS. All ills, however, cannot be blamed on tourism; they are as much the result of the spread of the mass media and international culture, mass marketing, commercialisation, materialism and changing values and attitudes. Public management have little power over these forces and international tourism movements.

THE FUTURE OF TOURISM

It is difficult to say what the future of tourism will be but trends in recent decades suggest that it will continue to grow both nationally and internationally and to be one of the biggest and most successful industries in the world. The WTO forecast by 2010 that international tourist arrivals will have doubled from the early 1990s, reaching 937 million. Tourism will continue to be of vital importance to countries economically, for foreign exchange, investment and employment. It will be the number one industry in the General Agreement in Trade and Services (GATS). In the early 1990s it was about 35 per cent of world service exports, including air fares.

While the industry will continue to grow, competition will become more intense and countries and regions will struggle to retain or increase their market share. Europe's market share has fallen, with a drop in arrivals of 7 per cent between 1980 and 1993. The industry needs to have more research and flexibility and responsiveness to changing market demands. There will be competition for customers but also to find and develop quality tourism products. That quality includes the warm interest and commitment of skilled personnel and efficient public services.

Tourism will become more international. The international segment will grow and become more important especially for national governments. There will be more international public and private organisations, multinational regions, agreements, conventions, expectations, and activities by organisations such as WTO. In 1994 WTO had 125 countries and over 250 affiliate organisations as members.

The size, economic importance, internationalisation and competition will lead to fewer but bigger, more powerful organisations. This is already seen in the agreements and joint ownership of airlines, and bigger resort and hotel chains. Increasingly these organisations will depend upon ever more sophisticated technology and information systems.

Increasing size can bring about more blandness and sameness in both mass market and up-market tourism. This can lead to demands for a more special tourist experience, which will be met by smaller organisations filling niche demands in the market.

The five factors of growth, economic importance, competition, internationalisation and organisational size could also be more intrusive, disturbing and destructive to social life and the environment. There could be increased tension and power conflicts. Resentment, alienation and heightened community and a nationalistic political climate can be brought about if tourism threatens, or appears to threaten, people, their culture and limited resources. As the Secretary General of WTO said at the ITB Berlin Travel Fair in 1996:

With very, very few exceptions, we are paying only lip service to the ideals of protecting the environment through sustainable tourism. At the same time, we are repeating the same mistakes of the past by going after the big numbers, regardless of their impact on the environment or social structures.

Our fragile planet cannot take it and our increasingly sophisticated travellers will not stand for it. How much longer will it be before a new generation decides to stay at home rather than deal with a crowded resort? The role of the public sector hand in hand with the private sector needs to go much farther than just marketing and prohibition – than just creating dreams.

We need to tackle the big issues of planning, sustainable development, security and quality, so that our dreams and the dreams of our customers can come true.

(Antonio Savignac 1996)

THE FUTURE OF THE PSM OF TOURISM

The future will involve, as always politics, power and policies. This is particularly so as tourism becomes more important economically and governments want to benefit from it. Therefore governments and industry will have to cooperate to retain or gain a greater share of the market. PSM will have to provide a more competitive, higher-quality infrastructure, resources, services, environment and management practice. The growth of the international segment of tourism could make the public and private sectors more dependent upon each other and deepen the relationship. A stronger interdependence could systematise the role of management and curtail the influence of government and ideology. Yet ideology could also be pressing governments to withdraw their financial support from the industry.

In the future, with the increasing importance, complexity and possible conflicts in tourism, management will require greater skills, resources and power. With greater competition and more powerful organisations managers will have to be more knowledgeable and sensitive to the needs of the industry, not least their need for freedom from 'unnecessary regulation and bureaucratic burdens' on tourism, and be the bridge agent between groups (Osaka World Tourism Forum 1994: 5). Management, however, must balance the freedom of industry with the need to protect the public interest. There will be increasing pressure from interest and community groups and politicians for managers to protect the environment, community life and the tourist, to stop tourism growth, and to get value for the dollar – for public expenditure. If the public and private managers have more power there will be demands for greater public participation, more negotiation, reconciliation with and responsiveness to the people. The more powerful active private organisations could require closer monitoring, or control. Management practice will have to give greater attention to standards and principles, and it is possible that principles will be increasingly enshrined in laws and international declarations to protect consumers, communities and the environment. The continual increase in information and technology will both support and place greater burdens upon managers.

Governments may begin to accept tourism as important, not just as an economic activity but for the benefits it could give to people culturally, physically, psychologically and spiritually. This acceptance could change the role of PSM. In a world where people in rich and poor countries are increasingly under stress, an enriching tourist experience can raise the quality of life, the experience can be educational, illuminating and recreative. Tourism can help in international understanding and goodwill and therefore be a factor making for world peace.

The World Conference of Tourism Ministers recognised the importance of PSM of tourism and politics:

Box 9.1 Declaration by the World Conference of Tourism Ministers, 1994

Recognizing that international tourism leadership bears the inescapable responsibility of bequeathing the beauty and abundant blessings of the earth to future generations. and emphasizing that aggressive efforts are needed to protect the natural environment and traditions from destruction caused by unplanned tourism development, so nations, international organizations and research institutions are called upon to reaffirm the importance of tourism in the promotion of international understanding, economic development, environmental conservation and peace, and to duly incorporate tourism in their development and assistance programs. Specifically, international funding agencies are encouraged to finance the tourism sector; and furthermore, all nations, organizations and institutions are urged to intensify international and interagency cooperation to aid developing countries, large and small, so that all aspects of tourism are effectively coordinated to achieve the best possible results.

(Osaka World Tourism Forum 1994: 2, 6)

Bibliography

ABC Radio (1989) 'Resorts, rorts and mirages', 25 April, Sydney: Australian Broadcasting Corporation.

Adams, I. (1990) *Leisure and Government*, Newcastle upon Tyne: Athenaeum Press Ltd.

Airey, D. (1984) 'Tourism administration in the USA', *Tourism Management* 5(4).

Albrow, M. (1970) *Bureaucracy*, London: Macmillan.

Amara, Raksasataya (1983) in Xuto, Somasakai (et al.) *Strategies and Measures for the Development of Thailand into the 1980s*, Bangkok: Thai Universities Research Association.

Anderson, J. E. (1984) *Public Policy Making*, 3rd edn, New York: CBS College Publishing.

Annals of Tourism Research (1983) Political Science and Tourism, Special issue 10 (3).

—— (1987) Tourism and Environment, Special issue 14 (1).

Ashworth, G.J and Tunbridge, J. E. (1990) *The Tourist – Historic City*, London: Belhaven.

Association of British Travel Agents (ABTA) (1983) *Tour Operators' Code of Conduct and Guidelines for Booking Conditions*, London: ABTA.

—— (1990) *Association of British Travel Agents* (booklet) London: ABTA.

Atkin, D., Jinks, B. and Warhurst, J. (1989) *Australian Political Institutions*, Sydney: Longman Cheshire.

Australia, Department of Sport, Recreation and Tourism (1984) *Annual Report 1983–84*, Canberra: AGPS.

—— (1985) *Australian Tourism Trends: An Overview*, Canberra: AGPS.

Australia, Department of Tourism (1992) *Program Performance Statements 1992–3*, Canberra: AGPS.

—— (1992) *Tourism: Australia's Passport to Growth: A National Tourism Strategy*, Canberra: AGPS.

Australia, Department of the Treasury (1989) *Australia's Foreign Investment Policy: A Guide for investors*, Canberra: AGPS.

Australia, Parliament (1977) House of Representatives, Select Committee on Tourism, *Interim Report* (November) Canberra: AGPS.

—— (1978) House of Representatives, Select Committee on Tourism, *Final Report*, Canberra: AGPS.

—— (1979) Senate Standing Committee on Finance and Government Operations, Statutory Authorities of the Commonwealth, *Second Report*, Canberra: AGPS.

Australian, The (1992) 26 October, Sydney.

Australian Government (1986) *Statutory Authorities and Government Business Enterprises: A Policy Discussion Paper*, Canberra: AGPS.

Australian Government, Ecologically Sustainable Development Working Groups (1991) *Final Report – Tourism*, Canberra: AGPS.

Australian Government Inquiry into Tourism (1986) *Report* in 2 volumes, Canberra: AGPS.

Australian Tourism Industry Association, *Annual Reports*, Canberra: ATIA.

—— (1990) *Code of Environmental Practice*, Canberra: ATIA.

Australian Tourist Commission, *Annual Reports*, Canberra: AGPS.

—— (1984) *Three Year Strategic Overview: 1985/86–1986/87–1987/88*, Canberra: ATC.

Australian Tourist Commission Act (1987) Canberra: AGPS.

Baldwin, R. (1985) *Regulating the Airlines: Administrative Justice and Agency Discretion*, Oxford: Oxford University Press.

Ball, A. (1991) *The Economics of Travel and Tourism*, Melbourne: Longman Cheshire.

Bhotivihok, S. (1994) 'Dr Savit speaks out on TAT's future', *Travel Trade Report* 17 (16), Bangkok.

Boutros-Ghali, B. (1994) 'Address to World Tourist Organisation', *WTO News* No. 3, Madrid: WTO.

British Tourist Authority, *Annual Reports*, London: BTA.

—— (1988) *British Travel Brief*, London: BTA.

—— (1992) *Corporate Plan 1992–93*, London: BTA.

—— (1995) Corporate Plan 1995–96, London: BTA.

Britton, S.G. (1983) *Tourism and Underdevelopment in Fiji*, Canberra: Australian National University.

Buckley, P.J. and Witt, S.F. (1985) 'Tourism in difficult areas', *Tourism Management* 6 (3).

Bureau of Industry Economics (1984) *Tourist Expenditure in Australia*, Canberra: AGPS.

Bureau of Tourism Research (1992) *Annual Report 1991–92*, Canberra: AGPS.

Burkart, A.J. and Medlik, S. (1981) *Tourism: Past, Present and Future*, 2nd edn, London: Heinemann.

Cady, J.F. (1964) *Southeast Asia: Its Historical Development*, New York: McGraw-Hill.

Caiden, G.E. (1991) *Administrative Reform Comes of Age*, Berlin: de Gruyter.

Callaghan, P. (ed.) (1989) *Travel and Tourism*, Newcastle upon Tyne, England: Athenaeum Press.

Cambridge City Council (1985) *Tourism in Cambridge – Positive Management Selective Development*, Cambridge, England: CCC.

Canada (1979) Royal Commission on Financial Management and Accountability, *Final Report*, Ottawa: Department of Supply and Services.

Carroll, P., Donohue, K., McGovern, M., McMiller, J. (eds) (1991) *Tourism in Australia*, Sydney: Harcourt Brace Jovanovich.

Cater, E. and Lowman, G. (1994) *Ecotourism: A Sustainable Option*? Chichester: John Wiley.

Cater, E.A. (1987) 'Tourism in the least developed countries', *Annuals of Tourism Research* 14(2).

Chapman, Richard A. (1988) 'Strategies for reducing government activities', in G. E. Caiden and H. Siedentopf, *Strategies for Administrative Reform*, Lexington: Lexington Books.

Commission of the European Communities (1994) *Report from the Commission to the Council, the European Parliament and the Economic and Social Committee on Community Measures Affecting Tourism*, Luxembourg: Office for Official Publications of the European Community.

Craik, J. (1991) *Resorting to Tourism: Cultural Policies for Tourism Development in Australia*, North Sydney: Allen & Unwin.

Crossman, R. (1977) *Diaries of a Cabinet Minister*, vols 1 and 2, London: Hamish Hamilton and Jonathan Cape.

Dahl, R.A. (1970) *Modern Political Analysis*, Englewood Cliffs, NJ: Prentice-Hall.

de Kadt, E. (ed.) (1979) *Tourism: Passport to Development?* London: Oxford University Press.

Diamond, J. (1976) 'Tourism's role in economic development: the case reexamined', *Development and Cultural Change* 25(1).

Doganis, R. (1992) *The Airport Business*, London: Routledge.

Dunsire, A. (1973) *Administration: The Word and the Science*, London: Martin Robertson.

Economist Intelligence Unit (1992) *The Tourism Industry and the Environment*, London: Economist Intelligence Unit.

Eddington, J. and Eddington, J.C. (1986) *Ecology, Recreation and Tourism*, Cambridge: Cambridge University Press.

Edgell, D.L. (1990) *International Tourism Policy*, New York: Van Nostrand Reinhold.

Elliott, J. (1983) 'Politics, power and tourism in Thailand', *Annals of Tourism Research* 10(3).

—— (1987) 'Government management of tourism: a Thai case Study', *Tourism Management* 8(3).

English Tourist Board, *Annual Reports*, London: ETB.

Faludi, A. (1973) *A Reader in Planning Theory*, Oxford: Pergamon Press.

Farrell, B.H. and Runyan, D. (1991) 'Ecology and tourism', *Annals of Tourism Research* 18(1).

Findley, C.G. (1985) *The Flying Kangaroo: An Endangered Species? An economic perspective of Australian International Civil Aviation Policy*, Sydney: Allen & Unwin.

Foreign Investment Review Board (1989) *Report, 1987–88*, Canberra: AGPS.

Forsyth, T. (1993) 'Traveller's tales' *Far Eastern Economic Review*, 6 May.

Foster, D. (1985) *Travel and Tourism Management*, Melbourne: Macmillan.

Grant, W. (1987) *Business and Politics in Britain*, London: Macmillan.

—— (1989) *Government and Industry: A Comparative Analysis of the US, Canada and the UK*, Aldershot: Edward Elgar.

Hall, C.M. (1991) *Introduction to Tourism in Australia: Impacts, Planning and Development*. Melbourne: Longman Cheshire.

—— (1992a) *Hallmark Tourist Events: Impacts, Management and Planning*, London: Belhaven Press.

—— (1992b) *Wasteland to World Heritage: Preserving Australia's Wilderness*, Carlton: Melbourne University Press.

—— (1994a) *Tourism and Politics: Policy, Power and Place*, Chichester: John Wiley.

—— (1994b) *Tourism is the Pacific Rim: Development, Impacts and Markets*, Melbourne: Longman.

Ham, C. and Hill, M. (1984) *The Policy Process in the Modern Capitalist State*, Brighton: Wheatsheaf Books.

Harris, Kerr, Forster and Company (1965) *Australia's Travel and Tourist Industry*, New York: HKF.

Harrison, D. (ed.) (1992) *Tourism and the Less Developed Countries*, London: Belhaven Press.

Hawkins, D.E., Shafer, E.L., Rovelstad, J.M. (eds) (1980a) *Tourism Marketing and Management Issues*, Washington, DC: George Washington University.

Hawkins, D.E., Shafer, E.L., Rovelstad, J.M. (eds) (1980b) *Tourism Planning and Development Issues*, Washington, DC: George Washington University.

Heeley, J. (1979) *Regional and Local Planning for Tourism: A Historical Perspective*, Glasgow: University of Strathclyde.

Hennessy, P. (1989) *Whitehall*, London: Fontana Press.

Hewison, R. (1987) *The Heritage Industry: Britain in a Climate of Decline*, London: Methuen.

Hitchcock, M., King, V.T. and Parnwell, M.J.G. (eds) (1993) *Tourism in South East Asia*, London: Routledge.

Holloway, J.C. (1994) *The Business of Tourism*, 4th edn, London: Pitman.

Hughes, O.E. (1994) *Public Management and Administration: An Introduction*, London: Macmillan.

Hunter, C. and Green, H. (1995) *Tourism and the Environment: A Sustainable Relationship?*, London: Routledge.

Industries Assistance Commission (1989) *Draft Report on Travel and Tourism*, Sydney: IAC Office, June.

—— (1989) *Travel and Tourism*, Report No. 423, Canberra: AGPS, September.

Insight 5(6) (1996) Australia, Department of Foreign Affairs and Trade, Canberra: AGPS.

Inskeep, E. (1991) *Tourism Planning: An Integrated and Sustainable Approach*, New York: Van Nostrand Reinhold.

Johnson, W.C. (1992) *Public Administration: Policy, Politics, and Practice*, Guilford, CT: The Dushkin Publishing Group.

Keyes, C.F. (1989) *Thailand: Buddhist Kingdom as Modern Nation-State*, Bangkok: D.K. Printing House.

Lasswell, H. (1951) *The Political Writings of Harold D. Lasswell*, Glencoe, IL: The Free Press.

Lea, J. (1988) *Tourism and Development in the Third World*, London: Routledge.

Liberal Party (1992) *Fightback! Tourism – A Key Industry for the Coalition*, Canberra: Liberal Party.

Lindblom, C.E. (1959) 'The science of muddling through', *Public Administration Review* 19: 79–88.

—— (1980) *The Policy-making Process*, 2nd edn, Englewood Cliffs, NJ: Prentice-Hall.

Lipsky, M. (1980) *Street-level Bureaucracy: Dilemmas of the Individual in Public Services*, New York: Russell Sage Foundation.

MacCannell, D. (1989) *The Tourist: A New Theory of the Leisure Class*, New York: Schocken Books.

McIntosh, R.W., Goeldner, C.R. and Ritchie, J.R.B. (1995) *Tourism: Principles, Practices, Philosophies*, 7th edn, New York: John Wiley.

McSwan, D. (ed.) (1987) *The Roles of Government in the Development of Tourism as an Economic Resource*, Proceedings of the Seminar held at Townsville, 1 October 1987, Seminar Series: No.1. Townsville: James Cook University.

Mathieson, A. and Wall, G. (1982) *Tourism: Economic, Physical and Social Impacts*, Harlow: Longman.

Matthews, H.G. (1978) *International Tourism: A Political and Social Analysis*, Cambridge, MA: Schenkman.

Matthews, H.G. and Richter, L.K. (1991) 'Political science and tourism', *Annals of Tourism Research* 18(1): 120–35.

Medlik, S. (ed.) (1991) *Managing Tourism*, London: Heinemann.

Newcastle City Council (1981) *Tourist Development in Newcastle*, Newcastle upon Tyne, England: NCC.

—— (1989) Economic Development Committee, *Activities and Initiatives 1987–89*, Newcastle upon Tyne, England: NCC.

Ogilvie, F.W. (1933) *The Tourist Movement: An Economic Study*, London: P.S. King.

Osaka World Tourism Forum 1994 (1994) *The Osaka Tourism Forum Declaration*, Osaka: Government of Japan, Ministry of Transport.

Page, S. (1994) *Transport for Tourism*, New York: Routledge.

Pearce, D. (1989) *Tourist Development*, 2nd edn, Harlow: Longman.

—— (1992) *Tourist Organizations*, Harlow: Longman.

Peters, B.G. (1995) *The Politics of Bureaucracy*, 4th edn, White Plains, NY: Longman.

Queensland Tourist and Travel Corporation (1990) *Report of the Committee of Review of the Queensland Tourist and Travel Corporation*, 3 vols. Brisbane: QTTC.

Richter, L.K. (1980) 'The political uses of tourism: a Philippine case study', *Journal of Developing Areas* 14(2).

—— (1985) 'State-sponsored tourism: a growth field for public administration?' *Public Administration Review* 45(6).

—— (1989) *The Politics of Tourism in Asia*, Honolulu: University of Hawaii Press.

Ronkainen, I. and Farano, R. (1987) 'United States Travel and Tourism Policy', *Journal of Travel Research* 25(4): 1–8.

Sampson, A. (1984) *Empires of the Sky: The Politics, Contests and Cartels of World Airlines*, London: Hodder & Stoughton.

Savignac, A. (1996) 'Tourism', *Bangkok Post*, Mid-year Economic Review, 2 July.

Shaw, G., Greenwood, I. and Williams, A.M. (1991) 'The United Kingdom', in A.M. Williams and G. Shaw, *Tourism and Economic Development: Western European Experiences*, London: Belhaven Press.

Soden, D.L. (1991) 'National park literature of the 1980s: varying perspectives but common concerns', *Policy Studies Journal* 19 (3 and 4).

Stewart, R.G. (ed.) (1994) *Government and Business Relations in Australia*, St Leonards, NSW: Allen & Unwin.

Stewart, R.G. and Ward, I. (1996) *Politics One*, 2nd edn, South Melbourne: Macmillan.

Swinglehurst, E. (1982) *Cook's Tours: The Story of Popular Travel*, Dorset: Blandford Press.

The Tourism Society (1989a) *The Tourism Industry 1988/89*, London: TTS.

—— (1989b) *Submission to Government Inquiry into Tourism*, London: TTS.

—— (1991) *The Tourism Industry 1990/91*, London: TTS.

'Tourism-selling Southeast Asia' (1981) *Southeast Asia Chronicle* 78 (7–8), April.

Tourist Authority of Thailand, *Annual Reports*, Bangkok: TAT.

—— *Annual Statistical Reports on Tourism in Thailand* Bangkok: TAT.

—— (1976) *Plan for the Development of Tourism in Thailand*, Bangkok: TAT.

—— (1989) *Exotic Thailand: Golden Places, Smiling Faces*, Bangkok: TAT.

Towner, J. (1994) *A Historical Geography of Recreation and Tourism*, London: Belhaven Press.

Travel GBI (1990) 'Comment', London: Travel GBI, March.

Travis, A.S. (1983) 'Leisure services in England and Wales: retrospective and prospective review', *Local Government Policy Making* 9 (3).

Trend, Michael (1987) 'The great Whiggery of tourism', *The Spectator*, 12 September, London.

Turner, L. and Ash, J. *The Golden Hordes: International Tourism and Pleasure Periphery*, New York: St Martin's Press.

United Kingdom, Cabinet Office (1985) *Pleasure, Leisure and Jobs: The Business of Tourism* (Lord Young Report), London: HMSO.

United Kingdom, Department of Employment (1988) Small Firms and Tourism Division. *Action Plan*, July, London: HMSO.

—— (1988) *Tourism '88*, London: HMSO.

—— (1989) *Tourism and the Environment – Into the 90s*, London: Department of Employment.

—— (1992) *Tourism in the UK*, London: HMSO.

United Kingdom, Department of Employment and Central Office of Information (1992) *Tourism in the U.K.: Realising the Potential*, London: HMSO. and Central Office of Information.

United Kingdom, Department of National Heritage. (1995) *Tourism: Competing with the Best*, London: Department of National Heritage.

United Kingdom, Parliament (1969) *Development of Tourism Act*, London: HMSO.

United Kingdom, Parliament, House of Commons (1971/72) *Debates*, 8 March, Col. 1454, London: HMSO.

—— (1974) *Debates*, 9 July, Col. 1319–1330, London: HMSO.

—— (1984) *Debates*, 7 December, Col. 670, London: HMSO.

—— (1985/86) HC 106, Trade and Industry Select Committee, *First Report: Tourism in the UK*, London: HMSO.

—— (1989/90) HC 18, Employment Committee, *Fourth Report: Tourism*, London: HMSO.

United Nations Development Programme (1991) *Tourism Development Master Plan: Vietnam*, Madrid: World Tourism Organisation.

United States, Congress (1977) Senate Committee on Commerce, Service and Transportation, *Ascertainment Phase: National Tourism Policy Study*, Washington, DC: US Government Printing Office.

—— (1978) *Final Report: National Tourism Policy Study*, Washington, DC: US Government Printing Office.

United States, Council of State Governments (1979) *Tourism: State Structure, Organisations, and Support*, Lexington, KY: The Council.

United States, *National Tourism Policy Act* (1981) Washington, DC: US Government Printing Office.

—— (1984) *National Study on Trade and Services*, Washington, DC: US Government Printing Office.

United States Travel and Tourism Administration, *Program Reports* (annually), Washington, DC: US Department of Commerce.

United States Travel Service (1978) *City Government, Tourism and Economic Development*, Washington, DC: US Travel Service.

Urry, J. (1990) *The Tourist Gaze*, London: Sage.

Vietnam Fair and Exhibition Centre (1992) 'Vietnam 5 years open to investment', *Panorama Magazine*, Hanoi.

Wilks, S. and Wright, M. (eds) (1987) *Comparative Government–Industry Relations*, Oxford: Clarendon Press.

Williams, A.M. and Shaw, G. (eds) (1991) *Tourism and Economic Development: Western European Experiences*, 2nd edn, London: Belhaven Press.

Wilson, G.K. (1990) *Business and Politics: A Comparative Introduction*, 2nd edn, London: Macmillan.

Wilson, J.Q. (1989) *Bureaucracy: What Government Agencies Do and Why They Do It*, New York: Basic Books.

World Commission on Environment and Development (1990) *Our Common Future*, Melbourne: Oxford University Press.

World Tourism Organisation (1994) *Tourism 1993*, Madrid: WTO.

—— *The Compendium of Tourism Statistics* (annually), Madrid: WTO.

Xuto, Somasakai (et al.) (1983) *Strategies and Measures for the Development of Thailand into the 1980s*, Bangkok: Thai University Research Association.

Young, G. (1973) *Tourism: Blessing or Blight?* Harmondsworth, Middlesex: Penguin.

Index

Authors cited